Sex and the Enneagram

"*Sex and the Enneagram* is an approachable presentation of the complex ways each Enneagram type may express or repress emotional openness in intimate relationships, and how deep-rooted issues of vulnerability, fear of self-disclosure or shame, and lack of trust can cloud and limit our sexual self-expression. In a warm, instructive, yet non-judgmental style, Ann also provides suggestions and reflections on ways an individual type might become more sexually, and therefore more completely, present to another in intimate connections. However, since we hold the potentials of all nine types within us, a studied consideration of each chapter in this book can collectively lead to a more abundant understanding and acceptance of the full range of our sexual lives and, in the process, to the even greater understanding that to be authentically present with another person serves to remind us, as Don Riso wrote, that we are always in the presence of the Divine."

— BRIAN L. TAYLOR, vice president of the Enneagram Institute

"Ann masterfully helps us hold the difficult aspects of this topic by gently guiding our own inquiry into what healthy sexuality really is. *Sex and the Enneagram* is a meaningful accompaniment to inner work. Culturally, this book makes conversations about true sexual freedom and intimacy accessible."

— MONIKA ADELFANG, certified teacher and authorized training and workshop provider at the Enneagram Institute and managing director of Quiet Insight LLC

"Ann Gadd, a prolific writer, counselor, and artist, infuses her visionary brilliance into this much-needed book, *Sex and the Enneagram*, as she describes the sexual and erotic dynamics of relationships through the lens of the Enneagram. Witty and easy to read, Gadd's must-have book for everyone interested in love is also filled with depth and rich wisdom for people at any level of familiarity with the Enneagram."

— LINDA CARROLL, psychotherapist and author of *Love Cycles: The Five Essential Stages of Lasting Love*

"Ann's courage to tackle sex and sexuality from an Enneagram perspective is courageous, and it pays off. I am personally grateful for her contribution to my understanding of myself and to the body of literature on the Enneagram."

—LUCILLE GREEFF, Enneagram teacher

"As the title suggests, this book explores each Enneagram style in its approach to sex and sexuality. Clearly a huge amount of research has gone into Ann's subject. She covers a wide range of topics from angles that illuminate sex and sexuality for each personality style. I discovered some gems about myself in this book, and I am now exploring what is and what is not working for me. This is a book I'll be gifting to friends who are open to learning more about themselves in a sometimes humorous, sometimes painful way, and I believe it will open up avenues for more meaningful and empowering conversations about sex and sexuality."

—CHERISE NORTJE, organizational development consultant

"Using the wisdom of the Enneagram, Ann Gadd boldly and graphically takes us into the sacred spaces of our sexuality. Her book inspires me with new possibilities and brings interesting ideas, textures, and latitude to explore in my relationship with my long-term partner."

— COLLEEN ANDERSON, clinical psychologist (MA)

"Ann Gadd's *Sex and the Enneagram* is an exciting and bold contribution to the growing body of Enneagram literature that focuses on the practical, daily application of this powerful sensemaking personality framework. Ann's insightful and challenging style encourages us to reflect deeply on our own sexuality and to notice how personality shapes our relationship with, and experience of, sex. This book will leave readers feeling delightfully laid bare and exposed by virtue of a veritable romp through the array of human fixations and behavioral patterns that lead us to engage with sex in such diverse ways. It comes at just the right time, as we continue to learn how to talk about sex and sexual identity in communities across the world. We recommend it to all readers who are ready to elevate their awareness of self, others, and society through the lens of sex and sexuality."

— AEPHORIA PARTNERS, leadership development firm

SEX
and the
ENNEAGRAM

A Guide to Passionate Relationships
for the 9 Personality Types

ANN GADD

FINDHORN PRESS

Findhorn Press
One Park Street
Rochester, Vermont 05767
www.findhornpress.com

Text stock is SFI certified

Findhorn Press is a division of Inner Traditions International

Disclaimer
The information in this book is given in good faith and is neither intended to diagnose any physical or mental condition nor to serve as a substitute for informed medical advice or care. The author of this book does not dispense medical advice nor prescribe the use of any technique as a form of treatment for medical problems. Please contact your health professional for medical advice and treatment. Neither author nor publisher can be held liable by any person for any loss or damage whatsoever which may arise directly or indirectly from the use of this book or any of the information therein.

A CIP record for this title is available from the Library of Congress

ISBN 978-1-62055-883-6 (print)
ISBN 978-1-62055-884-3 (ebook)

Printed and bound in the United States by Lake Book Manufacturing, Inc. The text stock is SFI certified. The Sustainable Forestry Initiative® program promotes sustainable forest management.

10 9 8 7 6 5 4 3 2 1

Edited by Nicola Rijsdijk
Text design, layout and illustrations by Damian Keenan
This book was typeset in Adobe Garamond Pro, Museo Sans and Calluna Sans with ITC Century Std used as a display typeface.

To send correspondence to the author of this book, mail a first-class letter to the author c/o Inner Traditions • Bear & Company, One Park Street, Rochester, VT 05767, and we will forward the communication, or contact the author directly at **www.anngadd.co.za**

To Anthony

Contents

Foreword by John Luckovich 9

Introduction: A Bit of Foreplay 12

1 So, What Exactly Is the Enneagram? 16

2 Getting Intimate with the Enneagram 23

3 Triads: A Different Kind of Threesome 28

Exploring the Sexual Types: The Conditional Group
Types One, Two, and Six 37

4 Type One: The Sinning Saint 39

5 Type Two: The Sexy Seducer 59

6 Type Six: The Loyal Lover 80

Exploring the Sexual Types: The Advancing Group
Types Three, Seven, and Eight 99

7 Type Three: Awesomely Orgasmic 101

8 Type Seven: The Spontaneous Suitor 120

9 Type Eight: The Lusty Lover 140

Exploring the Sexual Types: The Retreating Group
Types Four, Five, and Nine 159

10 Type Four: The Romantic Romeo (or Juliet) 161

11 Type Five: The Lonely Lover 181

12 Type Nine: The Sensual Sweetheart 202

The Type You Love 221

13 Why You'd Be Attracted to Different Types 223

14 How to Engage with Different Types 230

15 What to Expect When Things Go Wrong 238

Q&A with Ann 245

Acknowledgments 248

Notes 250

Bibliography 267

About the Author 270

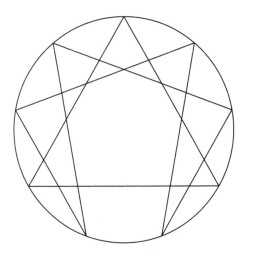

Foreword
by John Luckovich

The Enneagram is a sacred symbol. When George Ivanovich Gurd-jieff introduced the Enneagram to his students, he described it as "the fundamental hieroglyph of a universal language which has as many different meanings as there are levels of men." (P. D. Ouspensky, *In Search of the Miraculous*). This statement is no exaggeration. Rightly understood, the Enneagram can reveal the subtle connections between the higher and the lower, depth and surface, essence and form.

Therefore, the application of this profound system to the profane subject of sex and sexuality may at first seem irreverent to some, but it is precisely in such deeply human, carnal territory that the power of the Enneagram is able to serve in illuminating where the angel in us meets the animal in us. Sexuality unveils us. It renders us physically, psychologically, and emotionally nude to ourselves. Because of this, it remains one facet of modern human life that presents some of the greatest difficulty in hiding from ourselves or of maintaining the blinders and self-importance of the ego. This makes it exceptionally ripe territory for the work of the Enneagram: the fostering of ever-deeper relationships between our highest qualities and our most basic, vulnerable, and human.

In this book, Ann Gadd, combining humor and sensitivity, gracefully unveils some of the core human psychological knots and personality features that prevent us from intimacy with our embodied sexuality and with our sexual partners. Her compassionate treatment is balanced with sometimes stinging insights into the features of our personality that we unconsciously put in our own way of being present to our experience, and to the theme of this work, our sexuality.

She admirably traverses a huge range of subjects that fall under the umbrella of sex and that are prone to be emotionally charged with the psychological biases, blinders, and issues presented through the lens of the Enneagram Typology. This endeavor is so vast that no one book could contain it all, but Ann skillfully arranges the material as an invitation to begin a personal inquiry into what it means to be sexual beings with sensitive hearts and complex psychologies.

Meaningful confrontations with the personal and psychological dimensions of sexuality are few and far between, yet human beings are one of the most sexual animals on the planet. Our mating season is 24/7, and sex and romance occupy enormous proportions of our energy and have intense implications for our sense of meaning and identity.

Unfortunately, due to the taboo nature of the subject, there is very little representation in culture that offers mirroring or exemplifies the broad range of human sexual flavors and expressions. Generally speaking, culture tends to limit nuance of sexuality and expression in upholding a general view of how sex "should be" and presents contradictory images of what is "natural" or moral in sexual behavior. What this means is that, for the average person, there is very little guidance in the way of demonstration of what we may be overlooking or lacking integration of in our sexual expression. This can lead to a great deal of neurosis and psychological compartmentalization. Fortunately, Ann's work makes a valuable contribution to rectifying this lack.

We've all been trained by habit to regard a book such as this as a search for "what is my sexual style?" or a similar theme, but in reading this book, it becomes apparent that another sensibility is being asked of us as readers. Ann presents the Enneagram as a kind of palette of sexual self-understanding. While each Type has its own distinct constellation of sexual styles and psychological issues that may present themselves, it is important to always remember that just as much as finding our own type may be of benefit, we limit the scope of wisdom we have to gain if we don't take advantage of understanding the sexual styles of all nine types. The Enneagram invites us to be fully human, rather than living from only one ninth of our potential. In the same vein, why limit ourselves to one basic sexual stance when we could draw from and see our personal obstacles to integrating a fuller range of qualities of sexual expression?

Sexuality is an extremely personal, vulnerable, and sensitive topic, and many of us have suffered real sexual trauma. This in combination with the intensely personal self-disclosure the Enneagram can unlock can make this exploration, at times, a challenging confrontation with oneself. It can bring up strong emotions, difficult memories, and feelings of deep deficiency. We did not choose the bodies we were given, and neither did we choose our personality style. Similarly, we did not get to choose our sexuality, so in the work of understanding where our personality and our sexuality meet, be kind and gentle with yourself. The Enneagram opens up in layers, so throughout the experience of this book, the invitation is to try this material on and explore it for ourselves our own experience. Some things will resonate immediately, and some parts need to be worked with over time for them to be rightly comprehended. Thankfully, Ann holds a light to a wide range of universal obstacles to healing our sexual wounding while retaining humor and levity that keeps the inquiry from becoming too sentimental or precious.

In my own work on the Instinctual Drives and the Enneagram, I try to bring clarity to the difference between the sexual drives of the body and the intimacy we long for in the heart for the sake of inner work. In this, there is a great resonance between Ann's work and my own, and in the following text, she illuminates the doorway to free and vibrant sexuality offer a means to connect more deeply between the body, heart, and mind. Her insights make for a real confrontation with our type-related issues around sex, articulating the sexual territory with such spaciousness and non-judgment that evokes self-acceptance and curiosity for those of us on this path.

Accepting and inhabiting our sexuality is a major stepping stone on the path of inner work and the development of the capacity for presence. Mr. Gurdjieff said that a major contribution to the domination of the ego is the "abuse of sex" and that our delusions and self-deceptions around our sexuality are a major obstacle to the work of remembering ourselves with presence. A lack of accepting our sexuality as it is and imposing imagination or using sexuality to achieve or block emotional needs is a nearly universal, yet highly self-limiting condition of most people's sexuality.

Gurdjieff recognized that rather than setting oneself up to achieve an imagined or ideal standard of sexual behavior, as so many religions and spiritual traditions try to uphold, personal awakening, with the body as the foundation, necessitates presence with our individual sexuality as it is. Freeing our sexuality from our own judgments, shame, and fears is an enormous undertaking in the journey of inner work, and Ann's present contribution generously articulates a path whereby we can come to recognize what limitations we have imposed on ourselves while upholding a vision of what great sexual freedom can be through the lens of the Enneagram.

John Luckovich
April 2019

Introduction:
A Bit of Foreplay

*Your task is not to seek for love, but merely to seek
and find all the barriers within yourself that you
have built against it.*

—*RUMI*

Sex—it can carry us on wings of pure sensual pleasure, or crush and humiliate us. It can take us from the sacred sublime to the darkest, most depraved aspects of humanity. Sex presents paradox: pleasure/pain, love/hate, gentleness/brutality, spiritual transcendence/primal urge, unconditional giving/self-gratification, playful fun/serious offence... Only the essential survival needs of shelter, food, and water create as much desire in the human experience. Yet from the moment prehistoric woman first turned to face her male lover, sex changed from being a random, brief, and instinctual encounter to something more intense and pleasurable. Before then, taking the typical primate position, the female would present her rear; it was the new frontal position that created female orgasm. [1]

It did more than that, however. It created intimacy. When someone humps you from the behind, their facial features are of little importance. Face to face, it becomes impossible not to see your partner's expression and connect with their emotion. Are they happy, in pain, blissed out, or (heaven forbid) bored? The aim of this book is not to offer sexual technique suggestions, but rather to take your relationship with a partner or significant other to a deeper, more authentic level by guiding you to being more Present, rather than trapped in your fixations.

The external world is a mirror to our internal world. The late Dr David Daniels said that our sex lives reflect our lives—that how we engage with sex indicates how we engage with all aspects of living. [2] Discovering more about your sexuality opens the doorway to exciting transformative experiences, both in and out of the bedroom. A deeper understanding of our sexuality creates greater self-awareness and healing.

The Enneagram gives us a wonderful tool to reveal and explore our sexuality—to connect with our hidden shadow sides, and in bringing them to the light experience a deeper, more holistic expression of ourselves. By seeing all aspects of who we are, we see the potential of who we could be. Understanding our Enneagram type helps us to explore ourselves and the ways in which we can move beyond the restrictions of our ego. Because most of us hover around the "average" levels of emotional integration, I've focused much of the content of this book at this level, while also incorporating the potential of each type and the less integrated aspects. Most attributes within your type will apply to you, but not necessarily all of them. In describing each type, I create an overall picture of the type. It's also important to emphasize that we are each more than our type—we reside in all types—and that our types are the platform we can use to start our journey home to ourselves.

If I had written a book that focused only on the more positive aspects of each type while ignoring the darker aspects, it would create comfortable couches for us to sit on. But where would the growth be in that? All that would be achieved is a lot of ego-stroking, with no inspiration to shift and grow. To delve into these dark places is to liberate ourselves. That's why, in the words of Enneagram author and teacher Russ Hudson, I have occasionally used "strong medicine" [3] to get us to see beyond the limitations we see ourselves.

Some may question the inclusion in this book of topics such as erotica, pornography, fantasies, and divorce. With over 40 million USA adults watching porn regularly, [4] to write a book on sex and not to mention it would be, in my opinion, to avoid what has become part of the average person's sexuality. In their 2018 report, popular porn website PornHub claimed 33.5 billion visits—that's 92-million daily visits, [5] and enough data to fill every iPhone in use worldwide. [6] Clearly, we like to watch!

It's my understanding that we cannot embrace the light and ignore the shadow sides of ourselves—to transcend the polarity, we need to be able to hold both. It's often in the world of fantasy that we allow our shadow sides to come to the fore. Fantasy provides a safe space in which to engage with behaviors we may not typically use in our ordinary lives. In a book written with the intention of stimulating personal growth, it's important to acknowledge and include all aspects of sexual expression.

Presence is the essence from which arousal springs. If we are present in body, heart, and mind, we are more open to being aroused and also connecting with the sensual experience of the world around us. Being present doesn't mean we're always wanting sex, but when we are having sex, we'd always want to be present. In picking up sensations of smell, sound, and taste, our awareness expands, making us more connected to everyone and everything. In his book *Aware* as well as his talk at the Enneagram Global Summit 2018, Dan Siegel describes working with over 30,000 people: when in presence or knowingness, they reported experiencing receptiveness, sometimes together with joy and love. Presence also influences our health in general and our overall well-being.[7]

A.H. Almaas writes that we have the potential to access deeper aspects of consciousness when we are in real and open relationships. This mutuality means that in attuning to another person, we alter both our consciousnesses. Touching a lover with awareness of *their* needs opens us to a greater connection with *our* needs—and greater love for both of us. As we experience this love, so our own love deepens and expands, and so it spirals upwards. This is the greatest expression of sex.[8] Now, I ask you, how would you like to show up in the arms of your lover? As someone trapped in their ego, or someone who is authentically present and engaging?

A word of warning

It is tempting (and can be fun) to jump up behind your lover(s) and expose their inner sexual world. Remember, though, that we are all inclined to mistype people, and even if you are correct in your assumptions, this kind of exposure is seldom well received! People own information when they discover it for themselves. I hope this book takes you further on your own sexual journey, and in its gentle unfolding, opens the way for your partner to do the same.

A note on gender

One of the delights about the Enneagram is that it does not matter if you identify as male or female (or anything between), what race you belong to, what religion you subscribe to, or what continent you live on—your type remains the same. While the Enneagram types are not archetypically gender-related, some types do appear to have more traditional male or female characteristics. When you throw sex into the Enneagram mix, gender can have aspects of the types play out differently. Mountains of research and reading confirms that hormones play a big role in our sexuality. Take the simple idea of how many times a day an average man and woman think about sex. In one study, 283 psychology students were given a clicker to record each time they thought about sex. The women's median number was 9.9 times a day, while with the men's was 18.6 times.[9] A statistic from Covenant Eyes revealed that 68% of men used pornography every week, as opposed to 18% of women.[10] After an analysis of 400-million web searches from July 2009 to July 2010, researchers concluded that, irrespective of sexual orientation, men preferred images and graphic sex sites, while women prefer erotic stories and romance sites.[11]

Suffice to say that gender does influence our sexual behavior, and I have reflected this where possible. For ease of writing, I have some-times assumed male-female relationships, but the insights can be applied to a wide spectrum of sexual orientations in relationships. What we want to explore is how our sexual behavior unfolds within each type.

1

So, What Exactly
Is the Enneagram?

*A human being has so many skins inside, covering the
depths of the heart. We know so many things, but we
don't know ourselves! Why, thirty or forty skins or hides,
as thick and hard as an ox's or bear's, cover the soul. Go
into your own ground and learn to know yourself there.*
— *MEISTER ECKHART*

If you're fully up to speed with the Enneagram you can skip this
chapter. If, however, you only heard the word "Enneagram" when
you first picked up this book or you're needing a refresh, then reading this brief introduction is recommended. Your ability to understand the subtleties that go beyond the nine basic Types will greatly
enrich your understanding of this book.

Many people think of the Enneagram as personality profiling, but
the Enneagram of Personality is only an aspect of this remark-
able and complex system. When discovering which type you are, the
idea is not to go, "Yay, I'm a Type Six—I've found my box," and settle
comfortably into its confines. Rather, knowing your type gives you an
incredible source of information and a unique opportunity to move
beyond the restrictions of your type. Why? Because the parts of our
type with which we identify are mostly constructs of our ego-based
personality, and not our real soul selves.

George Gurdjieff—mystic, philosopher, and composer who brought
the symbol of the Enneagram to the West in 1916—is quoted as saying
that the deep understanding of the Enneagram makes all written knowledge superfluous. [1] One could say it is a blueprint for the universe. It is
not within the scope of this book to delve into these truths, but rather to
make the reader aware that understanding our Enneagram type is only

the first step on the road to reaching our fullest potential. Knowing your type is like having a personalized handbook for your own growth. Let's start with the symbol itself and its nine points, which represent each of the nine personality types.

The Enneagram Symbol in Brief

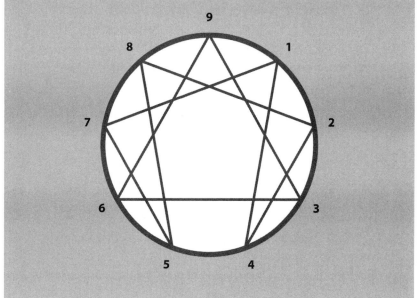

The Enneagram Symbol: A Nine-pointed Star

The symbol of the Enneagram (from the Greek *ennea* meaning "nine," and *grammos* meaning "figure") shows nine equidistant points on a circle, with each number representing a different Enneagram personality type. The lines between the types represent important aspects of our development—we'll get to that in a moment.

The symbol consists of three elements:

- A circle, signifying wholeness, unity, and infinity, and corresponding to the truth that "All is One."
- An inner triangle, which connects points Three, Six and Nine, and corresponds to Gurdjieff's Law of Three. [2]
  These three energies and the number on either side of them can be viewed in different ways, such as the Thinking, Feeling,

and Gut/Action centers, or active, passive, and reconciling/ neutral centers.

- An irregular hexagon (six-pointed polygon) connecting Types One, Two, Four, Five, Seven, and Eight. This responds to Gurdjieff's Law of Seven: if you divide 1 by 7, the result is the repeating decimal numbers 1-4-2-8-5-7-1, which reflects the movement along the lines of the hexagon. According to Gurdjieff, this law is used to explain processes of energy.[3]

Basics of the Enneagram

Here is a brief point-form overview of the Enneagram:

- Every one of us has a basic Enneagram personality style (a Type Five, Seven, etc.), with which we are born. This type remains the same throughout our lives.
- We have aspects of all the types within us.
- No type is better or worse than any other type. There is no desired type—a One is not higher up the consciousness pile than a Two, for example.[4]
- The types apply to all races, sexes, religions, etc.
- Each type has its own "cross to bear," meaning that each type has specific lessons to learn.
- The good news is that each type also has many positive aspects, and a unique gift to bring to the world.
- Your degree of consciousness or "integration" will alter your behavior, so people of the same type will behave differently.
- The "wings" (the numbers on either side of your type) Instinctual Drives, and the degree of your overall emotional health also ring the changes.
- There are several different triads or groupings of three that "flavor" the types and add further diversity and possibilities.
- Some people discover their type very quickly; for some it may be a long and winding road. There is no right or wrong way to discover your type—sometimes a longer journey provides for greater understanding, so don't get annoyed if you don't see yourself instantly. Tests, books, and feedback from others can all be helpful.
- Sometimes we resist being a certain type because we identify negatively with some of its attributes. (Personally, I did an

exploration of two types before accidently stumbling across my type.)

What are the Passions, Fixations, Virtues and Holy Ideas?

The Passions: In a book on sex, the term "passion" is (hopefully) to be expected! In the Enneagram, however, Passion is not what drives you into having wild, erotic sex, but is the wounding associated with each type that makes us act in certain ways. The Passions are based on the seven deadly sins of the Bible (anger, pride, envy, avarice, gluttony, lust, and sloth), along with two additional Passions (fear and deceit). Each of these nine "vices" relates to a different Enneagram type.

Oscar Ichazo used the term "Passions" to describe what happens when the Virtue of each Enneagram type becomes a vice: for example, in Type Two, humility can disintegrate into pride. [5] The word itself comes from the Late Latin *passionem* (*passio*) meaning to "suffer, or endure," based on Christ's suffering, and from the past participle stem of the Latin *pati*, meaning "to endure, undergo, experience." The term "Passion" was used to describe the suffering of martyrs, with its relation to desire only being found in the fourteenth century, and the connection to sexual love only appearing in 1580. [6]

The older use of the word, which implies "suffering," is more useful in the Enneagram context—we suffer because of our passions. The Passions are what hinder us from true Presence, and are how we lose our way. When we disintegrate from the oneness of all things into our egoic states, the Virtues we express when we are integrated or conscious (serenity, humility, authenticity, emotional balance, non-attachment, sobriety, action) become vices, the so-called Passions.

Claudio Naranjo also connects the word to "passive," [7] which derives from *passivus*. meaning "capable of feeling or suffering." [8] What this means is that we are passive to our Passions—oblivious of their influence on our lives. A Type Two, for instance, is normally completely unaware of how prideful they are about their good deeds—the Virtue of humility has become its paradox of pride. Becoming aware of the Passions can guide us to change.

The Fixations: These are the behaviors or beliefs that arise from the Passions. For example, in a Type One, the Passion is anger and the Virtue is serenity. Serenity (acceptance/"all is well") disintegrates to the Passion of anger when we believe all is not as it should be, and get angry and resentful as a result. We cannot be serene while being angry. The Fixation is the resentment we feel towards those who have made us angry by not doing things the way they "should" be done. Another example could be a Nine, whose Virtue is action. When we do not act, we become the Passion: lazy or slothful. This slothfulness can show up as simply being idle, but it can also develop into the Fixation of avoiding reality or action by daydreaming or indolence—an inability to show up for life.

The Virtues: The Virtues are the higher levels of expression of each type when they are integrated: serenity, humility, authenticity, emotional balance, detachment, courage, sobriety, innocence, and action.[9] They are counter to the Passions (for example, truthfulness versus deceit).

Holy Ideas: These comprise the reality of All-As-One, and are about Wholeness as opposed to the world of duality. Our nine Passions and their Fixations separate us from the experience of this Wholeness.

Lines of Movement
(Stretch and Release)[10]

It's important to remember that the behaviors of all Enneagram types are accessible to us. The Lines of Movement (see diagrams on page 21) are relevant because they are considered to be the *most* accessible points for each type: the lines connect your type with the type whose behavior you can most easily adopt to assist your growth. You can move to either or both of the points at the ends of these lines, so a Type One can "stretch" to a Type Four or "release" to a Type Seven, adopting certain behaviors according to their own degree of integration.

Lines of stretch: These move in the direction 1-4-2-8-5-7-1 and 9-6-3-9. In the past, this has been referred to as the direction in which we integrate, but now this movement is seen more as pointing towards the aspects of the type that provokes change or challenges us. So, we see that a Type One may be encouraged to connect with aspects of a Type Four by becoming more creative, expressive, and self-aware, although being more fluid and less rigid could prove a challenge for a One. You will move across to your line of stretch at that same level of integration.

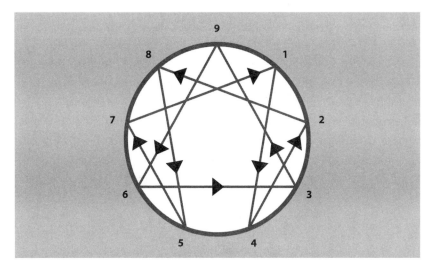

Lines of Stretch

Lines of release: These move in the opposite direction to the lines of stretch: 1-7-5-8-2-4-1 and 9-3-6-9. We use the aspects of our release type to release tension. So, a Type One releasing to a Type Seven may become more open-minded, spontaneous, and fun like a healthy Seven.

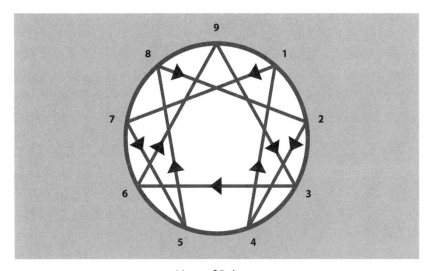

Lines of Release

Emotional Levels: Integration, Average, and Disintegration

The journey towards enlightenment or integration moves us away from a more ego-based state. Teachers, authors, and cofounders of the Enneagram Institute, Russ Hudson and the late Don Riso recognized nine different states within each of the nine types, which they grouped into three ranges of egoic behavior: Healthy, Average, and Unhealthy. These ranges they referred to as the Levels of Development (LoD).[11] In this book I refer broadly to the three egoic stages of Integration, Average, and Disintegration.

You will integrate or disintegrate depending on whether you adopt the higher or lower aspects of the type. We can (and do) move up and down the levels depending on our circumstances—our level is not fixed.

NOTE: If you find yourself in the disintegrated range, you are experiencing the most wounded versions of your type. You may require external support and dedicated holding in the form of therapy. Please seek the help you need.

2

Getting Intimate
with the Enneagram

A unique aspect of the Enneagram compared to other profiling systems is that it does not simply define nine personality types: the symbol of the Enneagram also explores various links *between* the types. The types do not act in isolation but comprize an energetic whole that goes far beyond the simple definition of nine unique types.

Making for ever more accurate descriptions of personality, the nine basic Enneagram types can be broken down further into various subtypes and subtleties. This means that although we are a particular type, we potentially contain all of the types within us. The idea is to overcome the limitations of your ego-restricted personality to move towards integration.

The Wings

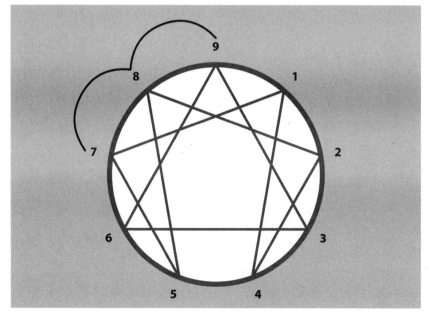

The Wings of Type Eight

One of the ways a type can vary is through its wings—the numbers on either side of that type. The Type Eight has a Seven- and a Nine-wing (as in the diagram on page 23). A Type Five will have a Four- or Six-wing, but not an Eight-wing. Unlike our basic type, which is fixed, the wings can alter—one or another of our wings may have a greater or lesser influence on us, and this can change with time. A Seven, for example, may have a strong Eight-wing in young adulthood, and move towards having a stronger Six-wing as they age. Wings can alter under different circumstances as well—you may draw on the strengths of different wings at the workplace or at home, for instance. [1]

Jerome Wagner writes that the basic types are a synthesis of their two neighboring types (their wings).[2] Because our wings are in close proximity to our basic type, their attributes are accessible to us, and hold potential for our growth and integration. For instance, a Type Nine is typically reticent about disrupting the peace, so doesn't value or voice their own opinions. If they connect with their Eight-wing, they may find that they're more able to confront an issue, as this is an Eight attribute. They could also connect with their One-wing by voicing an opinion instead of fence-sitting, and knowing the right course of action to take, as these are One attributes. A Nine may thus grow their sense of self by engaging with either or both of their wings.

The Instinctual Drives [3]

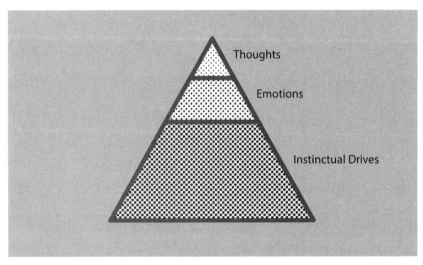

The Power of the Instinctual Drives

The Instinctual Subtypes are the animalistic aspects of human behavior that are hidden beneath personality. They are vital for our survival, and play a huge role in the ways in which we behave. Our instincts co-opt our personality towards getting our primary needs met. They create the drive and energy that allow us to fulfil our perceived need, be they basic resources such as food, or less tangible resources such as a sense of belonging or the buzz we get when we connect with someone.[4] As the diagram above shows, the drives are stronger in our subconscious motivation than either our thoughts or feelings. The Instinctual Subtypes are also referred to as Subtypes, Instinctual Orientations, Basic Instincts, Instinctual Variants, or Sub-orientations.[5] The Enneagram recognizes three Instinctual Drives.

Self-preservation Drive

The focus of the Self-preservation instinct is on the physical: *What do I need to survive in the world? What do I need to sustain my physical self?* This instinct urges us towards seeking protective resources such as food, shelter, warmth, money, and security, and it may be revealed in a person's ability to cultivate physical resources, or their skill at taking care of their physical needs. This might include exercising, pitting themselves against the natural elements (in outdoor pursuits like hiking or climbing) or against other people (in competitive sports), or simply taking physical care of their bodies. As they disintegrate, their behavior becomes more extreme.

This instinct helps us to avoid potential danger and be aware of health issues. It can create either a risk avoidance or an excessive desire to engage with risk, which makes us feel more physically alive. John Luckovich says that this instinct creates a personality that is more contained than the other two types because it is about self-preservation as opposed to interaction with others.[6] Disintegrated Self-preservation types can be physically neglectful, overly security conscious and risk avoidant, showing the need to hold on to what reserves they have acquired—like a squirrel hoarding nuts for years to come, instead of just for the winter.

Social Drive

The focus for Social types is on connection, participation, and how we relate to others. It creates a desire to belong to a group, a cause, or a religion. In animals this would be about being in a pack or herd, which is safety in numbers—a horse separated from the herd is more vulnerable to attack by predators.

The Social instinct is often misunderstood as being expressed as the need to constantly be with people or being adept at entertaining, but this is not necessarily true. Rather than being the life and soul of the party, types with this drive value a sense of belonging, having good standing within a community or group, or being community minded or part of a team. It's seen in what we present to the world (our clothes, tattoos, hobbies, and interests) in order to be accepted.[7] It's how we feel part of something, rather than alone. This instinct is less focused than the sexual drive (see below) but can also find expression in the relationship between two people, such as with a close and loved friend.

If we are disintegrated, the Social instinct creates the need for recognition, status, fame, control, or power over others. We speak of "social *media*"—we're telling the world about our latest travels, our humor, our stories, our lives (and sometimes also our breakfast!). I suspect people who post excessively on social media are Social instinctual types.

Sexual Drive

A Sexual drive is essential to survival. From the weird mating ritual of the male hippo who urinates and defecates on himself, using his tail to fan the excrement all over the place, to the spectacular and beautiful display of a peacock to a peahen, the urge to mate is a compelling drive that influences our behavior. A Sexual instinct is expressed in sexual relationships—both in how to attract and sustain them, and in the fear of not having the qualities to be able to.

Types with a Sexual instinct are excited by the buzz of human engagement. It's what inspires us to enhance our attraction through looks, what we do, or how we come across to prospective partners. It's the chemistry that's created when two people connect mentally, physically, or emotionally and the passion we have for living. Disintegrated Sexual types can disregard others' boundaries, or allow their own to be transgressed, which creates unhealthy dependence. They may also focus excessive energy into their appearance in an attempt to create a sexual connection.

Counterphobic Types

Each Enneagram type has one Instinctual Drive that is referred to as being "counterphobic," or going against the "Passion" of that type. For instance, a Type Six has the Passion of Fear. When counterphobic, the Six will move *towards* fear rather than run *from* it.

All three Instinctual Drives are found in each Enneagram type, making for 9 x 3 = 27 variants. We all tend to have a more dominant instinct, and the way the three instincts stack in order of strength defines much of our instinctual behavior. A balance between all three would be ideal.

The way our Instinctual Drives stack can have a profound effect on our primary relationships. For instance, irrespective of your Enneagram type, if you are a Sexual type married to a Social type, your basic needs are going to involve spending time as a couple, whereas they will be more inclined to mix socially. If it's your anniversary, you may imagine a romantic evening for two, while they may be inclined to throw an impressive party for family and friends. These varying needs can create conflict in relationships. If you were both Sexual types, then you'd probably desire the same kind of celebration, given your similar worldview.

Likewise, if you are a Self-preservation type, your Social partner's seeming indifference to issues of security and safe-guarding your home may leave you perplexed and even angry. Or, when planning a hike, you may feel resentful that while they're on the phone inviting rent-a-crowd, you're making sure you've packed water, emergency rations, a space-blanket, sunscreen, insect repellent, and just about everything else you could possibly need for any circumstance. Neither party is wrong or right, but the perception prevails that because they aren't sharing your needs, they must be wrong.

Understanding your partner's Instinctual Drives can go a long way to improving understanding and the quality of your relationships. First prize is if your instincts stack up in the same pattern. If the top two swop around, there will still be a level of understanding. It's when they are completely opposite that you may run into problems. As with everything, though, that more challenging situation can also provide room for growth. If you are Social–Self-preservation–Sexual and your partner is Sexual–Self-preservation–Social, your growth may come from understanding and developing your Sexual instincts. Your partner has then presented a unique gift for learning.

3

Triads:
A Different Kind
of Threesome

*That many-faceted thing called love succeeds
in building bridges from the loneliness on this shore
to the loneliness on the other one. These bridges can
be of great beauty, but they are rarely built
for eternity, and frequently they cannot tolerate
too heavy a burden without collapsing.* [1]
— *KAREN HORNEY*

The Enneagram is divided into several different triads—groups of three types that have similar motivations or expressions. Along with our wings and points of stretch and release, our connection to other types in various triads is one of the reasons why we see ourselves in different types—and ultimately why we have the potential to encompass all Nine types in our evolution beyond type. [2]

The most commonly used triad focuses on the centers of Body, Heart, and Head, with three Enneagram types falling into each center. This can also be called the Instinctive/Gut, Feeling, and Thinking triad, [3] and I refer to these centers in the general discussion about various types in the coming chapters.

For the purposes of our focus on sex and relationships, two other triads are particularly useful because they focus on the way the types relate to others, and what drives their desire to connect. The first is the Hornevian triad: the movement towards others (compliance), against others (aggression), or away from others (withdrawal). The second is Naranjo's description of three love types: Maternal, Paternal, and Erotic love, [4] which describe three different types or approaches to what we call "love."

Let's take a look at these three different triads.

The Instinctive, Thinking, and Feeling Triad

Triad of Body, Heart, and Head Types

All Enneagram types fall into one of the three centers of this triad: Body/ Gut (Instinctive), Heart (Feeling), and Head (Thinking). To function optimally, a person needs to draw on all three centers. Functioning in one center at the expense of the other two causes imbalance, and the degree to which we are disintegrated is the degree to which the three centers are out of balance. So, a more integrated Type Seven (in the Head triad) will have an imbalance in the Thinking (Head) area. If they become less integrated, there will be an imbalance first in one other center and then disintegration in all three. [5] Here is a summary of each center:

Body or Instinctive types:
- Body types are Ones, Eights, and Nines.
- They have issues with anger (common wounding), which can be expressed or repressed.
- These action-orientated types are focused in the present.
- Body types desire autonomy.
- Body types want to affect the world but not be affected by it. [6]

Heart or Feeling types:

- Heart types are Twos, Threes, and Fours.
- They have issues with shame (common wounding).
- Heart types focus on the remorse or sorrow of the past.
- Heart types have problems with self-image (actual self, idealized self, and shamed self).

Head or Thinking types:

- Head types are Fives, Sixes, and Sevens.
- They have issues with fear (common wounding).
- Head types are future orientated in being concerned with what could happen: "What if … ?"
- Head types have problems with accessing their own inner guidance and support.

In each center, one type represses, one expresses, and one does a bit of both. Twos, Sevens, and Eights express their respective shame, fear, and anger into the world. Ones, Fours, and Fives repress their respective shame, fear and anger. Threes, Sixes, and Nines both repress and express their respective shame, fear, and anger.

The Hornevian Triad: Compliant, Asserting, and Withdrawing Type

Karen Horney (yes, an appropriate name in a book on sex!) was a German-born psychoanalyst who later moved to the USA. She was known to disagree with Sigmund Freud's view on the psychological differences between the sexes when it came to sex, believing it was our biographies rather than our biology that created the difference. [7]

Arguably her greatest contribution to psychology was the naming of ten patterns or ways in which we get our instinctual needs met. These she later condensed into three groups: the Compliants, the Assertives, and the Withdrawns. [8] For the purposes of this book I have used the terms Conditional, Advancing (towards others), or Retreating (from others) to better describe the forms of sexual interaction experienced by these groups.

- Types One, Two, and Six form the Conditional triad (Horney's Compliants).

- Types Three, Seven, and Eight form the Advancing triad (Horney's Assertives).
- Types Four, Five, and Nine form the Retreating triad (Horney's Withdrawns).

While these apply to the way we get our sexual needs met, our general needs follow the same pattern.

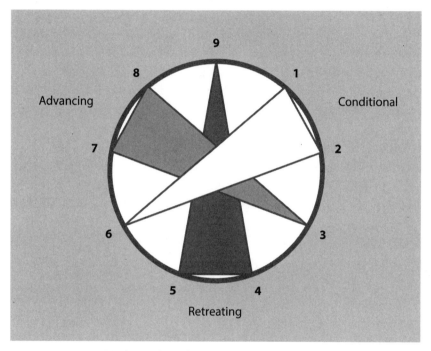

Triad Based on the Three Hornevian Groups

The Conditional Group (Types One, Two, and Six)

This group believes that to get their needs met, certain conditions need to be met first—such as earning affection and approval, adhering to their social or religious beliefs, being loyal, or even having a shower before having sex. These conditions differ according to their type. Some types impose conditions on themselves—"What is the right way to act?" "What are the rules I need to abide by?" "What should I do?"—and other types impose conditions on their partners.

Ones: Ones believe that being a "good boy/girl" (tidying the house, mowing the lawn, washing up, remembering a birthday, providing an income, or being faithful) earns them the right to conjugal bliss. They follow the ideals of the doctrine they believe in or group they belong to. They may (depending on their Instinctual Drive) apply these "rules" to themselves or to a partner. They set high standards and sex is conditional on these being met.

Twos: Twos find sex must be conditional on the needs of their partner. They may cater to their partner by preparing a special meal, doing things their partner enjoys (even if the Two doesn't), holding their hand, or running them a bath. Twos pride themselves on being needed (believing only they know what a partner wants). They feel that all the good deeds they do for their partner earns them the right to sex.

Sixes: Sixes impose conditions such as being responsible and reliable— such as being the dependable, loyal, trustworthy partner who pays the bills, attends school functions, and is supportive, faithful, and dutiful. As much as they desire support, they also fear becoming too dependent. They desire a partner who is as loyal and supportive as they believe themselves to be, and this becomes a condition of engagement.

The Advancing Group (Types Three, Seven, and Eight)

This group moves externally with thoughts, feelings, or physical distractions in an attempt to gain sexual intensity. These types believe they can only get their sexual needs met by inflating their sense of self and advance towards others by dominating or asserting themselves. They identify who and what they want sexually and engage in active pursuit: they can appear to hunt for a partner aggressively. Their needs tend to take priority over the needs of their partner, and they see themselves as the more important person in the relationship. In sexual terms, they would be the "doms" or dominant partner—the person "on top."

Threes: Threes attempt to get their needs met through personal success— they want to advance in status and as such need to advance towards others to receive recognition. They need the admiration of others, whereas the other two types admire themselves. (An exception is a Social Seven of the counterphobic Instinctual type, who does need the admiration of others.)

If they shine their lights brightly enough, Threes believe they will draw their partner of choice and the sex they desire: "I'm a star, which earns me the right to have you as my groupie."

Sevens: Sevens advance towards others with the believe that if they present an upbeat, exciting, interesting, and enthusiastic persona, people will be drawn to them and they can then start making demands: "The fun starts when I arrive!" They'll plan exotic excursions and wild parties, or prepare orgasmic food, all to demand attention. They enjoy risk-taking, so a quickie with a stranger could be wildly attractive.

Eights: Eights advance into the world with the strong belief that they are in charge. They need to be in control and can be brash and upfront in their approach, not letting any rejection appear to get to them. If they want sex, they will have no problem demanding it, even if they know their partner is not in the mood. They are the centers of their own universes. They aim for self-reliance and autonomy in all things, and they fear intimacy or allowing any vulnerability to show. They push against the world and those they are in relationships with.

The Retreating Group (Types Four, Five, and Nine)

This group retreats internally with thoughts, feelings, or physical distractions in an attempt to gain sexual intensity. In sex, these types withdraw from others or they submit to others' needs. Their retreating isn't necessarily physical but can be emotional as they withdraw into their own headspace or imagination. They want others to approach them, to "be sexed" rather than actively pursue sex. As such, they are seen to move away from others, to detach, or to avoid interaction (while secretly yearning for it). The Retreating group seeks security in their interactions and relationships.

Fours: Fours may attempt to get their sexual needs met by moving towards someone, only to move away again. In this game of hide-and-seek, they seek to appear mysterious, intense, and unobtainable, though they may also simply be aloof or reticent to engage socially. Keen to establish themselves as being different and therefore desirable, they may dress in a nonconformist way. They can also become self-absorbed and lost in sexual fantasies surrounding an imagined soul mate, rather than engaging with another person, which is another way of withdrawing from others. They can intensify their imagination in the hope of intensifying sex, but are in fact just shutting off connection from their Body center. [9]

Fives: Fives enjoy not being too reliant on anything or anyone—they may find it less hassle to be on their own than to engage in a relationship that could potentially overwhelm them. They try to master sex through the study of it, rather than emotionally experience it. Retreating can take the form of a preference for long-distance relationships or quick, intense sexual activity, where there are no lasting obligations, or they may simply retreat from sex into their own cerebral space or fantasies—observing rather than engaging.

Nines: Nines retreat from others into their safe daydream space in order to maintain their happy worlds, where the hostility of others cannot intrude. They are overly concerned with others' happiness and so may merge their partner's needs with their own. They can appear to be selfless saints, submitting to the sexual whims of their partners, all the while suppressing anger at not having their own needs recognized. Sex itself can become a way to zone out and disengage to reinforce their autonomy. [10] Typically more social than the other two types, they can be physically present but not actually engaged—there, but not really there.

The Love Triad: Maternal, Paternal, and Erotic Types [11]

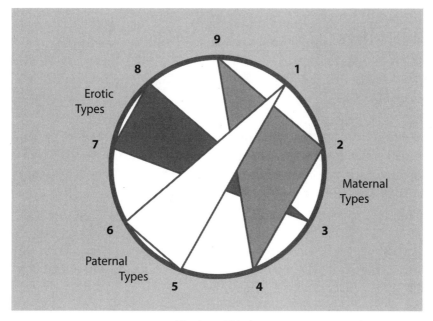

The Love Triads

We can also divide the nine basic Enneagram types into a triad that reflects three ways of approaching love. In a talk with Jessica Dibb at the 2017 Enneagram Global Summit, Naranjo described these three types of love as Maternal, Paternal, and Erotic. [12]

I was recently on safari, and was treated to a display of all three love types as I watched a pride of lions. A cub attempted to engage with his magnificent father—he looked up in awe at the great lion, who merely growled and dismissed him, showing a distant but protective Paternal love. The cub then started playing with the other cubs in a fun, spontaneous romp (Erotic love) before heading to the reclined lioness, who displayed Maternal love by allowing him to drink from her.

Of course, the names used for these approaches to love do not mean that a man can't demonstrate maternal love, or a woman use a paternal approach—these labels merely describe the kind of energy of these different styles of love, and are not about the actual gender of a person.

Finally, in mulling over these three kinds of love as described by Naranjo, I became aware of countertypes in the triad. Each group revealed one type whose expression of the style of love is different to the other two types. Note that these love countertypes are not to be confused with the counterphobic Instinctual Drives.

Maternal Love

This is the approach to love used by motherly, helpful Twos, deep-feelings Fours, and nurturing Nines. Their style of loving is warm, giving, and unconditional.

Maternal love countertype: In this group, Twos and Nines move outwards to nurture others, whereas Fours are self-nurturing. They may be kind to others, but they are the countertype because their focus is more on their own interior worlds.

Paternal Love

Types One, Five, and Six reveal a more removed or detached "North Star" [13] type of love. The paternal group include Ones, who have a fatherly, disciplined energy about them; Fives, who are inclined to observe rather than engage with others; and Sixes, who either desire to be an authority figure as with the other two types or who are attracted to authority.

Paternal love countertype: Here, Ones and Fives seek to be authority figures, whereas Sixes seek an authority figure, which is the paternalistic countertype.

Erotic or Childlike Love

Types Three, Seven, and Eight have a self-focused, child-like approach that's "all about me." The Erotic types include the demanding Eights; the joyful, playful Sevens; and the Threes, who want to be adored. [14]

Erotic or Childlike love countertype: In this group, Sevens and Threes want admiration from others, but Eights are self-admiring. They don't really care if you like them or not, so they are the Erotic love countertype.

This chapter has explained the terminology you'll find in this book. From here on, I've divided the book into groups that reflect the three Hornevian Triads. I also refer to Naranjo's love types in the discussion around each type. Now it's time to get naked!

Exploring the Sexual Types:
The Conditional Group

Types One, Two, and Six

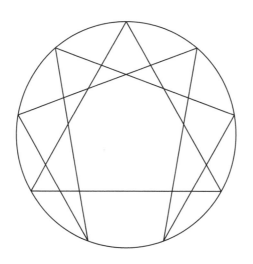

4

Type One:
The Sinning Saint

One's motto: "I do the right thing."

One as lover: The perfectionistic, conservative, and controlled lover who enjoys the same sex routine yet dares to be more wild outside their familiar environment. They often have a rigid outlook when it comes to sex, which can result in covert behavior to release tension.

Ones' sex is conditional: on them working hard, being reliable, and doing the "right" thing first in order for them to earn the right to sex. They would expect the same of a partner.

You may relate to aspects of a One even if it's not your type: if you are a Two or Nine (the wings), or if you are a Four or Seven (points of stretch and release).

Love type: Paternal. Ones enjoy being in an authoritarian or teaching role (to make the world a better place). As such, they see themselves as being morally superior in a relationship.

Relationship belief: "I am a good partner and I make love correctly."

Sexual frustration: "I try to be a better person and improve my skills as a lover, but my partner doesn't appreciate my efforts."

Understanding Type One's Sexuality

Brief Overview

Ones attempt to earn sex by doing what they believe is expected of a "good" man or woman: "I've worked hard to provide for the family/clean the house and sex is my reward." They feel that in order to be "good," their natural impulses (often viewed as "bad") need to be controlled. In a One's view, there is a right and a wrong way for everything. Forget *Fifty Shades of Grey*—with Ones, it's either black or white!

Pleasure becomes irrelevant when you're doing things correctly. As a result, Ones are the type most likely to become vexed and self-righteous about the "sins" of others and can adopt the moral high ground. Enjoyment is derived not from satisfying sex as much as the feeling that they have performed in the correct and expected way. Sex can easily slip into being a marital duty rather than an enjoyable expression of love.

Ones' views and values surrounding sex can be inflexible: "Come on, we're on our own," a partner may say to their One lover, "so let's try this." But if the One doesn't believe it's the right thing to do, the suggestion may be met with strong and even puritanical resistance. This inflexibility can disintegrate into distorted beliefs that "foreplay is unnecessary," "women are inferior," or "sex is my right."

Ones like to think that they do everything correctly and if their belief is that conjugal obligations are part of the package, then they'll try to do the job to the best of their abilities. They are, however, prone to self-judgment: *Was I good enough?* they may wonder privately. They can also be highly critical of others, and may not be afraid to tell a partner if their performance was not up to scratch.

Ones can try to control desire and can even express an authoritarian zealousness when it comes to sex, creating rules of engagement, such as how often and how to perform.[1] Mistrusting their own bodily desires can create inner turmoil—it is the instinct versus intellect.

Ones tend to be even-tempered (since it is "bad" to show anger), so it's unlikely that they'll be passionately flinging a glass across the room one moment and melting into their partner's arms for sizzling sex the next. At times, their anger just can't be repressed, and they can explode, only to feel mortified afterwards. Being Paternal love types, their love can be experienced as lukewarm and distant.

Ones see themselves as having a special or preordained role to improve the world as well as themselves. A typical response to asking a One to fill in an Enneagram questionnaire would be: "I'll do whatever I can if it will help me to be a better person."

Ones are also hardworking, truthful and dutiful. They enjoy order in the details in life and (when integrated) can be relied upon to act with integrity in all matters, including those of the heart. The early missionaries in the film *The Mission* reflects the trials of Ones: they want to make the world a better place and can't understand why other people just don't get it!

If Ones do fall in love and let go of their need to control and regulate sex, they can become intense and passionate lovers—explorative and open-minded like integrated Sevens.

The Arising of Type One

What gives rise to Ones' behavior? In the universal truth that "All is One," judgment cannot exist because it causes division. Criticism and perfectionism are dividing forces because by making something perfect (right), then another thing must be imperfect (wrong). The One's Fixation of judgment creates a world divided: "If I'm right, then you must be wrong."

Ones were raised to believe that love comes as a result of being "good." This is the child who was punished for getting muddy while playing, or who wasn't allowed to touch their genitals without recrimination. As a result, they felt they had to be prematurely sensible—like mini adults. They were the serious children on the playground who made sure the other kids played by the rules.

As they become disintegrated, Ones start moving away from the universal truth of wholeness (holiness) and begin to see the world in opposites, believing that to be loved one must be good (not bad) and do what is right (not wrong). They take on this judgment believing that it is up to them to "correct" or "improve" others' or their own behavior. As a result, they get angry and resentful towards those who won't toe their line. In sex, this can translate into a superior feeling that their way to have sex is the better way. When integrated however, they are serenely accepting and display great wisdom and integrity.

Ones in Love

Integrated Ones: Integrated Ones have high moral standards. They want to be fair and improve themselves—many Ones dream of changing the world. They are wise and impartial. They value self-discipline and taking the right path. Once they have learned to accept that their way is not necessarily *the* way, they become impartial and so can tolerate other viewpoints—becoming accepting of themselves and their partners, flaws and all. They have a great sense of the right thing to do in any circumstance, and are noble rather than seeing themselves as superior. Sternness has been replaced with warmth, and moralizing with genuine impeccability, once integrated.

As lovers, they are both kind and faithful. Integrated Ones no longer repress their desires and (if they draw on their Seven point of release) a woman One can be, as the saying goes, "a lady in the living room and a tart in the bedroom."

Integrated Ones look for the good in a partner rather than wanting to correct the "bad." They seek perfection in their relationships and they also want to be perfect themselves. It's a tough task!

Average Ones: Average Ones can be possessive of a partner. [2] They can also be a tad bossy and controlling towards their lovers, who never quite measure up to the One's requirements: "He did give me a massage, but it was too rough." "She did try to be more sexually active, but we still don't have sex often enough." "You'd look so much better if you cut your hair shorter." "He did go down on me, but it was like a puppy slurping its dinner." They can be unable to see or understand that their criticism of a partner is hurtful, rather than helpful.

Pleasing a One can seem like an impossible task at times, yet they themselves often battle to accept criticism. If the question "How was sex for you?" is not answered favorably, Ones can become very bitter and jealous: "Who've you slept with who was better than me?" "How did they do it?" "Were they promiscuous?" "How could you be attracted to them?" They want every minute detail—which is where the devil lies!

Natural desires can feel dirty—it's as if Ones feel afraid to indulge in anything that hints of pleasure and release. In this sense, Ones can be reminiscent of old religious orders who demanded frugality and saw sex as sinful, a way to denigrate rather than rejuvenate the body, or a process purely of procreation rather than a pursuit of pleasure—life begins above the waistline, or "lie back and think of England"-type thinking, reminiscent of the assumption in Victorian and Edwardian times that "proper" ladies didn't enjoy sex. (That was left to the prostitutes, who are estimated to have totalled some 80,000 or one prostitute for every 12 active males in 1839 in London.) [3]

If a partner does manage to persuade their One lover to have a quickie in the bathroom before the kids wake up, the One will immediately worry whether anyone saw anything, or if there is any remnant of their "bad behavior."

Disintegrated Ones: When Ones become disintegrated, they start becoming the opposite of what they preach. They may speak at length of kindness while acting cruelly. They can become like the grim, cruel nuns and priests featured in the Brontë sisters' books—seething with moral indignance, yet often committing the very sins they say they despise.

They may elevate their own actions while belittling the efforts of others, or they may strive to be perfect and end up being rigid or austere. Sexually speaking, this can result in condemning certain practices while secretly indulging in them.

Ones want their partners to share their need for exemplary habits and will criticize mercilessly to try to reign in certain "unacceptable" behaviors. They become increasingly small-minded and denounce anything that threatens their view of the world, particularly when it comes to sexual issues. Whatever their opinion—even free sexual expression or having multiple wives—they will zealously seek to advance their cause.

Disintegrated Ones can become self-flagellating, self-mutilating, and hypocritical, with a perverse and masochistic need to "purify" themselves and others. They can see no view other than their own. They may avoid masturbation, believing themselves to be above the lusty needs of us lesser mortals.

The weird contraptions designed in Victorian times to stop boys masturbating or ejaculating could well have been the inventions of disintegrated One thinking (with a Five to help with the design), which determined to rid the body of "sins of the flesh." [4] (In the late 1800s, masturbation was thought to cause blindness, insanity, and acne, among other ills.) [5]

Ones have the potential to be a joy to live with. They are inherently reliable, responsible, and truthful. They want to be the best they can be—in love, as lovers, and all aspects of life.

What One Dating Adverts Might Look Like

Joan, 56

I lead an active life. I'm a retired teacher and now work for upliftment charities—I'm currently organizing a fundraiser for cystic fibrosis by climbing a local mountain. If I don't do it, who will?

I enjoy hiking and the outdoors, coffee and camping. I love people who inspire me and would love to be the same for others. I'm old-fashioned in some ways, I guess— I enjoy a man with good manners. Definitely no drinkers or smokers. If you're looking for fun and a great smile, I'm your girl!

Noah, 40

I pay the bills. I wear socks that match and have no criminal record. I'm an upright citizen with a steady career. I crunch numbers, organize teams, and facilitate the smooth running of the company. When I'm not working, I enjoy cycling, trail running, and socializing. I help out at a nonprofit organization a couple of times a month. I enjoy traveling, so on holiday you'll find me walking the cobbled streets of old European towns or exploring the Greek isles (where I can nearly speak the lingo).

What I am looking for in a woman is a slim body and a broad mind! No seriously, I'd like someone sensible (no theatrics), with integrity, self-sufficiency, and a desire to make the world a better place. If you think you're that person, contact me.

The Passion of Anger and the Fixation of Resentment

Ones are part of the Anger Triad, together with Eights and Nines, but when you're focused on trying to be perfect, you can't (or feel you shouldn't) direct your anger towards others. The result is that it sits and boils in resentment. "Why can't you just do things properly?" Ones lament. While in the early stages of a relationship, Ones can be quite Sevenish in their behavior—fun, adventurous, and spontaneous. When the first flush of romance wears off, the more Oneish aspects can emerge. Partners "just don't get it," and anger and resentment follow.

A Peek into a One's Bedroom

Walk into a One's bedroom and you'll find everything clean and in its correct place. Woe betide the partner who forgets to make the bed, or who leaves undies on the floor—they may find themselves reprimanded or sex postponed as a result. Drawers will have clothes neatly folded and often organized by color, style, or season. The room may be cluttered, but everything will be dusted and aligned.

The room will be "tasteful," nothing over the top or too ostentatious. It might look like a page from a catalogue—neutral colors and pastels will rule, and artwork will be conservative and hung straight. Naturally, feathers fly if a partner fails to understand the importance of neatness and "cleanliness next to godliness"!

Fantasies and Erotica

Dressed in a pleated navy skirt and perfectly tailored jacket, hair neatly cut and styled, a One woman can be the very image of order and self-control. Yet people who are so controlled (and controlling) in their lives can find it a real turn-on to be out of control.

In allowing themselves to have fantasies (many Ones would consider this an indulgence), Ones are likely to visit parts of their imagination that their daily lives would not condone. Submissive sex fantasies may provide a release to all that pent-up resentment and rage. Desire can be driven by forbidden fruit—their best friend's partner, a religious leader, a much younger person, or anything they desire but don't usually allow themselves. It's "bad," yet so exquisitely delicious.

Ones can explore their shadow sides by fantasizing about what they consider to be "dirty" sexual acts—things that aren't "right," are against their religious or moral beliefs, or which others may disapprove of (rather than the other way around). In fantasy, vanilla sex is swapped for every other flavor, from chocolate to rocky road. Fantasies may involve same-sex engagements or having sex with multiple partners, if that's against what the One believes is "right." Another fantasy may see One's being punished for "bad" behavior—being beaten or tied up for being "wicked," so they don't have to own what happens because "He/she made me do it!"

Women may also fantasize about being damsels in distress, rescued by a Mills & Boon-type hero in a bodice-ripping escapade. It's conservative love and passion, potentially whimsical, without the messiness of actual everyday sex.

Believing that love is a respectable way to channel their sexual urges and that raunchy fantasies are a no-go area, Ones may engage their romantic Four aspect (line of stretch) and find themselves writing poetry or prose, rather than physically expressing their emotions. Because they are not Fours, however, the object of their affection may never actually get to read their heartfelt outpourings.

Many Ones have felt much torment over issues with sex and sexuality in contexts where life below the belt is deemed sinful and requiring suppression. It is sad to imagine what this type of thinking has done to sexual expression, as well as the polarity that has resulted when suppressed needs have been expressed in violent and invasive ways.

A sex therapist described a very religious client fantasizing about having her church minister observing her having sex or having sex with him.

The experience caused guilt and recrimination for the client, and instead of saying a silent prayer of thanks to the priest for livening up her sex life, she felt morally bound to confess her "sin" to her husband [6]—this is One-style behavior.

Typically viewed as "bad," erotica can be a way of stepping into one's shadow self. Ones strive to be so very good, but until they can reach a point of acceptance and let go of judgment, there is always an attraction to the opposite "badness." The desire to act out and rebel against "being good" can draw erotica to a hapless One like a moth to a flame. They may attempt to curb desire with rules such as: "If I do such and such, then I'll allow myself 15 minutes of porn a week," or "I'll watch porn, but only straight sex, and only when my wife's away."

When temptation becomes too much and they break their own porn-watching rules, they'll do penance by performing charitable deeds or emotionally flagellate themselves in whichever way they believe is suitable. Ones are strict with others, but can be even stricter with themselves.

Ones of Different Genders

Female Ones: Good girls are pretty and feminine; bad girls are sexy—at least that's what renowned sexologist Dr. Eve discovered when working with a diverse range of women's groups. "Feminine" attracted words such as "pure," "bride," and those reflecting a romantic view of women. "Sexy," on the other hand, elicited words such as "confident," "wild hair," "red" and "tight clothing." [7] Women who are Ones aim to be feminine rather than sexy.

Naranjo refers to Ones as being "over-civilized" and "overly virtuous." [8] There is a puritanical aspect to Ones of both sexes. Female Ones believe that if they work hard, are "good girls," help others, suppress their anger, and aim for self-perfection, they'll attract a perfect mate. When that doesn't happen, they can become confused and angry, and try harder to be better. They can then start to become judgmental of prospective partners, using criticism to avoid feeling the pain of neglect or rejection. The gap between their expectation of the "ideal" partner and reality widens. Having a partner arrive home horny, sweaty from a hike and covered in mud may not be appreciated—even though being ravished by a sweaty lothario may be a great turn-on in their fantasies.

A study of 457 couples revealed that One women most commonly marry Nine men, followed by Fives. [9] This makes sense from the perspective that easy-going Nines will withdraw from conflict or accept criticism to keep the peace, while Five men also retreat to the safety of their literal or figurative man-caves. Both types will allow themselves to be controlled.

A One woman may find work, child care, housework, or any other distraction more important than sex. Sex is scheduled. Only when the chores are done may they carefully draw the curtains, turn back the bed, bath, comb their hair, and finally allow themselves to enjoy sex. The need to do tasks first can become an obsessive and controlling defense against any form of sexual activity. Yet how can a partner complain when their One is working so hard? [10]

Disintegrated Ones can become incredibly jealous and controlling, but then have no outlet to vent their jealous rage: "What right has that slut to my husband?" Ones want to get revenge, but their impeccability prevents them from doing so, so the rage festers into grudges, often held for years.

Male Ones: Less integrated Ones can be cautious with cash, so don't expect the Ritz on that first date! Like their female counterparts, male Ones want to be good, respectable, and upstanding citizens. They tend to be conservative dressers and attempt to attract a mate through their reliable behavior. They can resist temptation when illicit sex is easily accessible to them—because it's the right thing to do.

According to a survey of 457 couples, male Ones are most likely to marry a Type Two followed by a Type Nine, followed equally by Types Seven and Four. [11] Two women would be looking to please their One partners and wanting to support their mission in life, and Nine women are more likely than any other type to tolerate criticism and being berated. Naranjo suggests that male Ones are less common than female Ones. He also comments that Ones frequently have a One parent. [12]

Some male Ones can obsess about their sex lives and their genitalia, studying the angle of erection, duration of sex, or depth of penetration. Behind this obsession is the fear that they may not perform to expectation—they may not be perfect. The harder you try to perform, the greater the stress and the less likely it is to get an erection or reach orgasm. Fearing failure, Ones may deny themselves the pleasure of sex, citing work, religious conviction, or any other "noble" cause as the reason. [13]

Ones are very aware of levels of seniority. Particularly if they have a religious affiliation that advocates it, Ones may easily see themselves as higher up the pecking order in a family or relationship. [14] Male Ones can believe that a woman has a role to perform, which just happens to be subservient to his role: "A man is the head of the family, so I get to make the rules." Because they feel they have the answers to all things including sexual norms, Ones may not take kindly to having their views challenged or criticized.

Like their female counterparts, male Ones feel that their impeccable behavior earns them the right to love: "You should love me, given all that I do."

Love Type: Paternal

As suggested by Naranjo,[15] Paternal love in Ones has a certain coolness, as if work and duty are the language of passion, rather than passion itself. Ones have a need to be approved of, to be seen to be a better person than their partner: "Look, I have standing. I am beyond reproach. You cannot reach this standing, but you can lovingly admire me for my (senior) position." "Respect me, even if you can't emotionally reach me." This can leave a partner feeling unworthy and frustrated.

Is Sex Dirty?

In an attempt to be a perfect partner, Ones may perform sexual acts for their partner that don't necessarily appeal to them and then feel resentment afterwards.

Ones can find it hard to decide what is sexually acceptable and what is not. Trying to do the "right thing" can create enormous stress as they attempt to live by their own rules: "It's over-indulging if I have sex/masturbate more than twice a week." "It's wrong to lust over somebody who is not my partner." "Pornography is evil." "Homosexuality is unnatural." They may compile ever more rules and judgments, making it almost impossible to live up to their own ideals.

When it all becomes too much, Ones may explode into some sort of perceived deviant behavior, only to vow to restrict their "lust" and be more self-disciplined in future. Moderation or suppression in all things, including sex, becomes the rule, irrespective of a partner's needs (or theirs).

They may condemn sex toys or gadgets as being "unnatural," all the while having secret fetishes—for instance, a husband may not allow his wife a vibrator, yet may covertly resort to phone sex. Ones might like to change the sheets immediately after sex or hide any sign that something has just gone down (literally and physically)!

Criticism

Ones also don't like any form of criticism. Because they are so self-critical, Ones find the criticism of others extremely painful; Something intended as a compliment ("Wow, you look great in that new negligee!") can be misconstrued (*I must have looked terrible in my old pajamas*). Likewise, during sex, a comment along the lines of "Could you slow down a tad?" could be viewed as an outright condemnation of performance. Because of their belief that "Anger is bad—I must rise above it and suppress it," Ones' fury will come out in snippy comments later. The way around this for a partner is to either apologize straight away, or to tactfully start with a compliment: "I love the way you massage me. Let's experiment and see what happens if we do it slower."

Being afraid of having their bodies criticized, combined with their sense that discretion is the right way to behave, Ones may opt for a "lights off in the bedroom" rule. When a partner dares to speak up and say, "I want more sex," the One response might be, "You should find out if you have a problem with your sex drive."

Being Positive

A One's tendency towards perfectionism and the need to do the right thing means that anything negative is viewed as unacceptable—including negative emotions. This is particularly true for Ones who have a Nine-wing, as the tender Two-wing can soften a One's approach. Complaining to a One about their lack of sexual technique (or offering suggestions as to how to improve it) won't be met with appreciation.

Take the distraught guy who, after his fiancée had just ended their engagement, was told by his One parent to "Cheer up—there are plenty more fish in the sea." If a One is told by their partner that they are sad or missing a loved one, feedback may well be along the lines of "But you've got so much to look forward to," or "Everything will work out fine—you'll see." Ones may even go so far as to tell others that they aren't really depressed when they are.

This need for positivity can translate into the physical—they want a "perfect" penis or vagina!

Holidays in Heaven

Here's an interesting thing about many Ones: take them out of their usual routine, away from anyone they see as a potential critic, and they can really let their hair down. On vacation, they can behave like spontaneous, upbeat Sevens, [16] which is probably why they enjoy travel so much!

Romantic and fun, a One's need to reel their partners in and point out their faults can fade as the sun sinks on a picture-postcard paradise. Their break will have been earned through hard work, which entitles Ones to at last enjoy themselves, and their sexual frustration, reigned in for so long, can then be given (almost) free reign. If a partner doesn't do anything horribly embarrassing, and the accommodation is clean and delivers as promised, all will be well.

On vacation, single Ones may do something completely unexpected, like have a one-night stand with a sexy Latin lover. Once back home, they will spend a fair amount of time recriminating themselves for having acted so "outrageously."

Under Pressure

A potential time bomb is created by Ones having to be permanently "good," being critical of others but unable to express their anger, as well as avoiding dealing with those they've upset. The less integrated the One, the greater the pressure to explode.

The more unwanted or "distasteful" the sexual desires that arise in their conscious minds, the more puritanical the One becomes. They will rid themselves of their own "evil" by projecting and becoming moralistic towards others.

Sex as an Indulgence

Believing that they have an important mission in life, Ones may view sex as an unnecessary waste of time—something that stands in the way of achievement. Frugality can also seep into sex with a belief that less is more—to let oneself go and succumb to desire is to head towards disaster.

Ones move towards Type Sevens on the Enneagram, so their frugalness is the opposite of the Seven's Passion of gluttony. Sevens want it all—Ones want none of it. Sevens want joy—Ones feel the need to inhibit spontaneity, free expression, and at times even the pleasure of others, which can be viewed as indulgence.

Sigmund Freud believed that children who were disciplined harshly for toilet-training accidents often became anally fixated or retentive, meaning that they came to desire extreme control and orderliness. [17] Defecating can be pleasurable, and it's this holding on to pleasure that typifies Type One:

they have an instinctive desire to delay gratification. In sex, desire, money, or anything that brings pleasure, Ones' impulses are sublimated and controlled, with delayed reward being seen as morally correct.

Rigid or Frigid?

Here is a description of a Type One husband, as experienced by his partner:

> *We were both strictly religious and were virgins when we married. He [Type One] appeared the ideal catch: good-looking, hardworking, sober, and dutiful. Yet when it came to sex, he believed it was his decision alone as the "boss" of the household, and that sex was primarily for a man's enjoyment. Inexperienced and inept at lovemaking (yet refusing to admit it), if he wanted sex, we had sex. I had no say. Without foreplay, sex was painful and uncomfortable. It was purely a way for him to release his sexual tension— I was just a vessel for his lust.*
>
> *"It's your role to satisfy me," he'd say. It made me angry, yet I had no recourse. He refused to believe that he was doing anything wrong. He started referring to me in derogatory terms: frigid, unfeminine, not a real woman. He had no desire for real intimacy. Eventually our marriage fell apart, despite our religious convictions. His self-righteousness wouldn't let him see how things could have been if he'd seen me as a sexual person with my own needs. I regret what could have been.*

What Ones mostly fail to acknowledge is that in the desire to do good or "improve" others, they often create hurt by being vindictive, critical, or overtly strict. Admitting the hurt they may have caused others means acknowledging that the cause did not justify the means.

Thankfully, while some Ones may negate sex or see it as the "root of all evil," many can see it as a path to pleasure and the glue to cement a relationship.

Righteous and Obsessive Ones

There is sometimes an aristocratic bearing with Ones, [18] as if the instinctual animalistic nature of sex is beneath their moral and mortal desires.

Mastery is not about mastering the art of lovemaking, but rather about mastering oneself: postponing or sublimating pleasure and natural sexual impulses is seen as a way of being a better person. This may be hard for a partner who doesn't share the same ideals, and who must endure righteous indignation if they dare to question the status quo. Once Ones establish *their* right way to perform sex, it becomes *the* right way.

Ones usually give the impression that they are self-righteous about religion, veganism, or whatever else is viewed as being a path of "right action." What is less common, but does occasionally occur, is that they follow a path that society in general sees as unconventional or even wrong, but which a certain One views as right. Hence, you may find a One who believes fervently that free love or having numerous wives is the correct way to behave. [19]

Should Have, Would Have

"Should" is a popular word used by Ones. They can feel obligated to do the right thing, even if it's the last thing they desire. It leads them to want to correct or "teach" others the right way of doing things, hence the number of Ones in the clergy, as well as teaching professions: "I earn love and respect by doing what's right."

If a One says, "We should have sex once a week," then once a week it will be, with little or no room for spontaneity. Impulses must be controlled. Tenderness is suppressed by rigidity. Like Fours, they can feel entitled, and this includes having sex, but their entitlement arises because of a perceived need to reward their exemplary behavior.

More liberated Ones still use the "should" word, if slightly differently: "You should have sex regularly with your partner." "We should relax more." "We should explore our sexuality." [20]

So many "shoulds" can lead to vanilla sex, with no exciting flavor (Flakey filling or cherry on top!). Sex may be repetitive, regulated, and even boring as Ones struggle to move beyond grinding routines and fixed ways of doing things.

The Instinctual Drives

Self-preservation Ones: This is the subtype most concerned with being perfect themselves. The emphasis and anxiety of a Self-preservation One is more around "Am I a good lover?" than "Is my partner perfect?", and whatever foibles their partner has or is seen to have will be excused. In a questionnaire regarding sex and love, a Self-preservation One responded with: "[Sex is] part of life, but do not sin." [21]

This subtype is the most anxious, particularly around self-preservation issues: "Are you sure the condom's guaranteed not to break?" "Have you had a shower—I don't want to dirty the sheets?" They put huge pressure on themselves, which can result in performance anxiety. Sometimes abstaining from sex is easier than believing they have performed inadequately.

Ones have a thoroughly decent approach to life and all matters of the heart. If a lover happens to fall pregnant, Ones will do the right thing and marry. But don't be fooled—just because Self-preservation Ones don't show their annoyance doesn't mean they aren't fuming. Anger often comes indirectly in bursts, which may not have any relevance to the actual issue.

In their desire to control things, they may preplan sex: "We always have sex three times a week. Wednesday, Friday, and Sunday are our nights." They may get secretly annoyed if a partner initiates sex on another night or initiates a different position, since this makes them feel unprepared and not in control.

Social Ones: Because of their focus on groups, Social Ones pride themselves on being role models for the rest of us mere mortals. As they become less integrated, the desire to be "right" means they may resort to making others "wrong."

They have strong opinions about the way people should do things—and this includes sex. How often, how, with whom … Social Ones have all the answers. They see themselves as redeemers on a mission to rectify the erroneous ways of the world, and can be almost evangelistic in their purpose. They are also the most cool and severe of the three Instinctual Subtypes, even to the point of limiting their own physical desires. The pursuit of "true love" can emerge as a respectable way to channel this One's sexual urges. "Love the ones you're with, as they are there to support you to be a better partner," [22] was a Social One's view on love and sex.

Underneath their righteousness is a genuinely noble desire to make the world a better place.

Sexual Ones *(counterphobic)*: These Ones want others to be perfect. Believing themselves to have accessed a higher state of being, Sexual Ones feel they have the right to insist that others act according to their set of rules. In a questionnaire question regarding sex and love, a Sexual One responded: "Love is shared from the heart and through commitment," while sex was regarded as "a release of steam." [23]

It's your performance rather than theirs that will be in the spotlight, and they want to rule and school you. Once over the heady early days of love and lust, Sexual Ones may start finding fault with how a partner prepares for and performs during sex. They set the rules others need to obey, because they believe others simply don't get it.

Sexual Ones may go after the person they desire with great zeal and intensity. Ones are very conscious of hierarchy and the Paternalistic expression of love is felt most strongly in the Sexual subtype: they can feel superior to a partner and motivated by justice to lay down the law.

I worked with a Sexual One who was having difficulties in her new relationship. She believed the problem centered entirely around her partner—it was him who needed reforming—and she simply could not see that she may have been at fault in any way. When I suggested she look at her own behavior, I hit a very stony wall.

Sexual Ones are also the more obviously angry and controlling of the One Instinctual Subtypes, feeling entitled to express rage and desires: "As your husband, I have the right to have sex twice a week." There's a zealousness and sense of entitlement about the way they set about improving others (who may not want to be improved).

In less healthy Sexual Ones, the desire for perfection in others often boomerangs in rather less than perfect behavior themselves: for example, the minister who preaches celibacy, only having sex with a married parishioner. "He/she just doesn't seem to want to improve," they may lament, while failing to see their own shortcomings.

The Wings

One with a Nine-wing *(Paternal and Maternal love)*: In this subtype, the perfection of the One meets the peace of the Nine. Ones with a Nine-wing can have an idealistic view of sex. When sex feels like it's not matching this ideal, they can become critical or resentful. This type can be more austere and dispassionate than the other wing type, knowing just what's "right for us." They may seek to elevate themselves and "educate" their partner in the "correct" way to have sex. They are more emotionally detached than the other wing type and are happy to be left alone.

With Nine and One both being Body types, they seek autonomy—as opposed to the One with a Two-wing, where the Two's Heart center creates a warmer type. Feeling they may not be performing well enough, like Nines these Ones may avoid sex with excuses such as "I have to clean the dishes first," or "I have to pay the bills." Unlike Nines, the One's tasks will typically be viewed as being of higher importance or purpose—they may involve education, community upliftment, or the fulfillment of household duties.[24] These Ones may also use the excuse that their partner has not upheld the standards or behavior they feel earns the right to sex, or that they themselves have not done so.

One with a Two-wing *(Paternal and Maternal love)*: Here, the One's perfection meets the Two's warmth. Less judgmental and somewhat more engaging than the other wing type, Ones with a Two-wing combine the One's desire to be "good" with the Two's need to be good to others. They may, however, also become critical and blaming of their partner's "faults." They battle to accept any form of criticism themselves, and don't enjoy being viewed as anything other than paragons of virtue and kindness (all the while harboring deep-seated resentment).

With the Two's influence, they are more focused on the needs of others and are less rigid and readier to engage with the world. As they become more integrated, Ones with a Two-wing will remember small details about their partner and look to meet these needs: showing up with the wine you enjoy or a bunch of your favorite flowers in an attempt to funnel their desire into what they see as a more acceptable or higher expression of love.

Moving to Sexual Presence

What Blocks Ones from Sexual Fulfillment

The kids are asleep at last, the couple has spent a loving evening together, and everything is moving towards having great sex. Just as the moment arises, however, the One will notice what's not "right"—the untidy bedroom, their own physical imperfections (*I'm too thin/fat*), the fact that their partner hasn't showered, that the painting needs straightening, there was too little/too much foreplay, basically anything that is not the way they believe it should be. This can turn a potentially wonderful evening into a disappointment, with both partners feeling let down, but for different reasons. The desire for perfection dampens the desire for sex. Ones may delay sex until things are "improved," or they feel they have worked or sacrificed enough to earn it.

Ones seek perfection: the perfect love, the perfect partner, and perfect sex. But unless they are integrated and have moved to a state of acceptance and serenity, they are going to judge what's going down in the bedroom. Criticism prevents arousal and pleasure from being expressed: *Was I good enough? Were they good enough? Was I a bit slutty? Was I not slutty enough? Did they orgasm too soon? Did they not manage to orgasm? Did our bodies make an embarrassing squelching sound?*

On and on this accusatory inner critic will play through the mind of a One, distracting them from Presence. Any tiny detail of sex may be viewed as a failure and hinder the desire for future liaisons. Instead of relaxing into the enjoyment and release of sex, Ones can experience sex as yet another arena in which they feel uptight and stressed, which limits their desire or ability to orgasm.

When Ones first fall in love, they are often able to move beyond judgement. If Ones give themselves permission to relax or they feel that their partner or environment is perfect (as well as when they are integrated), then they can be relaxed and willing lovers and enjoy sex.

In trying to do the "right" thing or what they believe is expected of them, they may experience performance anxiety, which results in erectile dysfunction, lack of lubrication, or frigidity. It can also lead to sex feeling "artificial," [25] coming from the need to fulfil requirements rather than from the One's own desires.

The best sex is a combination of ideas and ideals, rather than an attempt to dominate a partner. Ones may create rules or expectations not shared by their partner yet refuse to acknowledge that sex is a combination of viewpoints. From a male perspective this may take the form of "I'm the head of the household, so what I say goes," and a woman might become moody and uncommunicative, in a way that can't be argued against ("I have a headache").

If you're a One and recognize this behavior, then you can use your conscious awareness of when this is happening and ask if it is really serving you.

How Ones Can become Sexually Present

Accept yourself: If Ones can accept their foibles and those of others without the need to criticize or judge, they move to serene acceptance. They embrace their partners entirely, without the need to "fix" them. Likewise, they stop looking for what is "wrong," which brings them into Presence. In understanding that perfection is not limited to their own viewpoint, they can truly transcend the seesaw of right versus wrong, and become serenely all-embracing.

Achieve balance: When Ones can be with their own wonderful desire to do what is sexually right while at the same time holding the criticizing/judgmental shadow part of themselves, they achieve balance and transcend division.

Let go of being controlling and rigid: Ones can heal when they allow themselves to be more openly explorative and spontaneous, trying new positions or sexual roles without expectation or opinion. Control diminishes one's sense of self; letting go of the need to control expands the One's awareness.

Express yourself: Integrated Ones learn to express their true feelings of anger or upset *before* they explode in a rage or express their anger as cutting comments.

Let go of the idea that sex should be earned: You don't need to attach conditions to sex. Allow arousal to guide you, not a list of duties done.

Loving yourself for being, rather than being "good": If Ones can accept love for who they are (not what they do), they allow themselves to experience happiness and joy (the healthy attributes of a Type Seven).

Accept criticism: This is a tough one for perfectionistic Ones, but they can shift hugely when they don't see a sexual suggestion as a criticism and are able to accept when they're in the wrong without beating themselves up.

Let go of feeling morally superior: Sex can become perfect as it is when Ones accept both partners' viewpoints and desires. Rather than feeling superior and so needing to "correct" others, Ones can develop a true nobleness of self that inspires.

Questions to Journal

NOTE: It's useful to answer these questions no matter what your type.

- How does the need to judge others affect your and their sexual enjoyment?
- Do you desire to reform rather than accept your partner, and does this prevent the natural sexual flow between you?
- How does resentment show up in your sexuality?
- How could you work with this to improve your sex life?

5

Type Two:
The Sexy Seducer

Two's motto: "For you, my beloved!"

Two as lover: The sensual, seductive, caring lover who makes everything about you (while secretly hoping you'll reciprocate).

Twos' sex is conditional: on them being caring and earning sex by doing whatever they believe will please their partner: "I know what you enjoy."

You may relate to aspects of a Two even if it's not your type: if you are a One or Three (the wings), or a Four or Eight (the points of release and stretch).

Love type: Maternal. Twos are very caring and nurturing—they pride themselves on love being all about the other, rather than themselves.

Relationship belief: "I am a loving and caring partner."

Sexual frustration: "I am always the one giving in the relationship and my focus on my partner's orgasm and sexual pleasure is seldom reciprocated or even appreciated."

Understanding Type Two's Sexuality

Brief Overview

Many of the world's greatest lovers have been Twos. Their empathetic, romantic nature along with their desire to understand their partner's needs gives rise to the archetypal lover.

Twos earn sex by being of service. Male Twos will woo their lovers with flowers and seductive meals, and will know what perfume to give, what experiences will delight. Female Twos can fall into the classic role of seductress, knowing just which buttons to press in order to ignite desire.

Twos may be so invested in pleasing a partner sexually that their own needs are sidelined or even entirely neglected. Seduction can become interwoven with manipulation. They are extremely invested in being in a relationship; because they hate being alone, maintaining a relationship will be their attempt to meet their own needs. Unless they are emotionally healthy, all this giving will eventually take its toll, and a Two will reach a stage when they start feeling unappreciated. They want payback! Even though they may have seemed happy to give endlessly, at some point the pendulum swings the opposite way: they can tap into aspects of a lower Type Eight (line of stretch), and become threatening and vengeful, demanding attention or ending relationships suddenly. The once "selfless" giver can suddenly become cold and hard. It's from this behavior that the phrase "an iron fist in a kid glove" arises. They also tend to focus on a specific person and can at times be surprisingly disinterested or unhelpful to those who are not on their radar.

The Arising of Type Two

Somewhere in childhood, Two's sense of self was devalued and so they attempted to create a more loveable, idealized self. To make themselves appear more desirable, they tuned in to the needs of others and then delivered: "Look what I do for you—without me, you wouldn't cope." In sex this translates as "I know what will fulfil you, so you need me in order to enjoy sex." They have a prideful desire to inflate their self-worth by doing deeds for others, at the same time believing they are indispensable.

When a child understands that their needs will only be fulfilled if they first fulfil the needs of others, it creates the pattern of giving in order to get: "To be loved, I must first be loving to others." The belief that considering one's own needs is both selfish and sinful my have arisen out of certain religious doctrine, where martyrdom has not only been condoned but elevated as being desirable. Similarly, Twos try hard to fulfil the needs of others while often failing to acknowledge their own expectations.

Twos in Love

Integrated Twos: Being in a relationship with an integrated Type Two is a wonderful experience. They are open, loving, humble, authentic, deeply caring, warm, and generous. Nothing seems too much trouble for them. They give of their time and effort with a radiant, loving heart. They love themselves as much as they love the special person in their life and are appreciative of all their partner does for them.

Integrated Twos are very affectionate, yet respect others' boundaries. They have the strength of an Eight combined with the nurturing of a

Two, which is also the dynamic of an archetypal male with the archetypal female: power (Eight) with love (Two). They have the ability for deep connection and the intuitiveness of a Four (point of release). When they give themselves in love, they do so unconditionally, with a pure and open heart.

Average Twos: As Twos start to pride themselves on being good lovers, they start to believe that their presence is indispensable and that no romance can happen without them. Even a partner masturbating can start to feel like an affront to their sexual prowess: "Why don't you need me?" This can feel like a painful rejection and the Two may need reassurance that their partner's choice to fulfil a moment of desire alone does not mean the end of the relationship.

Twos seduce by delving into their partner's desires and fantasies, and then working to fulfill them. As such, they may have issues with respecting boundaries. They pursue love with ardor and persistence, and can sometimes even appear aggressive. "No" may be understood as "He *says* he's not interested, but I know him really well and I can tell he's just masking his real need for a relationship with me."

Relationships are the focus of Twos' attention. The object of a Two's desire may initially be the very embodiment of what they want, but Twos can become disillusioned[1] if their lovers do not reciprocate their adoration. They may disguise some sexual dysfunction with overtly flirtatious and sexual behavior.

Twos may increasingly desire constant ingratiating thanks and reassurance of their abilities and worth. If this need is not met, temper tantrums and "drama queen"-type behavior may emerge.

Disintegrated Twos: Unhealthy Twos are demanding, manipulative, and needy. They can become reactive and irrational if they feel their needs are being overlooked. Interestingly, they can say and exhibit aggressive behavior during an outburst, but may ignore or deny their tantrum and cruel words the following day, glossing over it as if it never happened.

Wanting their needs met can lead to feigning or exaggerating illness or acting punitively against their partners. If unable to attract love, Twos may even stalk those who have rejected them in the hope of getting them back. At their darkest, the Two's need to find a "perfect love" can have them delving into areas where they can act horribly and without remorse.

Complete denial of their motives can occur. The desire for love can have extremely disintegrated Twos, who were possibly themselves abused in childhood, looking for "love" in all the wrong places. [2] In a disintegrated mind, abuse can result from the need to rescue the abused—the focus of their "kindness" can be caught up in the Two's web of self-deceit, manipulation, sexual frustration, and need to dominate (like a Type Eight).

Being sensitive to their own and their partner's needs, Twos have the potential to make wonderful lovers. They are romantic, attractive, and affectionate, and are always looking for the very best in others. They are good listeners and genuinely want to help, without feeling the need for payback.

What Two Dating Adverts May Look Like

Big-hearted Ben, 38

I'll admit it: I love women. I'm an old-fashioned guy who'll bring you flowers and open doors, who knows what perfume you enjoy, and will remember your birthday. Relationships are the most important part of my life, so I'm looking for someone who wants to be loved and treated well. A warning though: I also love my dogs (I've got three rescues). I enjoy making a woman feel like a woman. So, if you're looking for a special relationship, swipe right! ♥ ♥ ♥

Isla, 42

I am not interested in most guys, just you—if you're a romantic gentleman who's emotionally, mentally, and financially secure. I'm looking for someone who knows how to treat a lady and is ready for a long-term relationship. (Happy to relocate for the right person.) ☺
Me: I'm a fun-loving, affectionate, sexy gal who knows what it takes to make a relationship work. I'm looking to meet someone to pleasure and please! I'm a great hostess who'll cook you your favorite meals with special care. You can rely on me to fulfil your fantasies and be the woman you're dreaming about. ☺

The Passion of Pride and the Fixation of Flattery

It was pride that changed angels into devils;
it is humility that makes men as angels.
— ST. AUGUSTINE

In his book *Mere Christianity*, C.S. Lewis writes that pride is the "anti-God" state, where the egoic self is most in opposition to God: "All the other sins are mere fleabites in comparison." [3] The late John R.W. Stott, Anglican priest and author, and rated by *Time* magazine as one of the 100 most influential people in the world, said: "Pride is your greatest enemy, humility is your greatest friend." Pride is frequently understood to be the "father of all sins," which led to the biblical fall from grace—though in the context of the Enneagram, it is no worse than any of the other Passions. [4]

Pride puffs us up, creating an inflated sense of self and exaggerating our deeds. You cannot boast alone, so pride seduces others with flattery, to create emotional dependence.

Twos need a partner to uphold their glorified self-image, to admire them, so they flatter those they desire to seduce. We all love being told that we're beautiful, sexy, or amazing in bed—it feeds our ever-hungry egos. Twos can use our need to feel recognized to their advantage by telling us what they intuitively feel we want to hear. [5] As the old saying goes, "You can catch more flies with honey than with vinegar."

Pride also has Twos believing that they have risen above their own needs and are indispensable to others. A Two said this to me: "I met a client on the plane and explained that due to health, I had had to downscale my involvement in the company some months ago. It was very hard to accept when he replied that he hadn't noticed my absence." Likewise, when a relationship has ended it can be hard for a Two to have an ex-partner declare how good it is to be on their own. Twos want their partners, on some level, to fall to pieces without them, so they can rush to the rescue.

The opposite of pride, humility is an authentic expression of our deeds, where we have no dependency or need for recognition. We act with pure altruism, with no need to brag or let slip about our "good deeds" to others as pride would have us do.

A Peek into a Two's Bedroom

Twos want their bedrooms to be appealing settings for seduction: whimsical pictures, sensuous textures, low lighting and extra-large beds may be common. Self-preservation types (counterphobic Twos) may prefer a cute and cuddly style (as in fluffy teddy bears or piles of pillows) over the dark and sultry look the other Instinctual Drives could enjoy. Twos particularly like candles.

Twos with a One-wing may have neater rooms with cooler tones, whereas Twos with a Three-wing may not be able to resist displaying the odd trophy or significant photo: "Me with the president," "Me at Harvard." Twos are not overtly neat, unless their One-wing is strong, so expect to find the odd sock tossed under the bed.

Fantasies and Erotica

In delving into their shadow, Twos may enjoy fantasies exploring their selfish sides—where it becomes all about them, rather than the beloved other. In fantasy, their own needs are being met or they are demanding sex, rather than earning it.

Bondage fantasies may be popular, where another holds all the power and the Two is at their mercy, absolved of any responsibility for "naughty" behavior. The shadow side of giving is that you can only receive—giving is not an option when you're tied up. Twos are then "forced" to enjoy whatever the other person decides to inflict. If the fantasy plays out with the Two as the person in control, then they can be openly self-centered (as opposed to having to feign their usual boundless giving). In particular, Self-preservation Twos can lose themselves in fantasies where they are the princess admired by all the princes in the land, or the favorite in the harem whom the handsome sultan cannot resist or they may enjoy having a lover destroy all opposition to win them over.

Behind these fantasies is usually the handing over of their power to the object of their desire. It could play out that she (the Two) is the typical female character in a cheap love story: strong, yet shy and reserved. He is famous, wealthy, or the boss—a bit of a bad boy. She tells herself she doesn't love him (although she does). He holds all the power. She feigns dislike. He eventually turns out not to be a modest good guy. He confesses his love and they have wild sex somewhere exotic.

The American Psychiatric Association defines characteristics of Histrionic Personality Disorder (HPD) as being:

- Excessive attention-seeking emotions
- Inappropriate seductive behavior
- Excessive need for approval and longing for appreciation
- Dramatic
- Enthusiastic
- Flirtatious
- Manipulative behavior
- Good social skills
- Pride of own personality
- Rapidly shifting emotional states that may appear superficial or exaggerated to others
- Tendency to believe that relationships are more intimate than they are
- Blaming personal failures or disappointments on others
- Being easily influenced by others, especially those who treat them approvingly
- Speech (style) wants to impress; lacks detail
- Emotional shallowness

HPD has been linked to Type Twos.[6] This does not mean that all Twos have the disorder, but rather that they have tendencies towards some of its characteristics. Interestingly, it has been suggested that there is a connection with HPD and Antisocial Personality Disorder, which has links to the behavior of a Type Eight (Two's point of stretch).[7]

What has this got to do with erotica? For a seductive Two who desires appreciation and loves a bit of drama, the thought of being a porn-star could potentially be a fantasy. Melodramatic Twos can often present as being sexually uninhibited, when in fact they may be the opposite[8]—an example would be the woman who confesses to having slept with numerous men, but who has orgasmed with none of them.

Because Twos typically get anxious when they are alone, they are inclined to move into the world to find a relationship to satisfy their need to be needed. That's not to say they won't stay in to watch a bit of porn, but it will seldom satisfy their deeper need for partnership and admiration.

Twos of Different Genders

Female Twos: If you examine the Enneagram symbol, you'll see that Type Eight (the most archetypal masculine type) sits opposite Type Four, which together with Type Two is one of the Enneagram's two more feminine types. If the Eight characterizes "advancing against" (as in aggression or masculine energy) and the Four characterizes "retreating" (as in being sexed or being the feminine container for sex), then the type Two is the balancing point between them, and carries both love and war in its makeup.[9]

That's not to say there are not male Twos (or female Eights), but rather that Two attributes of nurturing and caring are more typically associated with the feminine archetype, while dominance and control are typically associated with male energy. Carl Jung's definition of an "extroverted feeling type" fits comfortably with a Type Two and he describes this type as being "almost without exception, women." [10] While I have met many Two men, there is no doubt that Two women appear more plentiful.[11]

It's easy to see how perceptions of "feminine" behavior arose in the Victorian past, where disempowered women were viewed as sensitive, volatile creatures, who could become drama queens, and were more focused on feeling than thinking. The physical features of Twos also have a rounded softness, more easily identified with females. [12]

Interestingly, Two women are most likely to marry Eight men—the archetypes of female and male clearly create an attraction. Two men, however, have been found to be more attracted to Four women, followed by One women.[13]

Female Twos, particularly the Sexual subtypes, have been described as having seductress qualities: beautiful but dangerous. They can be charming to women they don't view as a threat, but are extremely competitive and even bitchy to women who are equally as attractive. Two women may exaggerate their sexuality to compensate for feeling sexually inadequate (for example, if they have a sexual or physical dysfunction).

Twos may have been "Daddy's little princess." Twos' fathers may have experienced their wives as argumentative, lacking in warmth or resentful of their attention of their daughter—as a result, father and daughter had formed a close bond, which could have become flirtatious as the daughter's Oedipus desire developed. As she became a teenager, the father may have felt uncomfortable with her behavior (cuddling and kissing, sitting on his lap) and withdrawn, leaving her feeling guilty, ashamed, rejected, and confused.[14]

Females Two will often dress in a revealing or provocative manner. Low cleavages and bright, sensual colors are favored, and they appear fun and frivolous. Ironically, after acting the outrageous flirt, when it comes to consummating the act, a Two may decide they simply can't follow through: "I have a headache." They may complain at length that their partners are a constant disappointment in the bedroom, lacking in technique or warmth—yet they themselves may lack the ability to initiate sex or reach orgasm. By blaming their "unskilled" lover, they coerce their partner to work harder to please them, which is what the Two wants.[15]

Male Twos: A less integrated Two man may adopt the softer, more emotive, theatrical, and needy aspect of a Two (more like a Type Four), while a less integrated Two woman may adopt the need to dominate and control (more like a Type Eight)—or vice versa. Being more in touch with their feminine sides, Male Twos may be attracted and relate to softer Maternal Fours or Paternal-type women such as Ones, Fives, or Sixes.

As in all types, there is tension in the polarities found in Twos' aggression and passivity.[16] Like Eights, Twos wills pursue a mate, but Eights do it to get and Twos to give. Skilled at reading others, male Twos can use their abilities to create instant intimacy: "I just knew you were going to say that. I felt you were feeling it." Suddenly the disinterested prey becomes interested: "How could you know that about me?"

Like Two females, male Twos (of any sexual orientation) may be overtly sexual—the Don Juans of the world—needing to hold and caress for reassurance, often to mask an underlying sexual dysfunction or even a sexual addiction.

Two men may project excessive manliness, even though in childhood their fathers were often emotionally or physically absent—meaning that they may not have actually participated in manly pursuits. "Yes, I loved football. Great days, great team we had in college," they may say, when in fact they were in the lowest-ranked team and avoided sport whenever possible. They may instead have been their mother's little confidant, providing a substitute for the emotional connection their mothers missed with their (absent) husbands. They like to see themselves as travelers or adventurers in a romantic way, as described by Jung's animus development level two, the "Man of Action or Romance."[17]

In general, male Twos may be harder to identify than their female counterparts. Society views women who sleep around as promiscuous, but men who do so are regarded as heroes by other men—it is therefore easier for a male Two to achieve the admiration he desires without social condemnation. Should he become impotent, his partner/s will be blamed. Homosexual or bisexual Two men widen the gap for a greater variety of lovers and thrills. [18]

Love Type: Maternal

Being nurturing, affectionate, caring, and focused on giving to the other rather than themselves, both male and female Twos demonstrate the energy of Maternal love. In integrated Twos, love is unconditional, warm, and forgiving—a caring and compassionate love that knows no bounds and is selfless in the higher levels of expression. In the less integrated Twos, it can become clinging, manipulative, possessive, and guilt-instilling, or involve martyr-type behavior.

Creating Dependencies

Twos need to woo others to get admiration. Unlike Type Fours, who will stand back and hope someone notices them, Twos go in active pursuit of a partner. They become highly attuned to the needs of a potential lover in order to seduce them into a relationship. [19] When the partner doesn't fulfil their desires, Twos can be very fickle and move effortlessly towards their next prospect and a more promising relationship. [20]

Less healthy Twos actively work towards making a lover financially, emotionally, protectively, sexually, or socially dependent, while insisting on maintaining their own independence. This gives them an air of entitlement and arrogance, as they believe they have the right to think and act on their partner's behalf and that they alone know what is best for their partner. This is why they are often attracted to fulfilling the role of rescuer or enabler for those they see as being dependent on their love and kindness. This can take the form of a codependent type being attracted to a narcissistically inclined lover. They may at times lash out in anger—"After all I've done for you!"—reciting all the good deeds they have been mentally taking score of. Twos like to be in charge, but often mask this need by appearing to acquiesce to their partner while subtly manipulating to achieve their desire.

Boundaries

Less integrated Twos typically have boundary issues. This may translate as them making themselves too much at home in a new partner's apartment on the first date—opening the fridge or cupboards, or checking their phone messages. A potential lover may agree to a date with a Two the following Friday only to find them uninvited on the doorstep on Tuesday, laden with food, flowers, and wine. Or they may come home to find their new Two lover happily tidying their drawers or fixing something in the kitchen. It would be hard to be angry as the Two was "just being thoughtful."

To get the extra connection and insight they desire, Twos may delve into a partner's emails or diary, or ask personal questions, such as, "How much do you earn?" In a relationship, they may have no qualms about prying into their partner's past love life, and may pressurize them into revealing their sexual secrets.

Over time this can be exhausting for the partner of a Two, who may become afraid to mention any need at all, knowing that it will be instantly fulfilled—but at an emotional cost. Twos may also cajole a partner into sexual acts they're not comfortable with.

Sacrifice

Twos are inclined to assume the role of martyr by sacrificing their needs for others. Take this Two's answer to a question relating to love and sex, which reveals their self-sacrificial approach to relationships:

> *I find myself as a very passionate person. I have a deep desire to please people around me, most importantly I have the deepest desire to please my family, be [it] in overall love and sexually. I often consider myself as the person that has to do the working, which I find is perfect for me. Love to me means being able to do everything in this world for those that are dear to me, those that are close to me with no expectation of anything in return.* [21]

In the above quote, the last few words show a higher level of integration. Compare that with the next quote, where we see the word "sacrifice":

> *Sex and Love are two completely different things. Love is about sacrifice; it's about the putting others' needs before your own; it's about kindness; respect; perseverance. Sex should be one of the means of expressing love. It could however also just be a physical act of satisfaction.* [22]

This Two has fallen into the trap of negating their needs, and while some may view it as admirable, this is not a balanced approach.

False Intimacy

Twos claim they desire intimacy, but they can subconsciously avoid it. Intimacy involves authenticity and, when they are not integrated, Twos fear showing up as themselves—if their partner doesn't enjoy their authentic self, warts and all, they risk rejection. Twos seek affirmation, so admitting that they give to get is painful for them to process. For this reason, they can lack commitment when going to therapy, or avoid it altogether. Real intimacy is replaced with boasting and inauthentic displays of "kindness."

Twos often report having "difficult" relationships, usually blaming a partner or series of partners for their experiences in love: "No matter how loving and thoughtful I am, I always seem to attract people who take advantage of me." Enneagram author, teacher, and psychologist Helen Palmer sees this as the need to avoid getting deeply involved and intimate. [23]

Giving to Get

Twos are strategically helpful and, if they aren't integrated, they may offer support that may seem to have no strings attached, although payback will be required at some point: "I set you up on a date that went really well! Now about your lending me your flat in France…" In a relationship, they may ask for nothing of you sexually, yet throw their toys out of the cot later, accusing you of making demands of them and never giving back, and shaming you into compliance. Fantasy and reality (lies and truth) may become intertwined if seduction requires it.

When you have spent your life focused on others' needs at the expense of your own, your feelings and sexual desires can feel distant and disconnected. You may not know what it is you feel or want sexually. As a result, Twos may not be willing to talk about something they find uncomfortable, such as their inability to ejaculate, the temper tantrum they threw last night, or the hurt they feel from a partner's rebuff. It also means that their partner's pleasure becomes *the* pleasure. Twos will often downplay their sexual needs and desires and focus exclusively on their partner: "See what a great lover I am, see how hard I work to give you pleasure." This can make them appear to be great lovers initially.

If a Two feels unappreciated or if their attempts to school a partner in lovemaking are met with resistance, they can quickly turn the tables and blame their partner for problems in the bedroom: "My ex made me orgasm every time and it could last for hours." "My last girlfriend really turned me on. My loss of erection is obviously your fault." Pleasure needs to be reciprocal and this is when Twos can come unstuck.

It can sometimes be difficult living with a Two if their idealized belief is that they are supremely kind, helpful, and loving. The nature of polarities dictates that the partner must assume the opposite role in the mind of the Two: being unkind, unhelpful, and unloving (a Two's shadow projection). This can result in the very thing the Two fears most: being alone.

I'll Be Whatever You Want

Twos adapt to an individual they wish to pursue or impress. The Two's ability to adopt roles and explore the fantasies of another creates the gateway to sexual gratification beyond the traditional. Author and Enneagram teacher Judith Searle suggests that Twos are likely to be sexually explorative, whether that involves swinging, being bi-sexual, or exploring sexuality in general. She suggests that the Type Four-Eight (female-male) dynamic divided by the Type Two (as discussed in the section on "Female Twos") may result in Twos exploring gender roles more readily than other types. [24] Naranjo suggests that for Twos, everything is permissible when it comes to love and when thinking is swept away by feeling.[25]

Skilled at tapping into the needs of others, Twos pick up on their desired partner's ideal partner: *Are they needing someone strong and decisive, or someone funny, sexy, and romantic? Do they have an interest in art? Music? Wine? Then I'll "develop" that interest myself, so we can be more intimate and share interests. If we both love the same things, that must mean we're close and good for each other.*

Their very identity resides in relationships.[26] These "interests" seldom remain once that partner has moved on. They also fit easily into sexual role playing. The partner wants a nurse, a dominatrix, the shepherd/shepherdess outfit, a stripper? Twos can easily accommodate. The payoff is more power and control.[27] When they are integrated, they can accurately mirror to a partner, when less integrated, they become a mirror of the partner.

The Need for Relationship

With Twos finding it hardest of all the Enneagram types to not be in a relationship, they will compromise their choices to secure a significant other: "Yes, she's pretty messed up," a Two confided to me regarding a new partner. "She's possessive, reactive, maybe even narcissistic, but then most people have some baggage."

If they don't get what they desire, they can switch to being rejecting and even aggressive, taking on the role of wounded martyr: "Women just take advantage of me because I'm such a soft target." "You'd have been nothing without me."

See Me, Feel Me

Twos need the constant reassurance of touch. Touch creates security. Their view would be "I'm being affectionate," when in truth it's more about ownership—control masquerading as romance.

Twos can pride themselves on their sexual feats and abilities: "Look how well endowed I am." "Look at how many times I could get you to orgasm." Women particularly can manipulate men with sex. The need for love can become so all-consuming that Twos can fly into a rage.

Twos may believe that getting their partner stimulated is stimulation for themselves. Psychologist Sandra Pertot describes two types of Reactive Lovers (closest to Type Two): those who really do enjoy making sex all about the other, and those who martyr themselves to their partner's needs in order to maintain the relationship.[28] In the language of the Enneagram, I would suggest that the first type is an integrated version of Type Two.

Happy Together

Twos, like Nines and Sevens, are one of the "happy" numbers of the Enneagram and can fake happiness to create excitement and stimulation. They commonly enjoy new experiences, which makes travel right up there on their list of things to do. It serves two purposes because it creates fun times and ensures a partner's full-time attention. At home, a partner may be focused on work or children, but on vacation, "I have you all to myself." Relationships to a Two can be polarized as either "wonderful" or "horrible," a fairy tale or a nightmare. Simply put, this translates as relationships that enhance their view of themselves as selfless and relationships that do not.

The Instinctual Drives

Self-preservation Twos *(counterphobic)*: Enneagram writer Beatrice Chestnut refers to Self-preservation Type Twos as playing out in a sense of "Privilege."[29] It indicates the focus inward towards self—a "me-first"[30] approach, which results in the countertype, as opposed to the typical Two's drive outward towards the other.

This subtype can resemble a child in many ways, as opposed to the more adult or worldly Social Two, or the wild and wanton Sexual Two. Take this bubbly Self-preservation Two's view of love and sex: "Absolutely beautiful! ☺ And they are free! When you give these freely, you get back even more than you could imagine! Beautiful.☺ "[31] (Twos just love smiley face and heart emojis!)

A child's needs are often met before an adult's, hence this "importance of me" belief. Historically, this dynamic has played out in traditional manners and customs—for example, a ("strong") man (archetypal Eight) must give up his jacket for a ("weak") woman (archetypal Two), or walk closest to the road to protect her, as one might do a child.

These subtypes seek a partner who will look after and protect them—a father or mother figure who will make them the center of attention and love them simply for being (as one would a child). Think of the wide-eyed child no one can resist, the teacher's pet, or the charming, cute child-person.[32] To do this, they adopt coquettish, childlike behavior that invites a rescuer. Their body language or childish way of speaking conveys the message "Take care of me." These Twos will often appear to be younger than they are, and may even dress in a childlike manner. Their seduction may play on the notion of innocence: "Will Daddy be gentle with his little girl?" Interestingly, the virtue of Type Eight is innocence, and the point of release is Type Two—so a Type Eight male may evoke this parody of an "innocent" adult in the Type Two.

These Twos also charm and disarm those they wish to seduce with humor, banter, spontaneous pleasure, uplifting energy, and a general sense of playful fun (which can make them appear like a hedonistic Type Seven). Like the kid who can't resist eating every cupcake at the party, Self-preservation Twos may be unable to stop themselves. This can also result in them sleeping with people they aren't particularly attracted to, but whose attention itself is desirable. They may not be able to resist spilling the beans about an illicit sexual encounter. Should the urge arise, they may act irresponsibly—like having unprotected sex in the office toilet. Like children, they may not want to take on responsibilities and commitments (such as three kids from a partner's first marriage), and may throw temper tantrums when their desires are thwarted or they feel rejected in any way or form.

For those used to seeing Twos as the compulsive helpers and givers of the world, it's easy to see how the Self-preservation Two could be mistyped. Sevens want fun to escape pain; Self-preservation Twos use fun to appear more desirable. Self-preservation Twos are more guarded in their connections, even to the point of shyness, and may be mistaken for a mistrusting Six—particularly because, like Sixes, they can be more ambivalent in love than the Sexual Two or the confident Social Two.

Social Twos: Here, pride is revealed in upwardly mobile ambition— Social Twos want to be recognized as people of standing. They navigate groups and societies with confidence and will easily slip into a leadership role to appear more desirable. They are often referred to by the name "Ambition" as they manipulate groups rather than individuals and pride themselves on being better than others. They know how to pull strings and influence others to get their needs met. [33]

They need to be seen to be important, so while chatting up a potential partner they will name drop, mention the prestigious university they attended (omitting to mention it was only for a two-week course), and casually let slip the number of lovers they've attracted: "Yes, I attended Harvard. Bill Gates was actually a friend of mine." "I found this stunning girl half my age, waiting in my bedroom for me. She just couldn't get enough." These Twos can also be typical enablers, using a partner's addictions and their acceptance of their partner's "faults" to ensure they won't leave. [34]

In relationships, they can be more possessive, exploitive, and controlling than the other subtypes, seducing with a hidden agenda and the currency of wealth, fame, and power. A less integrated Social Two may declare that they are feeling vulnerable, in love, or emotional, but this may be staged to achieve a desired result. In this sense, they often appear to be more Three- (goal-orientated) or Eight-like (bossy and controlling) in their approach. [35]

When less integrated, they like to feel that they are better than their partners—that they may have traveled more, achieved more, or have more money. It is very important to them to feel indispensable, while not wanting to feel their partner is indispensable to them. A Social Two, when asked about love and sex uses the word "achieve": "I am always yearning to either achieve or show love to those closest to me." [36]

Female Social Twos are nothing like their wilder Sexual sisters. They need social status and want to be seen as intelligent and accomplished.

There is a quieter, more adult and withdrawn aspect to them than either of the other Two subtypes. Their dress sense will reflect this by being less flashy and revealing.

Sexual Twos: This subtype is the most typical of the Twos.[37] If Social Twos seduce groups; Sexual Twos seduce individuals. Social Twos win attention through self-importance; Sexual Twos win attention through sexuality and seduction. As such, they are the most overtly sexual of the subtypes. Twos want to be confided in, and Sexual Twos in particular enjoy the intimacy of hearing their partner's secrets. To seduce, they can find themselves conforming to what they believe the other is looking for in a partner, or they may profess similar tastes and interests in order to create connection.

Sexual Two men tend to be more seductive, while women can be "femme fatales"[38]—aggressive when it comes to pursuing a love interest and fixated on the relationship. Sexual Two women can be irresistible, yet like female spiders they may eat up their prey when their goal has been achieved. The predator aggression of female Sexual Twos can be seen in the attractive woman who targets a wealthy elderly man, using every seductive trick in the book; such as being initially generous with her own money to con him into believing she has no designs on his fortune— giving to get. Or think of the "dumb blonde" act, which lures suitors with looks to hide canny intelligence. This behavior can include "cock-teasing" to lure a partner into commitment. When less integrated, Sexual Twos declare themselves to be lovers of love, in the name of which they may act in ways that hurt and harm, such as being exploitive, for which they take little or no responsibility.

With their point of release at Type Eight, where "you belong to me," the Sexual Two can be overtly possessive. They enjoy the power that comes from being adored and are also sensual, like Eights—a Sexual Two describes love and sex as being "like wine and food... all part of the sensual experience of being alive in our bodies."[39] To win over the object of their desire, they take pride in their appearance and like to convey that they have great depth of feeling (even if it is enacted). Unlike the more reserved adult and intellectual Social type, they are fun, irresistible, spontaneous, and flirtatious.

Even if they hold powerful positions in business, the Sexual Two's relationship and sexual needs will take precedence over everything else. There is a dangerous aspect to them and an insatiable desire to create passion in others to get what they want (which is everything); they gravitate to the rich and powerful, who can provide a limitless credit card. Yet, as this Sexual Two describes, sex and love can be extremely painful:

> *Love [makes you] vulnerable and is often times very difficult. My experience and expectation of love has evolved over the years and is a more beautiful picture than I imagined. Sex on the other hand is different—I think my expectations for it are still misaligned to reality; it is such a selfless act and yet there is so much of the self that you bring to it. Figuring out how to manage these tensions is pretty challenging.* [40]

The Wings

Two with a One-wing *(Maternal and Paternal love):* In this subtype, Two's warmth meets One's perfection. When integrated, this subtype can be truly motivated to improve the world without any agenda. You'll often find them as teachers, ministers, politicians, or in the field of health. They serve without the need for accolade or praise. This subtype is cooler and more reserved (the Paternal influence) than the Two with a Three-wing. Boundaries may be more established.

As they reach the average level of emotional health, this subtype more obviously displays the paradox between the Two's need for intrapersonal and emotional relationships and the One's rational, impersonal, and more controlled approach. There is a greater sense of obligation for what they do for a partner—the desire to be a "good" wife or husband. "Love/sex is the passion you should have towards your partner," [41] was the way a Two described their relationship—note the use of the word "should," a favorite word for Ones.

These Twos can take their need to give to their lover to the point of self-neglect. Their actions imply "It's all about you," yet resentment builds beneath that warm surface, and can be expressed as criticism towards the loved one.

Sex is also going to be more controlled and less expressive in this subtype. They may annoy a partner by feeling the need to improve them. Because of the One influence, they also have stronger morals and may be more self-righteous than the other type. [42] They don't enjoy being proved wrong and may deny or defy any attempt to do so.

Two with a Three-wing *(Maternal and Erotic love):* When integrated, the Two's desire to connect combined with a Three's authenticity results in genuine intimacy. The Three aspect makes them more charming, outgoing, and comfortable in company, and more demanding sexually. Relationships are foremost on their agendas. They are more likely to give of their gifts than to simply want to take care of others. When less healthy, they enjoy gossip, trading the intimate secrets of others for connection.

Both being shame types, Twos and Threes on the average emotional level create a double whammy of shame—but Twos want to mask their shame by *doing* more for others, and Threes by *being* more. Like Threes, they may use work achievements to avoid inner work, and can become workaholics as a result. There is greater ambition and a desire to social climb. When it comes to choosing a partner, their concern is, "Will he/she enhance my status?" Name-dropping and focusing on their achievements are important.

This subtype can be more demanding and direct about their needs (the Erotic Three influence). Because they lack the other wing type's critical One viewpoint, they are less likely to fault find with themselves and others, but more inclined to elevate themselves (like the Three). Above all else, they want to be desired and admired.

Moving to Sexual Presence

What Blocks Twos from Sexual Fulfillment

Control is very much a part of sex. When Twos are working to satisfy another's needs, they are essentially in control—they decide how much, when, where, and what to give. It is sometimes harder to receive than to give because receiving involves surrendering to whatever the partner chooses to give. Not being able to receive reflects a desire to maintain control and an inability to surrender, creating a power dynamic akin to that of a less integrated Eight. Twos don't enjoy it if you disregard or don't sufficiently appreciate their giving. As Naranjo puts it, Twos make love, but through their aggressive tendencies (and their Eight connection), they also make war.[43]

Focusing on pleasing another while sublimating or ignoring your own needs creates imbalance. When Twos let go of their prideful belief that it is always them who gives, they will learn to receive the many gifts that surrendering brings. True power lies in the vulnerability of surrendering or receiving. While Twos may talk about and act as if they are familiar with intimacy, the truth is usually that they have seldom experienced real intimacy. They need to learn that sex doesn't necessarily equal intimacy—the path to genuine intimacy is in being authentic.

How Twos Can Become Sexually Present

Acknowledge your needs: Twos become genuinely present if they allow themselves to be aware of and express their needs (sexual or otherwise), and see their needs as being as important as those of their partner's.

Allow yourself to receive: Don't make sex conditional on what you've given your partner. If Twos can start to recognize their motivations and why they feel compelled to give, they can start to show up more authentically in their relationships by being able to receive.

Move to humility: Twos should try to acknowledge the Passion of pride and where it shows up in their actions, and own their hidden need for reciprocation. This can move them from having codependent relationships to those of unconditional, genuine love, where superficial concern is replaced with genuine empathy and giving flows freely from the heart.

Allow genuine intimacy: It is helpful for Twos to consider the difference between deep, intimate love and superficial sex, and learn to differentiate between them. Love does not need to be a drama to be true, neither does it need to take the form of rescuing others and creating dependencies. Holding someone's hand or constantly stroking their arm is not necessarily an act of intimacy. It could be an act of possession or desire to hold on to another. Integrated Twos are neither possessive or needy.

Develop your own interests: Rather than attempt to mirror a partner's interests, Twos should develop their own. In this way they make themselves whole, rather than needing someone else to feel whole or fulfilled. This can mean that Twos need time alone to discover themselves when they are not in a constant giving role.

Get in touch with your own feelings: Instead of avoiding their feelings or understanding events as either "bad" or "good," Twos can attempt to acknowledge unpleasant events without needing to dismiss and deny them. Talking through arguments and taking ownership of their role in them (as opposed to blaming others) is hugely beneficial on the road to authenticity, and will also help Twos to create deeper, more authentic connections.

Let go of the need to boost yourself: To grow, Twos need to let go of the need to be admired to feel worthy of love. They are already enough.

Questions to Journal

NOTE: It's useful to answer these questions no matter what your type.

- What do you desire sexually?
- In sex with your partner, are you aware of how much easier you find giving than receiving? Why is this?
- Do you flatter a partner, as opposed to giving an authentic compliment?
- How does pride show up in your giving?

6

Type Six:
The Loyal Lover

Six's motto: "Finding the courage to love in the face of fear that it won't work out."

Six as lover: Funny, reliable, and engaging, Sixes bring welcome fortitude to a relationship, but their ambivalent natures can make them doubt love: "Does he/she really love me for who I am? What's their motive in the relationship?" As a result, they seek reassurance about a partner's love.

Sixes' sex is conditional: on duty, hard work, and taking care of or supporting a partner, and on being "safe" from potential hazards (STDs, unwanted pregnancy, etc.).

You may relate to aspects of a Six even if it's not your type: if you are a Five or Seven (the wings), or if you are a Three or Nine (the points of stretch and release).

Love type: Paternal. Sixes seek authoritarian figures whom they can admire or follow, while they doubt their own power. They can also be authority figures themselves. Being Head types, they are more inclined to think rather than feel emotions.

Relationship belief: "I am committed in my relationships. Partners can depend on me."

Sexual frustration: "My partner doesn't pull their weight—I always end up doing more." "No one is as loyal as I am." "Whatever I do when I make love seems to be wrong."

Understanding Type Six's Sexuality

Brief Overview

Sixes can be a bundle of contradictions—as much as one thing may be true of a Six, so might its opposite. They are one of the three Fear types, but the strong Sexual counterphobic Type Six goes against fear, meaning that anxious Sixes can sometimes appear courageous and fearless. While everyone else on a plane is dozing or reading the free magazines, the Six will have read the safety instructions and will know where the safety exits are, how to use the oxygen mask and where to locate the life jacket. If something does go wrong, Sixes will organize the evacuation because they've already studied the drill.

Six lovers are likely to be as cautious in their choice of partner. They want someone who can be trusted and who will make them feel safe, because loyal people don't leave you in the lurch—protective Eight men and fearful Six women are a common match. Likewise, Sixes may enjoy being part of a religious order, team or organization that offers safety in numbers.

Sixes have an ability to intuitively know stuff before it happens: "I just had this feeling I should cross the road, and as I did, this car came out of nowhere and crashed into the path where I'd been walking." The trouble is, Sixes don't always trust this intuition: *Is it really inner knowing, or just nagging doubt? When to act on it and when not to? Hmm... I'll ask my boss/phone a friend/check with the systems department/study the instructions again...* To the degree that they lack confidence (and unless integrated, they do), they struggle to trust their inner knowing and so seek input from others (who may not have the insight they do). It is hugely frustrating for a Six to follow the advice of a partner, knowing deep down that it's not the right advice. Yet they fear separating from the mothership and going it alone.

Palmer refers to this indecision as playing the "devil's advocate"[1] because Sixes can see both sides of the story. Doing so makes them able to walk in another person's shoes, and as a result they are the most potentially compassionate of the types.

Sixes are also ambivalent when it comes to authority figures. Some may intimidate them, while they may want to align themselves with others in order to feel protected: "If he says that's what needs to happen, then I'll have their backing and won't have to face the music alone." But doing so comes at the cost of a Six's own sense of knowing the right action. Along with submission to a higher authority comes the desire to rebel against it.

In a relationship, this can look like this: "I'll appear to go along with whatever you say, while covertly undermining the authority I've allowed you to assume." Sixes nevertheless enjoy being in a relationship—it's safer to stand together than be apart. They long for love, yet placing their happiness in the hands of a lover can itself be scary.

The Arising of Type Six

You're five years old, balancing on a wall you've been encouraged to climb by an older sibling. You look down and suddenly feel huge fear: you'll surely fall and hurt yourself, Mom will be furious, and your friends will laugh at your clumsiness. Suddenly the world looks very scary. You feel unsupported and alone. You don't trust yourself to be able to climb down safely, but you don't trust anyone else to help you either. You also don't want to look like a coward. Who to call for help? What to do? You've lost faith in your ability and the courage you had when you first stepped onto the wall has disappeared.

This is the world of Sixes. From a young age they lost trust, both in themselves and the world. When they wanted to jump to safety, a strong paternal figure wasn't around (emotionally or physically) to catch them or tell them everything would be fine. Without a strong father-like presence to guide them to independence, Sixes may have felt overwhelmed by a mother or mother figure. The absence of the father created a feeling that the world was not safe—and the attentions of an overprotective mother confirmed this. Fear and courage fought an internal battle. Now, life is about what can and can't be trusted. Loyalty is more important than love, because what is love if not trust and loyalty? In life, Sixes are always alert—looking for danger or what could go wrong. Other people just don't seem to understand the danger that's out there.

Sixes in Love

Integrated Sixes: When Sixes feel they have a partner who is the other pillar holding up their relationship temple, when they feel this partner is faithful, and when they can differentiate between imagined and real danger, they can relax into being. Their inner knowing becomes a consistent source of guidance, negating the need to seek outside reassurance. They trust their intuition and know the right course of action, engaging all three centers of gut, head, and heart to make their choices.

Letting go of the need to be suspicious of everything and everyone, as well as the fear of rejection, means integrated Sixes are more open to their sexuality and relationships. They can support a partner's ventures and be reliable companions who are honest and warm, with a playful sense of humor. Sixes are compassionate and good listeners, making them ideal candidates for careers in the healing arena. Integrated Sixes have dropped reactivity and replaced it with courageous action. They trust themselves and they trust others. They stop sweating the small stuff, and calmly and courageously embrace challenges.

Average Sixes: If Sixes feel safe in a relationship, they are easy to be with and their loyalty means marriages can be long-lasting. They are happy to meet a partner's needs before their own, but unlike Twos they don't expect anything but loyalty in return. There's a warm camaraderie that exists when they're not being doubtful and ambivalent.

As they become less integrated, Sixes may thwart their desire for a relationship because of the potential for rejection, or the fear that things may not work out as planned.[2] The answer to "What could possibly go wrong?" becomes "Everything!" One day they may appear committed to the relationship, the next day doubt and fear may set in, and they'll decide to end things. They also start to doubt how they feel: *Do I really love her? What is real love? She does this annoying thing of tapping her foot up and down—does that mean I'll just end up getting more irritated?*

Sixes look for motives: "I know you said you love me, but what do you really mean? Maybe it's only because I'm the breadwinner." They may become obsessive in their worry, their monkey minds[3] playing games with logic and the voices in their heads telling them different stories. Feeling insecure may mean that marriage becomes about security rather than love as the Six follows their head more than their heart. They can go into a marriage to escape an existing unstable relationship or an unhappy home life.

They enjoy routines and may become complacent, unwilling to step beyond the known. They may have no problem deciding to marry (big decision), but then may struggle to decide what to wear to the wedding (small decision).[4] Their protectiveness of a partner can be experienced as smothering, particularly to types who enjoy freedom. Sexually, Sixes may be less inclined to try anything new in bed and can even be prudish and conservative (unless they are the Sexual counterphobic type).[5]

Disintegrated Sixes: Feeling alone and left out, Sixes can easily become depressed and feel abandoned by those they felt were loyal—like deer in headlights, paralyzed by fear and expecting the worst. Therapy may help, although a Six might doubt the integrity and motivations of the therapist.

As Sixes disintegrate, they become more reactive and reason flies out of the window (together with a piece of china or two). They become increasingly unpredictable and prickly: "I should never have gone into this relationship. It was doomed from the beginning. I should have known you weren't to be trusted." In this headspace they can be suspicious, controlling, paranoiac, opiniated, inflexible, and sarcastic. They want to divide and rule, and will vacillate between regarding a partner as friend and foe.

When the head and heart no longer communicate, Sixes live in a state of anxiety and panic, where no one can be relied upon or trusted. They swing between dominance and submission. Those they trusted are now sent packing.

Sixes have the strength of being to be able to maintain marriages and relationships—if a partner has walked a rocky relationship road, this can be a comforting and endearing quality. They are devoted to their partner, and whatever causes or career their lover embraces.

What Six Dating Adverts May Look Like

Rashid, 43

Hi. My name is Rashid. I'm a SM, 6'1, with a reasonably good build (a tad lanky perhaps). I've been told that I'm nice looking, intuitive, funny, and that I communicate well (but that's by my mum, so you'll have to believe her!). I'm tired of playing games—what I want is to find someone who values the words "loyalty" and "sincerity" as much as I do. I have a willingness to give 100% in a relationship. I battle to open jars and am afraid (really afraid) of spiders, so that'll have to be you. I hope we can become friends. In the meantime, smile—and remember we all deserve love.

Nurse Olivia, 32

Before you read further, I should tell you that I somehow manage to spill ice cream (Rocky Road, mostly) on myself every time I eat it—which is often. If that hasn't put you off, read on… I'm a nursing sister and I love what I do. Mostly, I love the people I work with at the hospital—we're a great team. I'm no supermodel, but I enjoy sport (endurance running). I love cooking and do a great Julia Child impersonation. (One day I'll have my own restaurant.) My special skill (other than cooking) is standing on one foot while balancing a bottle

on my nose. Scoff if you like, but it occasionally wins me
free drinks at the pub! So if you're chilled, don't mess around
in relationships, and at least 72% awesome (and if you can
tolerate my Nutella addiction), drop me a line!

The Passion of Fear and the Fixation of Worry

Because they can imagine every possible outcome, Sixes are the scenario planners of the world: *Why couldn't he see me tonight? Is he really tied up at work? He's been cool lately—maybe he's not into me... Hang on, we didn't have our usual Thursday sex because I was at that school function... Maybe he's met someone else?* On and on the possible scenarios play out in the Six's brain. Her man was probably just working late, but in the end the Six is almost certain he's found love elsewhere.

Sixes also worry about future events that seldom manifest:

It's six months since Dave and Jill ended things. I'd really
like to ask her out, but will Dave be mad at me? Or maybe
Jill will think bad of me for trying to date a friend's ex.
Maybe our friends will think it's odd. What if I called and
she refused? Or, if she did accept, wouldn't the first date be
awkward? Can I trust her after what Dave said about her?
Maybe I should phone Ted to see what he thinks.

There is a belief among Sixes that if they think up every possible thing that could go wrong, then they'll have created a barrier against those things going wrong. (Often the one thing they didn't imagine is the thing that actually happens!)

Fears can take all forms, but in relationships fear tends to center around rejection, betrayal, impotence, premature ejaculation, loneliness, losing control during sex, falling out of love after committing, not being a good lover, or not being performing as well as their partner's previous lover... You get the idea. It's not surprising that these fears create more stress, which can lead to the very issues that created the stress.

Sixes also project their thoughts, motivations, desires, feelings, and fears onto others—accusing others of things of which they themselves are guilty. So, a Six who does not trust him/herself to be faithful may project mistrust onto a partner, imagining the partner is having an illicit liaison. Sixes' own guilt can convert to blame in the process: [6] "He's deliberately having premature ejaculations, so I can't be fulfilled." "She won't allow herself to reach an orgasm just so that I feel like a failure as a lover."[7]

A Peek into a Six's Bedroom

Sixes are relatively ordered. Unlike Ones, they are not neat because it's the "right" thing to do, but because they feel safer when there is order in the universe (or their bedrooms). Following the decorating "rules" of their community or childhood, a Six's style may be traditional or conservative, and will likely incorporate family memorabilia. They often have natural taste, knowing just what to match with what. They're also sure to have a good security system!

Fantasies and Erotica

"I seldom have fantasies," said a Six woman. "I would feel disloyal to my husband if I thought about another man—as if someone else was in the bedroom—so I'd rather focus on what's happening in bed right now. It doesn't feel right any other way."

Sixes may avoid sharing their fantasies for fear of either being rejected by a shocked partner, or they may be afraid that a jealous partner will seek revenge for their imagined indiscretions. Paranoia and projection inhibit sexual communication and expression.[8]

Fantasies may involve situations where they explore what sex (and life) would be like without fear and responsibility; where they stop being so worried about what their partner is thinking or the negative aspects of sex ("Will I get an STD?" "Will my affair be discovered?").

In the Birnbaum study, the fantasies of 48 couples were studied over a three-week period. It found that the fantasies of individuals high in "anxious attachment" focused on being supported, intimate, and showing affection. Fantasies on days of relationship strain mirrored their desire for security and safety, but also revealed a powerful partner (representing safety) in whose control the individual felt helpless and who derived pleasure from humiliating them (revealing their insecurity).[9] The desire for safety and security then can come at the cost of autonomy.

Our sexual beliefs are often molded in our childhoods, and depend on the environments in which we were raised. Sixes are often drawn to religious groups, who provide a higher authority to guide decision-making. These "rules" can play havoc in the lives of Sixes, who fear breaking them yet equally desire to rebel against them. This can result in a constricted, repressed sexual view. Some of these rules, found across many different belief systems, could include disapproving ideas about sexual orientation, premarital sex, sex for pleasure (rather than procreation), masturbation, or erotica.

Sixes can be filled with the dilemma between their own desires and the ideas of the doctrine they subscribe to. What to do? This could well be why states in the USA who are known for being religious or having more conservative values have been found to purchase substantially more porn subscriptions [10]—the tension between these poles drives sexuality "underground."

Sixes who are traveling or afraid of contracting diseases through sexual contact may opt for porn as a safe way to get aroused. One Six said:

> *My desire to have sex means I would like to have hook-ups regularly, as I'm not in a committed relationship. But the problem arises because unless I'm with someone I know and trust, I don't feel I want to have sex. My attempts to overcome this fear and just do it anyhow have failed miserably and resulted in my feeling more unsafe.*

Sixes of Different Genders

Female Sixes: The archetypal 1950s woman was portrayed in the media as mysterious, fickle, dutiful, anxious, respectful of authority (her husband), needful of protection, a homemaker, and keenly desirous of a good marriage (security). There are many similarities with Six women, who may choose strong, dominating Eights in order to feel safe (while male Sixes commonly choose attractive Twos and Nines). [11] Yet having a strong partner often comes at the price of freedom and having to prostitute their own needs and desires for security. Sixes want to please their partners but may become so fixated on this idea that they become tense. Women in particular can believe that voicing their needs is likely to result in rejection or humiliation. A paranoid Six woman can, as a result, become completely victimized by a partner, yet be afraid to act.

While they may fantasize about sleeping with different people, Six women may resist actual sex because of fears around health, pregnancy, or being discovered. Oral sex may feel degrading or humiliating. Women may fear being hurt or in some way "dirtied," or that her partner just wants to use her. [12]

Male Sixes: There can be an old-fashioned correctness about male Sixes, as this Six man suggests:

> *Sending an SMS to ask someone out just feels wrong. I'd rather pick up the phone than hide behind new technology. Best would be for her to call me, because then I won't risk rejection, but I know that's a cowardly way out.*

Six men will want to know that the care and protection they offer is valued and appreciated, and that you're on the same team, although some may see sex as a trap designed to lure them into a lifetime of providing. Generally, though, they want to be the ideal partner. If they marry a type who likes to travel, they will want to please by going along, even though it pushes them out of their comfort zones; alternatively, they'll offer little resistance to staying at home alone. They worry their partner might leave them if they don't comply, but at the same time they don't want a partner to have authority over them. Some Sixes enjoy being pushed out of their comfort zones and choose partners who do this:

> *At work I'm in a leadership role, so sexually I find it more relaxing to be in a submissive role. I enjoy my partner taking control. But it's tricky finding someone who is prepared to take the lead in the bedroom but be submissive in the relationship otherwise.*

They enjoy routines in a relationship. A comment from a Six with a strong Five-wing is that: "I enjoy our regularly scheduled sex. I enjoy seeing how our bodies work together and then thinking up ways to improve that."

When less integrated, Six men can become paranoiac regarding their sexual exploits, particularly if they overlay their desires with religious "rules": "I can masturbate," a Six man told me, "as long as I don't think about women."

Sixes can be known to take articles in the media too personally because they provoke fear: "Can you believe it?! This guy slept with this woman, and while he was orgasming she murdered him!" (*Could that happen to me with Fred?*) Seeking the sanctity of a safe and supportive marriage may ultimately feel like the best option—"It's us against the depravity of the world." [13]

Love Type: Paternal (Countertype)

Sixes are the Paternal Love countertype, seeking out authority figures, powerful people, heroes, or others they can admire and look up to. (The other paternal types, One and Five, like to be the authority figures themselves.) An exception is the counterphobic Sexual Six, who may be more inclined to assume an authoritarian role, and so is less of a Love countertype.

Sixes are one of the three Head or Thinking types of the Enneagram, together with Fives and Sevens. Like Fives, they can appear somewhat cool and remote in relationships. Although the Self-preservation type is often described as being "warm," there can be a feeling of "internal coldness"[14] even in this type. Romance can be lost in their search for loyalty.

Paternal love-type Sixes may hero worship rather than choose to be the hero themselves (or vacillate between the two roles). Powerful people make them feel less afraid:

> *My husband could not understand why I was drawn to powerful men. Not sexually, but I enjoyed their company and would go out of my way to accommodate them. Through the Enneagram, I realized it was just because I felt safe with them. As if I wanted the reassurance that if anything went wrong, I'd have support.*

In our imbalanced society, where paternal interests typically take precedence, the role of the father or paternal figure frequently becomes distorted in the following ways:

- He/she may have been absent.
- He/she may have been a tyrant, which caused a Six child to fear them.
- He/she may have abused their position of power and been overly authoritarian or abusive.
- He/she may have been overly afraid, making a Six's worldview one of suspicion, fear, and caution.
- He/she perhaps went the opposite way and became overly protective, making a Six child feel smothered and afraid of life in general: "If they are so protective, there must be a lot of bad things they need to protect me from."[15]
- A child might have had to forgo their own needs to cater to the demands of the parent.

Ambivalence

Because they fluctuate between obedience and disobedience, leading and following, fearing aggression and being aggressive, being dominant or submissive, and a host of other contradictory behaviors, Sixes can be hard to gauge.

The Fear of Being Taken Advantage OF

In marriage, Sixes will work long and hard to create a successful relationship. They have a fear of being abused, abandoned, or taken advantage of, so all runs smoothly if their partner is equally tethered to the cart. Feeling they are carrying the load alone will not work. [16]

Sixes may get into a loop of complaining endlessly to friends about their relationship, sex life, or lack thereof, and yet do very little to alter the situation. [17]

What Could Possibly Go Wrong?

Sixes often overcommit and are then afraid of letting people down. When less integrated, they can have a depressed view of the world and relationships, expecting the worst while forgetting all the good times. They are fearful of messing up or of what could happen if they don't please their partner. The smallest tiff can have them feeling that the relationship is doomed. Sixes can go crazy with these scenarios, stressing for ages about decisions before they act. At times when things go pear-shaped and others get annoyed, Sixes will seek reassurance: "I know we had an arrangement, and I'm sorry I didn't pitch. Do I still mean something in your life?"

This fear of what could go wrong has them vacillating when it comes to dating, like this Six:

The prospects for long-term relationships seem bleak. I haven't been on a date in four years! I'm not sure why men are attracted to me. My friendships with my colleagues are great, yet nothing ever seems to move beyond drinks after work. Dating makes me anxious and so, rather than look for an online prospect, I've resigned myself to having friends, sport, my cat, and my career. It's not what I want, but I don't know how to move beyond the fear of engaging with a stranger and so I have to take care of my own sexual needs.

Afraid that they might be betrayed by a partner, they may break off a relationship rather than experience rejection (as Threes do). They may also decide to have several relationships, being unable to decide on one: "There's the person I enjoy debating with, who intellectually inspires me (Head); the person I really love, but fear being with (Heart); and the person I have sex with (Gut)."

Suspicious Minds

Remember the Elvis song? It could have been written for Sixes. They make great detectives because they are constantly looking for clues and are naturally attuned to picking up on things many others would miss: "Does it mean anything that you've worked late five nights in a row?" "Your car smells different. Someone else's perfume?" "If you say you worked late and ate at the office, then why are you eating that slice of toast?"

Sometimes it can seem that whatever a partner does to reassure a Six of their love just creates more doubt. (It's a bit like trying to answer the question: "Do I look fat in this?") Fear makes Sixes inept when it comes to accepting compliments: *By saying I'm great in bed, is she saying I'm useless at everything else? Or maybe she just wants to have sex more often?*[18] Because of their self-doubt and insecurity, Sixes may question their relationship: *Does he really love me, or do I just offer security and a well-decorated home?*

A conversation with a Six could start like this and go unsteadily downhill:

> *"Do you honestly love me?"*
> *"Yes, of course I do, otherwise I wouldn't have married you."*
> *"You don't sound too convinced...?"*
> *"I am absolutely convinced."*
> *"Then why did you look at that guy riding past on a bike yesterday?"*

If you're in a relationship with a Six, understanding their need for reassurance can go a long way to calming their insecurities: "Honey, I know I've been working away a lot, and it's horrible because I really miss you. Let's have dinner out to reconnect." Like Fours, they may focus on what's not in the relationship rather than what is. Although they want their partner to be open with them, they may not be able to reciprocate because being guarded is their way of protecting themselves.

It's a fine balance: a Six may confuse their partner by appearing to distance themselves because of their need not to feel smothered, only to feel abandoned and need their partner to reassure them that they are loved.

Sex to Relieve Tension

Particularly for women, it is difficult to have sex and reach orgasm when anxious, distracted, or worried. Yet according to Professor Gert Holstege, anxiety is reduced through orgasm [19]—creating a catch-22 situation. For the Six, particularly in a new relationship, the nervous expectation of healthy, anxiety-reducing sex can itself create stress. Sport is a great way to relieve this tension (as is sex!).

If Sixes get used to sex as their way of stress relief, not having it can make them grumpy. A partner may feel pressurized into have sex just to keep things happy, and so may themselves feel more like an instrument than a lover. Sixes need to be aware of the tendency for things to become automated and impersonal, and make sure they appreciate and honor their partners as much as they need to be appreciated and honored.

Scheduled Sex

Sixes often struggle with decision-making, so regular sex dates will relieve them of the need to figure out the right time. As one Six said: "We schedule sex three times a week. I like to know ahead of time what nights to prepare. I'm not spontaneous about sex—we'd rather mark it on our calendar!"

This can come at the price of excitement: "same old, same old" isn't the script for hot sex. Partners can become bored: "She only wants to do missionary style. I'd like to try something different." Sixes could benefit from understanding that while loyalty and steadfastness are great things to have in a relationship, a little deviation from the road well traveled can enhance a relationship. [20] In contrast, Sixes who are able to easily access their counterphobic aspect will be keen on wild, explorative, unplanned sex—anything to show to themselves and their partners that they aren't afraid. When Sixes are with people they can trust, they may be happy to become explorative, particularly if their partner is more adventurous:

> *I will try new things, so long as I can be in control and I*
> *trust the person I'm with. I'll know if it's working for me or*
> *not, so I need to feel I can make the call to stop things if I'm*

feeling uncomfortable. I'll often watch the kink on a porn channel first, so I know what to expect.

The Instinctual Drives

Self-preservation Sixes: This is the warmest of the three subtypes and these Sixes especially desire connection: being engaging and funny reassures others that they mean no harm. They want to help: "I'll be there for you—but will you be there for me?"

Self-preservation Sixes look for a strong and capable partner or group of friends who will satisfy their need for safety and security, even if it takes them a while to trust people before getting close. They love being part of a group and may get very upset if they feel they've been left out. Self-preservation Sixes fear abandonment—being alone in the world. They can experience others as excluding, which is often their own projection:

> *When I'm dating someone and I ask them out, if they don't respond within a few minutes, when they do reply, I've already convinced myself that they want to end things—that they've found someone else. When they tell me happily that they were just in a long meeting, then I feel pretty foolish for having given up on them so quickly without any real cause.*

Like Fours and Twos, they can become depressed and feel their loneliness deeply when they don't have a partner. Nevertheless, their loyalty and need for security can have them staying in toxic relationships, becoming more insecure and needy as the relationship deteriorates.

They are cautious when it comes to spending[21]—this could create friction if they are married to a type who enjoys lavish shopping.

Social Sixes: Social Sixes look neither to dominate others or to be protected by them. Rather, they look to the social arena for a cause or impersonal authority to whom they can give allegiance[22]—this could be a corporation, a religious leader, an organization such as the army, or a philosophical belief system that provides their rules of engagement with the world.

They are the more family orientated of the three types. It's important to them that a prospective partner will fit in with their family—even if they really like someone, family acceptance could determine whether they continue with the relationship. Once they have a family of their own, they will work hard to support it.

They tend to be precise, cerebral, neat, and philosophical. Much like a One, they abide by the rules—although their motivation is fear of what could happen if they don't, rather than doing the "right" thing. When asked about sex and love, this Six used the word "committed," which is integral to a Six's relationship need: "Sex and love are part of committed relationships." [23]

Sexual Sixes *(counterphobic):* The Six is often the most obvious of the Enneagram counterphobic types. (A counterphobic type moves *against* the Passion of the type.) In this case, Sexual Sixes move against fear—they want to do scary things to prove they are not afraid. This can show up in certain areas of their lives and not in others. Rather than being generally compliant as with the other two instinctual drives, Sexual types demand submission and obedience from a partner rather than being obedient and submissive themselves. They may try to quell their fears by taking charge in the bedroom or exploring new positions, but they need to see that this is just another way of avoiding their deep-rooted fear.

When you feel helpless, the natural inclination is to work at being the opposite. Sexual Sixes put work into their bodies and are concerned with their appearance, wanting to attract and maintain a strong partner with attributes that others will admire. Palmer refers to this subtype as "Strength and Beauty." [24] They are the Six type most likely to fight rather than take flight, and as a result, are typically physically stronger. [25]

Interestingly, these Sixes often display a mixture of gender roles in their appearance. [26] Women may appear to be quite masculine or androgynous, even tomboyish, yet may dress in girly dresses and be enticingly sexual. Men may appear to be masculine in certain respects, but effeminate in others—possibly to the point of giving out the confusing signals about their sexual orientation. This type is also more intense. When in a relationship, Sexual Sixes may feel the need to test a partner's commitment. Their need for reassurance means they can feel powerless because their sense of self is determined by their partner. To a Thinking-type Six, logic rules love and being cautious in love is the sensible thing to do. [27]

The Wings

Six with a Five-wing *(double Paternal love):* In this subtype, Six's fear of lacking support meets Five's fear of being inept. This combination makes for a more withdrawn subtype, combining knowledge with the courage to pursue causes and take a stand. The Five influence may mean they are less engaging than the other wing type and may be inclined to challenge ideas and systems—this is the reactivity of a Six with the iconoclastic aggression of a Five. As a result, they are less likely to be in a relationship than the other, warmer wing type.

Six with a Seven-wing *(Paternal and Erotic love):* In this subtype, Six's security meets Seven's risk-taking. This double-fear subtype (both Six and Seven are fear types) comes across as warmer, more extroverted, spontaneous, engaging, and open than the other wing type. As a result, sex may be less routine and more explorative. They are committed to relationships and family, and are generally fun to be with. A partner's input in decision-making will be important to them.

As is the case with many of the wing types, a polarity occurs between the desire for fun and experience (Seven) and the need for security, responsibility, and routine (Six), which can play out as ambivalence between a desire for adventurous sex, with the fear of the consequences, or wanting to initiate a relationship yet procrastinating.

Moving to Sexual Presence

What Blocks Sixes from Sexual Fulfillment

In sex, looking ahead to possible problems (unwanted pregnancy, premature ejaculation, sexually transmitted diseases, disappointing a lover) can be crippling. Being anxious about performance may be a self-fulfilling fear. Psychiatrist Anodah Offit, a pioneer in understanding the psychological basis of human sexuality, suggests that a man who projects his own sexual dissatisfaction onto a partner, believing her to be unhappy with his efforts, could become impotent as a result. [28]

When it comes to matters of the heart, and life in general, there are no guarantees—yet doubting Sixes want to know that a partner is there forever: "I trust them now, but how will it be in five years?" Once they can accept not knowing and be at peace with the way things are, they are able to let their guards down. If Sixes can be in the moment, rather than focus on what might happen, they can enjoy their sexuality to the full.

How Sixes Can Become Sexually Present

Learn to trust: Sixes show up sexually (and in their lives in general) when they start to trust themselves. They start to heal when they acknowledge their own loyalty and at the same time accept the part of them that is disloyal (to themselves or others).

If they're with someone and have mutual trust, they should see that that's what counts—not tomorrow's sex, not how long this relationship will last, not what happens in five minutes' time. Then they can simply enjoy the now.

Let go of fear and become accepting: Occasionally things will go wrong during sex. When they do, less integrated Sixes may be mortified while integrated Sixes can find humor in the situation, accepting that it's just part of life. Rather than focusing on fear (anxiety is not an aphrodisiac), it is healing to be present with what is.

Become conscious: Use the arising of depression, doubting, dark thoughts, or pessimism in yourself to act as a warning that you are moving away from being fully present. Consciousness brings choice. You have a choice to either carry on slipping into that space or to find the courage to move out of it.

Conditional Sex: Let go of the need to feel sexual exploration needs to be conditional. Give yourself permission to enjoy your and your partner's bodies without feeling that you need to earn love. Let go of over-thinking. Relax and go with the orgasmic flow.

Understand that security is inside you: Security comes from having faith in yourself, not from finances, buildings, careers, or partners. It starts with you. Find that space within you that knows and trusts, and is courageous and strong.

Be present: There is so much beauty in the present moment—it is where intimacy is felt. When your thoughts are focused on the future, you aren't connected to your heart. A moment that is fully experienced can endure as an exquisite memory, but when we are focused on the future, we miss both the moment and the intimacy it holds.

Questions to Journal

NOTE: It's useful to answer these questions no matter what your type.

- In overthinking or being anxious of what could go wrong in sex, do you hold yourself back from relaxed sexual expression?
- Does the safety of predictability thwart sexual excitement for you and your partner?
- What does loyalty mean for you?
- Explore the conditions you feel need to be met in order for you to have sex, and then ask yourself which are truly valid.

Exploring the Sexual Types:
The Advancing Group

Types Three, Seven, and Eight

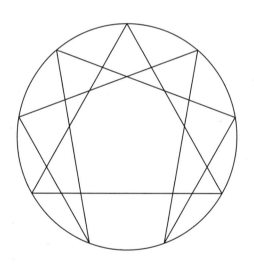

7

Type Three:
Awesomely Orgasmic

Three's motto: "Fake it till you make it."

Three as lover: The goal-orientated, top-performing, self-enhancing, status-orientated, career-focused lover, who feels that love is earned through their achievements. Threes look to "solve" intimacy issues the same way they solve problems in the workplace.

Threes advance their cause: by impressing others with perceived or actual success and/or drawing attention to themselves to overcome their feelings of shame. Threes want to be the center of attention to attract a lover. Sex can feel like putting on a performance: "Wasn't I great?" "It's taken quite a few partners to get this technique wired, I can tell you!" Threes want to shine the light of their success to seduce others (externally) but may feel less fulfilled inside.

You may relate to aspects of a Three even if it's not your type: if you are a Two or Four (the wings), or a Six or Nine (the points of release and stretch).

Love type: Erotic. In wanting to shine brightly, they are child-like in their self-focus: "Look at me! Look at what I've achieved!"

Relationship belief: "I'm better than the others. I'm a super-lover because I achieve more in bed."

Sexual frustration: "My partner just doesn't get what an amazing catch I am. I bet they've never had sex this good!"

Understanding Type Three's Sexuality

Brief Overview

Threes focus on achievements—life is about *doing* rather than *being*. Somewhere in feeling disconnected from the Divine, Threes create the subconscious belief that they need to emulate the Divine within themselves. In less integrated Threes, this manifests as a need to project success and accomplishment to feel OK—as if who you are is somehow not good enough, and you must be a god/goddess to avoid shame. Threes feel the need to be "more than" (*better* looking, *more* skilled). Overlay this need with sex, and you get a person who needs to perform rather than one who simply experiences. Claudio Naranjo refers to Type Three as "The Marketing Orientation" type [1]: the type who must head into the relationship marketplace and sell themselves to be worthy of love.

Magazines offering articles on things such as "10 Tips to Being a Better Lover," or "21 Mind-blowing Sex Moves to Master," or "Achieving Orgasm Every Time" will appeal to Threes because they want to be remembered as "The best lay I've ever had!" It can start feeling for Threes like being a rat on a treadmill. How many more books on goal-setting and self-improvement do they need to read? How much more do they need to be? Enough is never enough.

Threes live for success and the accolades they hope will follow. They are great at multi-tasking and organizing social and business get togethers—Naranjo refers to them as being "ego-go." [2] The so-called chameleons [3] of the Enneagram, Threes change according to their environment in order to best sell their skills and themselves. A hipster Three selling homemade vegan chocolates (with ethically sourced cocoa and recycled packaging) may dress in skinny jeans and a vintage top, but will change to Armani suits and a tie when they switch to working in a legal practice.

Twos, Threes, and Fours make up the Heart or Feeling center of the Enneagram, the triad that has feelings of shame and worthlessness at their core. It must be remembered that the centers are indicative of where we are wounded, rather than where we are healthy. [4] So, Threes are most wounded in their Feeling center, which manifests in a fear of being worthless, [5] resulting in a sense of shame. To cover up, disintegrated Threes may feel the need to lie about achievements or became vain (Fixation and Passion). That is why, although Threes are in the Feeling center, they can mask their authentic feelings and work hard at creating an impressive persona: "Me as a great success;" "Me as superior and more significant than others;" "Me as the man among mice." This can lead to what Horney refers to as "Neurotic Ambition" and "Vindictive Triumph": the need to shame others with your success. [6]

Threes uphold their persona by disconnecting the superior or idealized self from the authentic self or, more often, completely dismissing their actual self and focusing only on the idealized self. [7] In less integrated

Threes, the idealized self starts to become more real to them than the true self. [8] Arrogant and ambitious, the idealized self looks down on those who don't earn as much/aren't as attractive/haven't achieved/are less sexually experienced. There is a strong belief that anything can be achieved through talent. Threes who aren't integrated can be aggressive in their desire to be acknowledged and need constant praise: "You're amazing in bed, honey—best ever." In bed they feel they need to already know what to do. They cannot ask for help and are reluctant to ask what their partner wants as to do so would raise the issue of their self-sufficiency and success.

In contrast, the Three's shadow self is helpless, needy, incapable, and failing, and it desperately seeks attention and affection to compensate. The authentic self has transcended the need to hold success in the one hand, while pushing away failure with the other. The true self acknowledges and is okay with both success and failure—with just being, rather than doing. That's the integrated Three. [9]

The trouble with the average Three's polished outside persona is that the authentic inner self feels neglected and empty—something to be ashamed of. In less integrated Threes this can develop into narcissistic behavior. (Narcissism is also viewed by some Enneagram experts as relating to Type Seven). Horney's view of narcissism differed from Freud and other mainstream psychoanalysts in that she believed it arose from nurture rather than nature: she proposed that the environment that gave rise to narcissism was defined by indulgence rather than deprivation. [10]

I'd speculate that Threes are the fastest-growing Enneagram type in the Western world and China. Think of what *Time* magazine called the "Me Me Me generation"—with their use of *self*ies, and *my*opic use of social *me*dia ("my experiences/moods/thoughts/vacations..."), this is a generation that wants easy excellence and instant fame. Authors William Strauss and Neil Howe ascribe the following traits to Millennials: special, sheltered, and achieving. [11] In her book *Generation Me*, Jean Twenge found millennials to be confident, entitled, and narcissistic. [12] All of these traits describe Type Threes, with the exception of "special," which applies more to Type Four.

The Arising of Type Three

From a young age, Threes search for role models: popular bloggers, movie stars, people with status, or whatever their society looks up to. They start to believe that love is earned through success: "I have to achieve to be loved." As children they often excelled and were admired—the little heroes/heroines of the family.

Threes may have found their early sexual explorations were thwarted by repressed parents, or that a parent (mostly of the opposite sex) may have rejected the child's attention. Alternatively, the opposite-sex parent (or person who played that role) was absent (physically or emotionally) during the formative years, or the child may have tried to compensate for the father (or paternal figure) in the eyes of the mother (or maternal figure): "I'll achieve what he did not." [13] They often go into the same field as a parent, perhaps to impress, please, or outshine them.

They typically have a close bond with the nurturing figure, and in wanting to be validated by this person they look for ways to attract strokes. Inevitably, this means sacrificing what they want to be for acknowledgement: [14] "I really wanted to be an artist, but Mum felt accounting offered better prospects." Threes soon lose touch with their own hearts' desires and feelings, becoming alienated from their authentic selves. [15]

Threes in Love

Integrated Threes: At their best, Threes are authentic and open to true depth and beauty, as opposed to superficial performances. They recognize they have a natural right to love and be loved. Here is the response from an integrated Three on sex and love: [16] "They create and permit [a] platform for a wonderful experience of vulnerability and authenticity, intellectual and physical fulfillment."

Integrated Threes are modest, accepting, and no longer resist loving by refusing to surrender to it. They are open to asking for help, and can see that life is more than a list of achievements and a substantial bank balance. The split between loving response and sexual response has been healed, resulting in an ability to connect deeply with a partner—they are sincere and emotionally truthful. In relationships they are not afraid to step into the fire and commit.

Accepting their so-called "flaws," they drop the need for an idealized self. They may acknowledge their accomplishments, but they present them graciously because they've realized that no accomplishment is greater than a true and open heart. They are lovers of beauty in an appreciative rather than an acquisitive way. They fall in love with others, as well as life itself, and lose the need to be the best.

Average Threes: At this level, a Three's choice of partner may be strongly linked to social status. The long list they have compiled of a potential mate's desired qualities must be checked off before any advance is taken: "It's called being efficient, right?"

In turn, they start to market their abilities to impress their potential "catch." Banter may replace genuine conversation and Threes may "play" with several prospects at the same time, often over social media (because they're too busy to actually hook up). They often assume a role in a relationship as if they were the star in a movie—acting the part of the perfect partner. Because they can maintain control while they have the edge or upper hand, they can hold back aspects of themselves rather than feel vulnerable. Admitting to being a virgin may, if they are not religious, be seen as being humiliating.

As they disintegrate, they can find it harder to maintain long-term relationships. Sex becomes about feeling desired and admired rather than pleasure and emotional connection. If celibate, they will throw themselves into yet more achievements. Relationships start to feel like a surrender of "freedom." Rather than risking troublesome love, they will hold themselves back instead of sharing their accomplishments, and remain cool and aloof.

Disintegrated Threes: Disintegrated Threes start being unable to see partners as individuals with their own hopes, desires, and feelings, and will view them either as devoted admirers there to serve the Three's needs, or scheming enemies. While the Three sees themselves as succeeding, the partner is viewed as failing. [17] Likewise, while they believe that they are skilled and gifted lovers, partners are likely to be seen as sexually inadequate.

Threes are highly unlikely to admit to any form of sexual dysfunction. It can't be about them, right? If they do seek help, it will be more about showing what a great person they are for accompanying a "problem" partner than admitting they themselves may have an issue: [18] "I went into couple therapy because Sue needed the support." "Men just can't resist me. It's so annoying. So, I went to see what I do about it?" If, for example, a Three is experiencing premature ejaculation, they may blame their partner: "You shouldn't have given me fellatio first." Failure is not an option. If a partner leaves them, their view may be: "The idiot doesn't know what he's missed out on!"

To the world they may appear cheerful and successful, yet the disintegrated Three's idealized self-image becomes distorted: life is all about the Three, and they need their partners to pander to them and accept a subservient role. After blaming others for their problems, Threes will feel annoyed with themselves for showing symptoms of stress. The need for glory can be so insatiable that truth is lost along the way if things don't work out as planned, causing huge frustration.

Threes start to have no regard for their own best interests—no longer is it "I want to be the best," but a compulsive "I must be the best at all costs." Disintegrated Threes can end up sleeping with a boss or powerful person, even if the person physically revolts them, if it gets them closer to their goal. They will completely alter their personalities if it helps them achieve, whether that means marrying into wealth or seducing the CEO. [19]

They often have the unconscious desire to humiliate and defeat others so that they can rise above them, acting cruelly and maliciously with no empathy or remorse: [20] to emerge victorious, others must lose. [21] This can be devastating to the partner of a disintegrated Three.

To maintain their belief of being a great sexual performer or a sexual magnet, disintegrated Threes may seek outside validation through affairs and brief sexual encounters. Though they may ultimately find themselves alone, they will still appear upbeat, creating a fantasy of the "next big thing."

The gap between the actual self and idealized self widens as they feel increasingly emotionally empty and unhappy. The strain of pushing themselves to hide this gap can mean they reach burnout and give up the battle entirely. Alienated and with no interest in maintaining themselves on any level, they can become ineffectual, even catatonic.

Threes as lovers can be genuinely loving and self-accepting, often using their skills for the betterment of mankind. When they no longer need to act the perfect lover, they discover that they are already. Accomplished and outstanding, they inspire others to be the same.

What Three Dating Adverts May Look Like

Ron, 35

Hello, gorgeous! I'm a SWM, 6", with a muscular build (yes, I do work out a lot). I've been told that I'm good-looking, communicate well (I've just completed a public speaking course), and am fun to be with (I have loads of

*friends). I love people. I work and play hard—some describe
me as an all-round "winner." I own my own apartment and
drive two luxury sportscars (bit of a petrol-head, I admit).
I look forward to taking you to some amazing restaurants
and exotic places. It would be nice if you were as beautiful
physically as you are emotionally. I hope you'll send a recent
photo. In the meantime, smile, and remember: Your life is
about to change!*

Batya, 34
*College educated, smart, fun, and sexy. Looking for a guy
between the ages of 35 and 45 who ticks these boxes:*
- *You must own your own home and car (business
  would be great)*
- *Your income must meet or exceed mine ($60,000)*
- *You must be single, preferably never married*
- *You must not have any kids or pets*
- *You must be healthy*
- *You must be well groomed*
- *Looking like Ed Sheeran would be a big bonus!!!*
*PLUS: For one weekend, you'll need to be my date at a
family reunion. (All expenses paid.) Must be either religious
or willing to pretend. Please don't respond if you don't think
you match these requirements.*

The Passion of Deceit and the Virtue of Authenticity

The Three's Passion of Deceit arises with the demise of Authenticity—
being deceitful about the self as opposed to lying (although they can do
this when disintegrated). [22] Threes can alter to become whatever their idealized self requires.

Huge inner tension is created when you are heavily invested in maintaining an idealized version of yourself as superior and successful, while
suppressing the version you see as unsuccessful, compliant, and needy.
Because every shortcoming is viewed as a failure, Threes will tell themselves, "I'm an amazing lover" (idealized vision) to hide their fear of being
sexually inept. The real self embarrasses; the contrived self excels. The
fear that someone will see the real self and its perceived failings leads to a
greater dislike of self. The real self must be hidden from others, concealed

for fear of detection, which is why connecting can prove difficult. In their fear of being found out, disintegrated Threes become increasingly deceitful, lying about achievements, claiming ownership of success that isn't theirs, or even repeatedly having plastic surgery—whatever it takes to uphold the idealized self.

A Peek into a Three's Bedroom

Particularly if the Three is single, their bedroom can be a temple to their success, displaying trophies, medals, degrees, and photographs of themselves with the rich and famous, or vacationing at exotic playgrounds. This is particularly true of those with a Two-wing, whose style aims to impress. Those with a Four-wing may display a unique and arty approach to décor, with minimal but beautiful furnishings. Self-preservation Threes may not put huge effort into décor (as they're too busy working)—unless they can afford to pay someone else to "sort it out."

Fantasies and Erotica

In exploring their shadow sides through fantasy, Threes may find themselves enjoying thoughts of sex where they don't need to perform, or where they allow themselves to feel insecure and be led by a partner rather than take charge. Being hit on by someone else takes away their feeling of responsibility—it's not their fault if they were seduced—which relieves performance anxiety.

Social and Sexual Threes, who spend their lives looking great and frequenting expensive clubs where they're the life of the party, find that all this "being nice" gets tiring. What if, in fantasy, they allowed themselves to be bad, yet remain in control? They may enjoy fantasies (or realities) where they become the dominatrix rather than playing to the social needs of others. When they rule, the other must submit and adore them! Or they could entertain the sleazy "good girl gone bad" fantasy, where the sweaty trucker wrenches off designer underwear with lusty haste.

Fantasies, particularly for Sexual Threes, may involve people finding them so attractive they are not able to resist the temptation. The more lovers glow with adoration, the better the Three will feel and the more it will mask their insecurities.

Ever been on vacation and done something outrageous because no one knows you? Sex devoid of emotional engagement is popular for Threes: you meet, you have sex, you part. In the fantasy, the stranger's face is sometimes hidden, or a Three woman is taken in a crowded place from behind, reducing the chance of intimacy. There is a raw primal aspect to this fantasy that Threes may not allow in their otherwise controlled lives. The tendency for an Oedipus complex can make Three women fantasize about sex with a strong and powerful father figure in whose presence they can experience themselves as weak.

Like the affirmation and adoration required by a Type Two, some Threes may enjoy the fantasy of being a stripper. Flaunting is sexy but involves no intimacy and being desired can be arousing. It also helps keep at bay the fear of not having a perfect body in real life.

For male Threes, a fantasy could center around seducing a virgin (perhaps a cheerleader or young teacher)—corrupting innocence is very compelling. Virgins always remember who deflowered them, a point that high-achieving Threes will enjoy. Being in control as the more experienced partner allows a Three to feel superior and assured that criticism is unlikely.

Threes of Different Genders

Female Threes: In her controversial book, *The Power of Sexual Surrender*, Marie N. Robinson writes that "orgasm is the physical act of surrender."[23] A Cornell psychiatrist who devoted her life to treating women who were frigid, Robinson claims that frigidity is suffered by millions of American women—and I'd suspect many of them are Threes. Female Threes are on the increase, particularly in U.S., where they are the most common Enneagram Type.[24] Frigidity can become an issue where there is the need to contain free sexual expression for fear of being rejected. That's not to say that all frigid women are Threes, or that all Threes are frigid, but the tendency is there.

The reason Robinson gives for the rise in female frigidity[25] is that, "the frigid woman has learned to fear physical love, to run from it, and this fear has profound repercussions on her relationships with men. The reasons for her fear are hidden from her, are locked in her unconscious mind."[26] Speaking closely to a Three women's need to achieve in a traditionally male-orientated environment, she says, "the feminist credo thoroughly discredited feminine needs and characteristics and substituted male goals for female goals"[27]—an idea not popular with feminism ideology.

Robinson goes on to explain that if a woman mistrusts her own femininity and her partner's love, she will desire to be in control. In contrast, "in real orgasm a woman must be out of control; must willfully, delightedly desire to be so." [28] A Three women I knew admitted to having slept with loads of men, mostly before her marriage, but certainly quite a few after it. Yet she confessed to never having had an orgasm; it was the feeling of being desired and the power over her conquests that she craved.

Trying so hard to not need others, to appear strong and to avoid asking for help, Three women can find it hard to surrender control—feeling that they will fall apart if their entire self is swept up in a sensual experience without reservation. They are more likely to be so-called ice maidens or temptresses, who create and control desire by promising sweet sexual treats—but rarely deliver.

If faking orgasms make them appear more skilled lovers, they'll yell in feigned delight. They will stroke a lover's ego to conform to the idealized image of themselves as good lovers—yet it's just another form of deceit. Repressing their own sexual desires can manifest in stress and psychosomatic symptoms.

The focus of the Social and Sexual subtypes on appearances can result in stylish, impeccably dressed women who dazzle the world with the promise of being best friend, lover, wife, or employee. There is, however, frustration in needing to be independent while being dependent on others' approval, and the Three's tendency to dress for others can create a hollow interior with a glamourous façade. (The Self-preservation Two can show similar behavior, but the motivation is different.)

Three women may have a deep longing for a relationship, yet the fear of rejection can have them scorning any offers, even when they are attracted to someone. Many Three women have Oedipal complexes; they were "Daddy's princess," the daughter Dad could relate to and coach to be successful. Rejected by Dad as they became sexually mature, they can experience all men as rejecting. [29]

Some female Threes may find themselves attracted to married men or in long-distance relationships. I've encountered several attractive and intelligent Three women who would have been able to win over many single men, but who would repeatedly go after married men (who weren't interested in divorcing their wives), or much younger men (who enjoyed the attentions of an older woman but had no desire for a permanent bond). If things did change, and the men showed an inclination to form a lasting relationship, the Threes lost interest. "Love" in this sense is about attracting someone of status and the affirmation of being seen and adored.

Three females can be intensely jealous of any competition. I recall a Three friend saying that if she went to a party and felt there was someone more attractive than her, she'd leave. Threes want to be "The Best" and can use their sharp minds and wit to belittle their opponent.

Male Threes: Male Threes project a successful image. Searching for love but fearing intimacy, they may confuse sex with love. Men may be addicted to the thrill of seduction, but can easily move onto the next best thing when desire diminishes. They are in love with falling in love.

Although they may appear to be the ideal partner, in time their lack of emotional depth may prove to be frustrating, especially to certain types such as Fours: the (romantic) candles are lit, but no one is (emotionally) home. Three men desire success and all that accompanies it, including the eye candy on their arms. They can adopt the role of successful entrepreneur or celebrity with ease and style, yet may also complain that relationships are too demanding, costly, and take up too much time.

Pressure to be the idealized Lothario or to perform sexually can create anxiety, and this stress can lead to erectile dysfunction. What they see as failure may be humiliating enough that they distance themselves from meaningful future engagements, opting rather for casual or paid-for encounters (while believing that prostitutes enjoy engaging with them).

Disintegrated male Threes may be so focused on themselves and their appendages that they show no concern for a partner's enjoyment, unless it's a way to boost themselves: "I got you to orgasm four times—what a man!" [30]

In her book *The Sexual Self: How character shapes sexual experience*, Offit suggests that religion has been relentless throughout history in enhancing the view that masturbation is the cause of blindness as well as a host of other preposterous suggestions. Offit identifies "Sexual Egocentricity", which links most closely to the Type Three. One could expect that Three men would enjoy self-gratification, to those with Sexual Egocentricity, it's embarrassing proof of failing to be sufficiently desirable. [31]

Love Type: Erotic

Naranjo suggests that Threes' love tends to be self-focused, [32] making them one of the three Erotic types of the Enneagram. It is more of a childish, demanding self-focused love.

In Ancient Greece it was believed that Eros (the Greek god of love), together with his pals Pothos and Himeros (longing and desire) and his sidekick Cupid, shot arrows to create desire in men and women. In Alexandrian poetry, Eros degenerates and becomes not a youth, but a mischievous child. Over time, he was portrayed as being ever younger until, by the Hellenistic period, he was seen as an infant. Eros is now associated with a child-like love—a love of self, and the love-type associated with Threes (as well as Sevens and Eights).

Relationships Aren't My Concern!

Threes are vulnerable when it comes to relationships because their outer façade of brilliance and achievement masks the fear of letting anyone see the emptiness they feel inside: "What if someone sees I'm a fake?" Threes are also super-sensitive to criticism and rejection. Natural sexual urges may be controlled and redirected into work. The contempt they feel for themselves becomes the contempt they fear from a lover.[33]

Threes fear that they could be exposed as shallow frauds.[34] In both sexes there is a lurking fear: "Am I loved for who I am or for my cash/the lifestyle I offer/what I do/the sparkle I add to my partner's ego?"

Narcissism

In psychiatry, narcissism can be viewed as either a tendency, a condition, a stage of development, or a disorder[35]—and as Threes disintegrate, they move through this list. More men are full-blown narcissists than women.[36] The narcissistic aspect of Threes results in sexual egocentricity, which drives them to want to be desired. They see themselves as more than they are, like a dating app profile that reads: "Better-than-average looking, great sense of humor, and financially well off." Even though they see themselves as exceptional and gifted, they still have hidden self-hate and tend to beat themselves up for not having performed to their ideal.

In loving themselves less, narcissistic female Threes may cover up their "flaws" with makeup and surgery; in contrast, disintegrated male Threes may wear badly cut clothes, be overweight and have bad haircuts, yet still believe they're irresistible and that their penis is a gift to their partner. They may limit their sexual expression if it threatens their exalted view of themselves.

Partners of narcissistic Threes are unlikely to receive praise for a performance well-executed. A disintegrated man may refer to a woman as a slut if she is multi-orgasmic, while praising his skill as a lover. If he can barely manage a single orgasm himself, he'll be inclined to deflect: "There's nothing wrong with me—it's your fault."

Shame

Shame is commonly associated with sexual experiences and can be hugely damaging to a relationship. While shame affects all the types, a deeper association may be held by Twos, Threes, and Fours.

Childhood sexual expression can be fraught with humiliation—from tough toilet training, to scoldings for playing "down there," to outright abuse. With the onset of puberty, a whole new range of potential humiliating and shameful experiences arise during our teenage years—leaking during menstruation, erections at inappropriate times, wet dreams, being caught masturbating—which get triggered repeatedly throughout our lives and add to the loss of our sexual confidence.[37]

Dr. Donald Nathanson, psychiatrist and author of *Shame and Pride: Affect, Sex, and the Birth of the Self,* claims that it's not just a sexually repressed upbringing that creates shame: deeper still is the shame of not being loved. Shame starts with any experience where we are rejected, or see ourselves as unattractive, lacking in courage, having failed, or being inadequate or unworthy—and sex can trigger all these potential points of shame. Nathanson suggests that we respond to shame with one of four coping strategies, which he called the "Compass of Shame": Withdrawal, Attack self, Avoidance, Attack another.[38]

Withdrawal would be hiding away from others, such as a Type Five might do. *Attacking self* would be a masochistic way of belittling the self, such as self-harming. *Avoidance* plays out in drug or alcohol use, seeking experiences to gain thrills or denying that there is a problem. *Attacking others* would be about blaming and shaming others, either verbally, or physically and sexually, or by damaging another's property as might be expected from the Advancing Enneagram types.[39]

I would suggest that Threes mostly use three of these techniques to deal with their feelings of shame. Sexual type Threes, being upbeat like Sevens, would act out the avoidance of shame.[40] Self-preservation types would possibly withdraw to seek autonomy.[41] Being the most aggressive of the Threes, Social types would be most inclined to attack others.[42] Research for the Compass of Shame Scale revealed that men exhibit more Avoidance and women more Withdrawal. Attacking others was slightly, but not significantly, higher for women.[43]

Not wanting others to discover their lack of self-worth or "defected" self, Threes work hard to deflect attention from what they perceive to be a lack by displaying their achievements, or beautifying themselves or their bodies. Nathanson says that people experiencing shame commonly find a hero or heroine to emulate. They also become extremely competitive. Whichever strategy or combination they use, they show an external image which is at odds with the defective person they feel themselves to be.[44]

Competent, confident, sexy, and desirable attributes will mask the incompetent, weak, unlovable, unattractive, shameful, sexually inadequate, and undesirable person they subconsciously feel themselves to be. Work allows them to feel worthwhile.[45]

The Instinctual Drives

Self-preservation Threes *(counterphobic)*: For the other two instinctual Three types, an excessive amount of time, energy, and cash can be poured into narrowing the gap between the idealized and perceived self. But the counterphobic Three does the opposite, telling themselves that they're above petty concerns, and that it's their performance rather than image that counts. As such, they pretend not to care,[46] but secretly do—the counterphobic type creeps in, not wanting others to realize.

The Self-preservation Three is often depreciating of their looks because the idealized self is not staring back at them through the mirror. They don't want to be seen as being fixated on their image—being vain about not being vain, they're more modest about their appearance.[47] So, women Self-preservation Threes may not wear makeup, and Three men may scoff at going to the gym (but work out at home).

They are the most likely of the Threes to be workaholics, desiring security through financial well-being and their work-related abilities: "If I'm the best at my job, I can't be fired." "I've got so much stashed away that even if I lost my job, my investments would keep me."

They are the least likely of the Three types to ask for help or to show their stress. As one Self-preservation Three said to me: "Until I had a meltdown, I had no idea that I could be affected by stress. It came as quite a shock to discover this vulnerability—to learn I was not invincible and needed help."

Self-preservation Threes can be modest and are counterphobic because they appear to be unconcerned with image.[48] They desire to be "good" people, and good people aren't concerned about image—that would be vain and unacceptable. This tendency means they can be mistyped as Ones. In relationships, Self-preservation Threes may send out these kinds of messages: "I'm not particularly interested in dating. I've got other interests." "Flirting is for dumb blondes who have no other way to attract attention."

Self-preservation Threes want to be good lovers and partners, and inspire admiration for their financial and career achievements. They're practical, resourceful, and able to take care of the financial needs of their families, although the desire to accumulate cash can mean they seldom have time to enjoy it. Partners may find it hard to connect with them sexually or emotionally because they're so caught up in striving, often for financial security.

They find it harder than the other two Instinctual drives to connect with their feelings and may demonstrate their love by doing things for others or by meeting obligations rather than free-flowing love. Efficient functioning can destroy emotional interaction—partners themselves may be judged according to whether they "tick all the boxes." Despite being one of the Feeling types, thinking can rule over feelings. Naranjo describes Threes in general as being Dr Alexander Lowen and psychologist Stephen M. Johnson's "rigid" character—people who split loving from their sexual responses.[49] Chestnut describes Self-preservation Threes as being the most rigid of the Three types:[50] efficient at the cost of all else. A Self Preservation Three said, "Sex for health reasons needs to be done."[51] (Yet another task to be ticked of a long to-do list!)

Because they like to be in control and don't want to connect with feelings of weakness, it can feel to partners that their Three seeks out sexual contact, only to withdraw from it. Splitting love from sex translates as an inability to experience true love; something is always missing. Some Threes attempt to overcome this by having a partner they care for but feel no sexual attraction towards (love), and a lover they desire but for whom they have little feeling (sex). Getting Threes to relax may be tricky and reaching orgasm may take some effort.

Self-preservation Threes may, according to Naranjo, have experienced some kind of chaos[52] where their need for attention was thwarted by parental illness, alcoholism, or a needy or emotionally unavailable parent. Young Threes then learn to take care of themselves and find other ways to get attention.

Unlike the other Instinctual drives, not only do they move against vanity (their Passion), but also deceit (their Fixation). Ask if they've been unfaithful and they're more likely to reveal the truth about their infidelity than the other two subtypes.

Social Threes: Like the child who was always putting on plays and demanding a parental audience, Social Threes enjoy being center-stage. As a result, they're the most vain yet also most adaptable of the three subtypes. They're socially skilled and can work the room, shining at social events and creating admirers and connections. [53]

They're smooth operators and can coldly use their emotional connections to achieve their goals. Threes can "claw their way to the top," demonstrating vindictive triumph [54] over those beneath them. An ex-partner of the Three's new love may find themselves humiliated in their defeat, hurt be seen as a necessary part of the Three claiming their prize. "Sex," a Social Three stated, "is a need that has to be scratched and then it's over." [55]

When life is about dangling your achievements as bait for would-be admirers, there is little true self remaining. Two beautiful, successful female Threes admitted to me that they found being a CEO a lonely place to be. Both questioned if the corporate ladder was really the one they wanted to climb.

Sexual Threes: These Threes desire sexual admiration rather than admiration in a career. They may market themselves as great lovers and put effort into studying sexually attractive role models, emulating them to enhance their appeal. They can also become people on whom others project their desires, and can merge with their partner's fantasy: "You want me to be a naughty shepherdess so you can follow me?" Their dilemma then becomes "Do they only love me because I play along?"

Sexual conquests affirm their success. Like sirens, they lure and enchant those who fall into their spell, and bewitch them into taking care of them (unlike Self-preservation Threes, who want to take care of others). They are happy to be out of the limelight, and can be the "power behind the throne," like Napoleon's Josephine. This allows them to be more introverted and focused on creating a pleasing presentation of themselves, rather than a presentation in the office. [56] Their idealized self is being the perfect wife/husband/lover in the perfect partnership with perfect kids—the stuff adverts are made of.

When the idealized version of love falls apart, it can be traumatic to search through the debris for an authentic self. It's as if the mask is there, but the actor has left the stage. In bed this can feel as if the person with whom you've slept many times still feels like a stranger—physically present, but emotionally absent. This Sexual Three's response is typical: "Both [sex and love] are important, but at times I'm too stressed to devote much time to this area of my life." [57]

The Wings

Three with a Two-wing *(Erotic and Maternal love)*: In this subtype, the Three's ambition meets the Two's warmth. When integrated these Threes are outgoing, charming, fun, and have a gentler approach when it comes to relationships than the other wing type. They balance work and relationships and are connected to their emotions. Relationships are as important to them as the desire to achieve. When less integrated, they want to project themselves as being the perfect partner and lover. In bed they may want to be on top physically and emotionally. In public they'll want to woo the room to gain the admiration they feel they deserve.

Three with a Four-wing *(Erotic and Maternal counterphobic love)*: Here, Three's ambition meets the artistic Four. More introvert, cooler, and private than the other wing type, they are more attuned to their emotions, much like integrated Fours. When less healthy, this can translate into moodiness and emotional distance. They may be awkward and self-conscious in the bedroom, and uncharacteristically unsure of themselves. Fear of rejection plays an even larger role in their relationships, so short-lived flings may be seen as an easier option.

Moving to Sexual Presence

What Blocks Threes from Sexual Fulfillment

Advancing towards others waving flags of their achievements means Threes can disconnect from their authentic selves. Being focused on their performance and the praise they hope to receive, they lose connection with the here and now. It can feel as if they are acting a part. If bragging about their past conquests makes others feel inadequate and grateful for their attention, less integrated Threes will go there—all the while missing out on the beauty of truth. Being real requires valuing their true selves, and sex becomes about intimacy and mutual care, rather than seeking to impress.

Allowing themselves to be vulnerable requires a huge amount of trust in a partner, which, if broken, can be emotionally destructive. As a Three described it, "I feel as if having broken down part of the wall to finally let someone in, should they reject me, I'd never allow myself to break down the wall again."

Another way to deceive themselves is through self-talk, as a Three once told me: "I'm way too busy for a relationship. It wouldn't be fair on my partner. I work such long hours, and I fly such a lot."

Threes can find it safer to keep partners at arm's length, flitting like butterflies from one affair to the next. A string of lovers means never having to reach depth with anyone, as well as boosting the façade of their sexual prowess. Some may choose unavailable partners, or simply remain celibate: "My friend's partners are all complete losers—it's preferable to be single than be hooked up with someone like that."

How Threes Can Become Sexually Present

Connect to your authentic self: As Threes connect with their inner self, they become aware of their real feelings. Sexuality becomes an all-encompassing experience, rather than about performance, and achievement is authentic rather than self-aggrandizing.

Love, intimacy, and sex unite when Threes can hold the paradox of their need to be great lovers with their fear of being empty. Sex is not about being the best or competing with a partner. Losing the need to be a "love super-star," they can become genuinely extraordinary—a person who loves and is loved.

Accept: Threes need to release shame and guilt from past sexual encounters, as well as any self-judgement and embarrassment about early sexual longings for a parent. They no longer feel the need to reject to avoid being rejected.

Open to your inner world: When the mask of success is dropped, Threes confront the fear of exposing their inner world to a loved one. By losing the constant need to improve their outer appearance, they can adopt a more natural approach and discover their inherent beauty.

Create a healthy work-life balance: Threes should allow their work to occasionally take a backseat. Stress is reduced when life comes into balance.

Let go of fearing failure and the need for control: Integrated Threes can laugh at bedroom failures and ask for sexual help and feedback. Through this vulnerability, they learn trust. True winning involves surrender, which becomes a strength rather than a perceived weakness.

Questions to Journal

NOTE: It's useful to answer these questions no matter what your type.

- Do you believe that sex is something that requires hard work?
- Do you deserve to have a good sex life. Why?
- Are you stressed out by the need to be a great sexual athlete?
- Do you ever fake orgasm? If so, why?
- How could you be more authentic in your sexual expression?

8

Type Seven:
The Spontaneous Suitor

Seven's motto: "Passion, pleasure, and the pursuit of love!"

Seven as lover: Sevens want excitement, a new stimulant, or something to give them an extra blood rush: "I need something to fulfil me, *now!*" Sevens dislike their freedom being limited, so long-term commitment can be difficult. They are inclined to avoid dealing with problems in a relationship—they want it all to be fun.

Sevens advance their cause: by moving into the world with the belief that their presence will liven up the group—that they are the main attraction. As such, they direct their energy outwards. They live in the future of possibility, planning sexual engagements in an attempt to fill the gluttony of desire. Their external focus results in them losing inner connection.

You may relate to aspects of a Seven even if it's not your type: if you are a Six or Eight (the wings), or if you are a One or Five (the points of stretch and release).

Love type: Erotic. Sevens usually see themselves as being more important in a relationship—child-like eroticism arises when sex is mostly about having *their* needs met.

Relationship belief: "I'm more exciting and open-minded than others in bed."

Sexual frustration: "Partners become too predictable and boring. They can't keep up with me."

Understanding Type Seven's Sexuality

Brief Overview

Gluttony, the Passion of Type Seven, is not simply about the desire for food and alcohol, but the desire for experience: "What's going to give me the biggest high?" To Seven's, happiness lies in a new experience, just out of reach.

Freud coined the term the "pleasure principle" or *Lustprinzip* in German, which he saw as the driving force behind the instinctive seeking of pleasure to avoid pain. This contrasts with the "reality principle," which develops with maturity, when we learn delayed gratification. Freud postulated that "an ego thus educated has become 'reasonable;' it no longer lets itself be governed by the pleasure principle, but obeys the reality principle, which also, at bottom, seeks to obtain pleasure, but pleasure which is assured through taking account of reality, even though it is pleasure postponed and diminished." [1] It's like the famous "Marshmallow Test," where children are given a marshmallow and rewarded with another one if they delay the gratification of eating it immediately. Like the children who choose the immediately available marshmallow, Sevens dive right in to life's sweet promises.

Because they are hedonists who experience love as pleasure, it stands to Seven reason that without pleasure, love is lost. [2] The danger with this thinking is believing that a "happy," pleasure-seeking demeanor is seen as an enlightened state of being, rather than a focus on pleasure. In this way, the Seven's belief in being their idealized self creates an "exquisite" human whose faults are themselves divine. [3]

Sevens desire quick-fixes—they can't tolerate long learning processes, and want to believe that they already are what they want to be. If Eights are into lusty primal sex, then Sevens want the high it potentially brings, along with being high on life (or with a substitute drug). They are an advertiser's dream—dangle the word "new" in front of them and they'll be whipping out their wallets. Websites like lastminute.com are their delight, because spontaneity is their passion. They are great visionaries and entrepreneurs who enjoy seeing potential.

Sevens are typically intelligent, widely skilled and diverse in their interests. They are fun to be with and sharp-witted. Naranjo relates the Seven to the Fox in fables—the clever, witty schemer. [4] I see this type as the archetypal trickster or court jester, who is outrageous at times yet avoids any adverse reactions to his performance.

Have you ever been talking to someone at a party who's not really listening because they keep glancing behind you to see if someone more influential, famous, fun, or popular has arrived? That feeling of "the next best thing," is typical of a Seven. Their restlessness means that the now is never quite enough—the grass is greener on the other side, the real thing is just around the corner.

Confident and charismatic Sevens tend towards exhibitionism and love being the center of attention. I recall going out with a Seven female friend who, stone-cold sober on entering a club, thought nothing of leaping onto the bar and sprawling seductively, to the hoots and cheers of an adoring crowd. They are also the "playboys" [5] of the world, who break the rules, take risks, and make and lose fortunes—all with seeming indifference. Think of the handsome man on a luxury yacht surrounded by *Vogue* models and champagne—smooth movers and shakers, who often fake goodness. Like Twos and Nines, they make life appear rosy.

This type could be related to aspects of stage two development of Jung's animus, the "Man of Action," an adventurer like Ernest Hemingway, who "possesses initiative and the capacity for planned action." [6] Sevens see the bigger picture and unless integrated to their One point of stretch, may ignore the finer details. They are innovators who use their Five point of release to join the dots between different concepts, to envision a different way of doing things (including in the bedroom).

They are Fear types, however, and mask it by pitting themselves against the world through adventures and entrepreneurial activities. Sevens don't sweat the small stuff and they also have no time for fancy titles, rank, or hierarchy. Sexually this means that they will easily hit on someone famous or above their standing, not in the self-ingratiating way a Two might, but rather because they really don't see social divides.

If Type Ones see life in terms of should/should nots, Sevens have removed the word "should" from their vocabulary. To a Seven, to live is to choose from a smorgasbord of tantalizing options. In sex this means that what *could* happen may be more enticing than what *is* happening: "I wonder…?" "What if….?" "How would it feel to…?" If sex is disappointing, or if rejection happens, there's always something new to look forward to. While Fours don't want to be boring, Sevens don't want to be bored, believing that, "Others don't see the possibilities—they're too constrained in their thinking."

Tolerating a partner's "negative" emotions can also prove hard for a Seven. As they run from their own fearful feelings, they may want to run from a partner who evokes those feelings in them. "When I get down, I just read a book or have a cup of tea and then I feel much better," was how a Seven described "dealing" with troublesome emotions. Pursuing potential lovers or fantasizing about sexual liaisons can become another form of distraction.

The Arising of Type Seven

To deny feeling unloved and unappreciated, Seven children learned to avoid emotions such as fear, anger, and pain. Feeling separated from a maternal figure (because of travel, ill-health, work, or a sibling) and ultimately from Being itself, young Sevens focus on external distractions. [7] As they get older, it's only the nature of the distraction that differs. This creates a state of constant anticipation and planning—living in the future and as a result not being present.

Because they don't tolerate hierarchies, Sevens tend to rebel against their fathers (or father figures), who are commonly perceived to be higher in the ranks in the family and form deeper relationships with their maternal figure. [8]

Sevens in Love

Integrated Sevens: Sevens in their healthier levels genuinely want to make the world a better place and are happy to serve a cause that will do this. As a result, they're often drawn into professions where they can advise and influence others. [9] They are great motivators and life coaches, and are good at public speaking, so will inspire others to action no matter what their profession.

They've learned to savor each moment and that includes making love, while being fully present to the experience. The need to look to a more tantalizing future has been replaced by the joyful appreciation of the now.

Sevens are passionate, enthusiastic, and youthful, which, together with their curiosity and self-confidence, can make for fun times in the bedroom. Making love is an exquisite gift, rather than an act for their gratification. [10] The sensual world beckons them. If something happens that is not ideal, such as premature ejaculation or the loss of an erection, they're not self-conscious and can laugh it off and try something else. (They have an outrageous [11] and sometimes bawdy sense of humor, which can relieve any performance anxiety.)

In same-sex relationships, if something has worked pleasurably for them, they will thoroughly enjoy sharing the technique with you.

Average Sevens: Sevens are fast talkers. Even if they're discovered in bed with the babysitter, they can charm their way out of accepting responsibility, shifting blame onto a partner: "Sex was so predictable I had to try something more stimulating." If this approach doesn't work, then Sevens can become angry and accusatory, and generally throw their (sex) toys out of the bed.

In focusing on their own needs, they can be uncaring or unconcerned about others. If Sevens are married to one of the compliant or withdrawn types who don't challenge their behavior, they can quickly feel superior in both intellect and skills. Equally, however, if engaged with a more confronting type, they can feel inferior. [12]

Setting boundaries within a relationship may proof tricky for Sevens. They don't want to be limited and will look for any space to slither through. They may feel torn between a sense of duty towards a loved one, and a desire to be free and escape the constraints of a relationship. As they disintegrate, they can become increasingly unreliable, or overpromising ("I'll take you away to a luxury spa for the weekend") and then not delivering.

Sevens fear aging because they believe age will limit their sexual prowess and attractiveness. As they disintegrate, they can become less discriminating in their choice of partner, [13] desiring variety, excitement, and new experiences. Relationships become more about a fear of being alone than genuine interest.

They become increasingly self-interested and superficial—consumers who fail to appreciate what they consume. Those close to them start getting exasperated by their constant avoidance of dealing with painful issues. To support this excessive lifestyle, they need increasing amounts of cash, which can sometimes mean choosing a partner for wealth rather than for love.

Disintegrated Sevens: Disintegrated Sevens become increasingly self-centered or narcissistic, and view their own enjoyment as of paramount importance. They can become scattered and erratic, chasing risk with serious addictions. As such, they can become "above the law," confrontational, and irrationally demanding [14]—"I want sex now. I don't care if you don't feel like it. You're my partner, and you owe it to me to service my needs!" If their needs are not met, they can throw hissy fits and become completely unreasonable, demanding from others what they are not prepared to give.

They show no remorse or responsibility. If anything or anyone threatens to constrict their enjoyment (including their own children), disintegrated Sevens can lash out in petulant anger; dependents are restricting. Anyone who doesn't support their idealized image of being fun and fabulous becomes a target for humiliation and derision. Sevens also have an idealized view of the world and those close to them (unlike Threes, where the idealism relates to themselves only)—it's essential to maintain optimism. Everything and everyone close to them needs to be amazing. Any form of criticism or attempt to deflate this view creates fear and feels threatening.

The idealized, upbeat version of themselves conflicts with the inferior, insecure version. Even though they can appear optimistic, with a casual, self-assured breeziness even in the direst situations, it's a fragile state and can quickly turn into depression and dejection.

Sevens feel above the necessities of living [15]—the tedium of everyday life gets rejected or must fall onto a partner's shoulders: "Bills are a bore!" "Paying tax is a complete waste of time and resources!" "Responsibility is for those who don't know how to enjoy themselves." Sexual promiscuity increases along with alcohol intake or drug usage, particularly drugs such as cocaine that give a high—anything to feed their insatiable appetite for stimulation. [16] Seeking the next new experience becomes compulsive.

Sevens become increasingly irrational, making irresponsible decisions, often with negative financial implications, which can be extremely trying for their partners. Morals and law are pushed aside in the process. People become objects to be used and often abused.

Sexual acting out is common, along the lines of "I couldn't control myself. X was there, and it just felt like a wild thing to do at the time." Discipline disintegrates into self-indulgence, both sexually and financially. They become increasingly scattered, starting projects yet seldom completing them. In relationships too, commitment becomes an issue, and they may coldly get rid of the very person who has been supportive. Life is solely theirs to enjoy.

Disintegrated Sevens become increasingly exploitive of their partners and others, [17] feeling entitled to take love and care as they please, without limits or restraints. As fear increases and it becomes harder to escape pain, Sevens can become completely debauched, experimenting with increasingly depraved sexual acts and manipulating partners to comply. Nothing is fun anymore. Paradise is lost. Angry and uncontrolled, they lash out at those who have tried to help them, and seek thrills to escape the anxiety that threatens. [18]

Having stopped to smell the roses, Sevens have the potential to find true inner joy in the experience in the moment. Staying with a lover rather than projecting away from them allows the Seven's creativity, spontaneity, and deep sense of appreciation for their partner (and life in general) to emerge.

What Seven Dating Adverts May Look Like

Silas, 24

If you're looking for laid-back, that's so not me. If you're after a fun time, be it trying out the gnocchi at a new Italian restaurant, bungee jumping off a bridge, or meandering through a remote region in Africa, then I'm your man! (Even my cat is hyper—he climbs up the drapes and chases his tail.)

I'm spontaneous, so weekends roll out in a series of adventures and explorations—there's always something new to try. I love the outdoors and WARNING: you'll have to share me with my kite-board (and cat). Suburbia doesn't work for me, my rooftop apartment in the city center does. Together we'll create loads of fun, where laughter and new experiences ensure we don't ever get bored. If you enjoy the great side of life and trying new things, hey, we're already a match!

Cora, 38

To date me you've got to enjoy life to the maximum! A sense of humor is also pretty essential. Life is for living and I want to live it all! If there's a mountain you've yet to climb, a country you've never visited, or that new eatery you want to try, I'd love to take you there! I drive way too fast, believe music is best enjoyed at full volume, and love to party. I've ridden an elephant, base-jumped, spent three months exploring India on foot, walked to base camp at Everest, and gone to sleep in the bush to the sound of roaring lions. I don't do depressives, couch potatoes, or people who are old before their time.

I own an advertising agency and do a lot of freebie work for various charities. I'm not necessarily looking for a man to match all of my interests, but having someone to share some of them would be great. I offer a fun, upbeat relationship, where we can explore life together, before we hit Shady Pines (with a bang!!).

Fear

When less integrated, hedonistic Sevens cut off from much of their emotional depth. They can come across as superficial—someone people can know for a long time, but don't really know at all. Some people, particularly the Feeling types, might find this apparent lack of emotional depth frustrating.

Sevens' self-growth is limited because they're not able to experience "negative" emotions for fear of giving up their idealized self-image. This can also make it hard to approach a Seven as a partner when you're having problems, as their hyper-positivity can make you feel unheard and misunderstood, [19] creating unintended alienation. A Seven can lack empathy and is predisposed to slapping us on the back and telling us to "chin up, it's not that serious."

When life doesn't work according to their envisioned plan, Sevens rework the event into something more positive: "I went on this Tinder date. After five minutes he went to the restroom and didn't return. But that was so lucky, because this hot guy came into the bar and we started chatting. He's married, but it made for a much more fun evening." Being upbeat is easier than facing the pain of rejection.

In wanting to affirm their superiority (in the nicest way), Sevens enhance their abilities, becoming Jack and Jills of all trades, but mastering few when they're less integrated. They also don't really enjoy studying a subject—it takes too long. To a Seven, attending a weekend workshop makes them an expert in the field, and designing their own website turns them into a software developer.

The Passion of Gluttony and the Fixation of Planning

Being Fear types, Sevens create a future-orientated mindset (the fear of what could happen), hence the Fixation of Planning and Anticipation. [20] Paradoxically, Seven's Passion of Gluttony (from the Latin *gluttire*, meaning to gulp down or swallow) creates the need for immediate gratification of what is anticipated. Sevens feel invincible because they exist in a future where what they have conceived has already happened: "I'm already what I plan on being." They take the fast track to everything, including romance.

If they can't woo you straightaway, they'll move on to someone else.

Gluttony manifests as a desire for new experiences and instant gratification. Planning provides a way to map their sexual desires: "I'm having two-way sex now... I wonder what it would be like with three of us?"

A Peek into a Seven's Bedroom

Decor won't be painstakingly pondered. It will be more a case of "Hey, I like that—let's make it happen!" "Maybe a bedroom revamp will increase the apartment's value and we can sell for a profit!" They'll want their space to be comfortable and trendy, with great contemporary artwork on the walls. Sevens are both generous and lavish, so budget won't be much of an issue when it comes to creating a stylish, seductive haven. If less integrated, they may be more inclined to flashy luxury—think exotic fabrics in the form of red satin sheets, gigantic beds, and garish art.

Fantasies and Erotica

Sevens can become fascinated by the idea of having sex a certain way, and the fantasy can become as clear and well-planned as if it's already transpired. Their natural curiosity and great imagination can have them dreaming up new and innovative ways to have sex, often enjoying the potential more than the act. Watching pornography may be a way to stimulate their planning. But although they may take time to imagine a sexual liaison, they can spontaneously deviate from the plan if that feels more exciting!

They are open to exploring new ideas—all fantasies will be entertained. Sevens are self-indulgent and will take the time they need to explore their desires. They can be extremely permissive with themselves and their partner, and may enjoy openly exploring a partner's sexual exploits.

Consequently, they're the most likely of all types to be found in a swinger's club, even if their partners don't share their enthusiasm. This Seven expresses many of these elements:

> *Being a Seven, I get why people have kinks and I also find I don't have the same level of judgement that other people have. It's all part of a creative, explorative process. I'm less emotive about sex and more rational, which allows me to be open to more sexual exploration, because I don't get hooked on feelings. I like to plan these encounters and think of ways to perfect the new move.*

Sevens believe that somewhere out there is a sexual utopia. They may enjoy indulging in fantasies of what would it be like to sleep with someone from every continent/country, or how would it feel to have sex with the boss's wife.

They may also bring their shadow selves into their fantasies, seeking pain and constraint rather than avoiding it—this could include bondage and S&M. They can enjoy dominating, with some raunchy yelling to liven things up (because silence is boring).

Sevens of Different Genders

Female Sevens: The mind is the largest sex organ, and a lack of erotic thoughts and fantasies during sex affects the body's ability to orgasm. A study found that women who are distracted by thoughts unrelated to sex were less likely to reach orgasm.[21]

As a Seven woman described: "I sometimes have a hard time reaching a climax. My mind is full of ideas—a new start-up concept, the neighbors, my partner's experience, work… I just can't relax." Bringing a partner to orgasm is important, because their pleasure affirms the Sevens' abilities. From another Seven woman:

I live in my head! Maybe that's why despite the limitations,
I've always been monogamous. If I let a man into my
head, then I trust enough to allow myself to be free and
uninhibited. As a result, I'm not into casual sex, although
having sex with an ex definitely works!

With their imaginative, expansive minds, female Sevens often fantasize about seduction before they engage. They enjoy wordplay as a type of foreplay—having partners try to figure them out from the subtle clues they give (both verbal and demonstrative). Follow the clues, and the Seven can be a passionate and skilled lover, particularly when intellectual stimulation is added to the mix.

Male Sevens: Male Sevens tend to be creative and vigorous lovers, who often don't seem to have many of the sexual hang-ups associated with other types. Most tend to be monogamous, despite issues with commitment. Even a crisis may do little to quell their desires.[22] Boredom, however, will mean sex becomes unappealing:

*I enjoy powerplay during sex. I enjoy dominating women, even
if I myself don't orgasm. But after a while with the same person,
and when I feel I've achieved my goal of being a great lover
to them, it's hard to sustain interest. So much of my focus goes
towards that aim, that I can often overlook the more emotional
aspects of our relationship. I can also view sex as purely an
instinctual function—we're horny, let's do this and move onto
something else exciting.*

Like their female counterparts, Seven men can find that intimacy, genuine affection, and the sharing of emotions is hampered during sex by a future-orientated busy mind. To focus on sex, some Sevens report smoking marijuana or having a drink as helpful; others take time to unwind after work and give themselves a chance to catch up with their partner. As one Seven says:

*If I don't find some way to still my busy brain, I'll be having
sex, but thinking about an email I need to send. If my
partner realized where my head is much of the time, she'd be
very unhappy. I have to try to be in the bedroom and start
focusing on my partner and her body.*

Male Sevens, particularly those with an Eight-wing, may try to woo a prospective partner with lavish gifts, expensive dinners, and the finest of everything—wine, champagne, jewelry, and vacations, seldom realizing that genuine love can never be bought.

Love Type: Erotic

The compulsion for new experiences can result in sexual infidelity. Books such as *Mating in Captivity* by Esther Perel may help Sevens understand the difference between a partner's need for the familiarity and safety of intimacy, and a Seven's need for the risk-taking, eroticism, and freedom of desire. (Perel sees intimacy and desire as two distinct things and examines how to sustain desire in the familiarity of marriage.)

Being one of the Erotic and asserting types, Sevens won't beat around the bush when it comes to fulfilling their desire. If they want it, they want it. If you're not prepared to fill their demands, Sevens may become angry, or simply seek pleasure elsewhere.

Erotic love is self-satisfying and childlike—restless, like a kid whose attention span is fleeting. The Seven will be thinking, *I'm here in a romantic restaurant with my new lover… but I need to text my next engagement.* After shooting his arrow, Eros is already setting the next in his bow.

Being the Star

Sevens enjoy being the center of attention, so a partner will be valued if they don't upstage them but stands back and lets them shine. Should you restrict a Seven—such as question the facts of a story they're telling, making them look foolish as a result—expect a cutting, humiliating, sarcastic, or derisive retaliation, if they don't completely gloss over the issue.

Seduction

Sevens are great at rationalizing, so unacceptable behavior, lies, or a string of affairs can be glibly and convincingly explained away. They can also have unrealistic expectations of others: "Why can't you just accept that my having sex with other women is just sex, nothing more? Why do you insist on imposing limitations on both of us?" This can make a partner begin to feel as if they're the one with the problem.

While many Sevens are faithful and monogamous, for some Sevens, saying no to an illicit romp may be almost impossible. The allure of new sexual opportunities can become a fixation.

A Seven I knew made it his business to seduce any number of women simultaneously, even though he was married: the babysitter, his wife's friends, his employees, old women, young women… Interestingly, sex was not the key motivator—it was the chase that brought excitement and the ego boost he craved. Seduction over, he would quickly lose interest and move on. Straying Sevens may force their partners to have to make difficult decisions as to whether they're prepared to live with these indiscretions. A polyamorous relationship might work for a Seven, but is it what their partner really wants?

Boring!

It can be very hard for a Seven to commit to a single person. "Give me life!" a Seven said when asked to comment about sex and love. Another Seven responded with: "Fun and *dangerous*." [23]

Sevens want to know more about their partner's body and desires. They seek what is different—unexplored new territories, including sex. Partners wanting to keep a relationship with a Seven alive, may need to look at ways of spicing things up. Same-old, same-old might feel comforting to some types, but in a Seven it'll result in restlessness and possibly a wandering eye. Boredom in the bedroom is suffocating. A position that was greeted with enthusiasm last week may be abandoned the next. (Hint: The 245 positions of the *Kama Sutra* may help!)

The only way to feel free is to cut the tie that binds you: Sevens love to experiment, which can cause friction if their partner is adverse or has religious taboos towards certain practices. Some Sevens may be more focused on achieving the end goal of orgasm and less concerned with the journey there.

Sevens can also mess with your head. A partner can start to feel uninteresting and restricting, while the Seven projects a spontaneous, fun, adventurous, and open-minded view of the world and your relationship. Any hint of not being upbeat—feeling sad, irritated, depressed, or not fired up over an idea—can have Sevens accusing you of being less spiritually or emotionally evolved: you're the one with the problem. Unable to own that they are avoiding painful emotions or their narcissistic self-interest,[24] Sevens don't get that exuberance doesn't always equal integration.

Seeking freedom at any cost, they love to hop on a yacht here, discover a new island there, fly back when yachting gets boring, and then drive 800 miles to a party in the desert… It can be exhausting for a partner to keep up.

Exhibitionism

Naranjo writes about Sevens as being "hypomanic."[25] Hypomaniacs have a "positive temperament, impulsivity, and detachment (negatively)," as well as "predisposition for mania, including tendencies towards elevated mood, novelty seeking, interpersonal dominance, and high self-confidence." His research concludes that "an exploration of abnormal personality traits revealed that hypomania is also associated with personality dysfunction, including entitlement, exhibitionism, and eccentric perceptions"—traits that fit comfortably with what we know about disintegrated Sevens.[26]

Psychologist Michael Bader states in an article that the practice of exhibitionism has to do with anxiety, and not only power. It's likely that the exhibitionism can result from the Seven's underlying fear (particularly as they disintegrate) combined with anxiety, a lack of empathy, self-centeredness, fantasy, and the relief from enacting a fantasy (the high made real).[27]

Thinking Versus Feeling

Being one of the three Head or Thinking types, Sevens are inclined to think rather than feel their emotions. Given their natural focus on themselves, this means they can be experienced by others as uncaring and inconsiderate—in tune with neither their partner's feelings nor their own—which can inhibit intimacy. They are intuitive, but may combine with their One aspect (point of release) to make them believe that they are "right." Their minds may become scattered and they may battle to stay focused.

Sevens will debate convincingly that their failure to stick to an agreed plan makes them "open to change" rather than unreliable, and that letting you down at the last moment is because they value "freedom of choice" but "felt cornered" into agreeing to the plan. Tell them they are thoughtless and insensitive, and you'll awaken an angry dragon—with their One influence and Seven self-confidence, they seldom accept criticism.

Sevens will hide their fears and insecurities behind a mask of confidence and even arrogance. They demand constant growth from a relationship yet fail to see that their thinking (as opposed to feeling) may be the cause of a problem.

The Instinctual Drives

Self-Preservation Sevens: The Seven passion of Gluttony manifests in this subtype as a desire to create favorable and often very ambitious opportunities for themselves. Self-preservation Sevens are the go-getters of the three subtypes. They are skilled at negotiating and networking.

A Seven will stop at nothing to get the partner they want. Having achieved their goal, they can get frustrated with partners who aren't as intelligent or quick-witted as they are. In their relationships, behind their friendly and upbeat façade, they're busy controlling what experience you will both explore next. They are confident lovers, who seduce with ease. Sex can become an acquired skill, like appreciating a good wine—something to be planned, considered, and savored. Their self-preservation needs mean that money is an important part of feeling OK. People are drawn by their natural warmth, generosity, sense of fun, and lavish entertaining—partners, may find themselves lost in the crowd listening to the Seven's next intriguing story (they love to tell stories). Security comes from creating a group of loyal and adoring fans who they trust.

It tends to be their house where friends and family hang out, which feeds into the Seven's desire to be the benevolent benefactor. Drinks, excellent food and even drugs may flow freely (in the case of illegal drugs, Self-Preservation Sevens can feel that they are above the law).

These are the warmest, most flirtatious, seductive, and sensual of the three types, hence their association with being "playboys" [28] or party animals—there is more of a physical love of things than the ethereal love of the more spiritually driven Sexual Sevens. Despite this, Self-Preservation Sevens can stay in committed relationships. It's as if their security needs require a backup plan—someone who is there for them if everyone else rejects them.[29]

As they disintegrate, they push their limits by overspending and overindulging: "I have a healthy green shake in the morning, but from then on I indulge in whatever alcohol and food I please. I see it as being in balance."

Social Sevens *(counterphobic)*: This warm and engaging Seven's interests are more directed at relieving others' pain than running from their own. Less narcissistic and exploitive than the other two subtypes, they are altruistic and their self-interest is more hidden. Gluttony is suppressed in favor of uplifting others. According to Naranjo, they are often vegans.[30]

You'll find them working as dedicated social activists, alternative healers, laughter yoga teachers, or life coaches, often in charity organizations. They are dutiful and loyal in love like a Six, even to the point of minimizing their needs and being self-sacrificing for a partner or the greater good. They can become too focused on their goal of enlightenment to the detriment of their relationships. Partners may find it hard to understand their intense desire for betterment, and Sevens can lash out and blame others for thwarting their spiritual inclinations.

Like Sixes, they also display greater guilt than the other two subtypes, and they are often the most intellectual and idealistic. In relationships they are more accountable for their actions and display a greater conscience. They can also be fiercely protective of those they love, yet at times see them as a burden.

They want their partner to share their enthusiasm, be it for a client whose physical pain they have alleviated or a project that's making the world a better place. They like to see themselves as helping or sacrificing for others (without acknowledging that it's a way of avoiding their own pain).

Social Sevens often fail to acknowledge their own needs and shortcomings. In a relationship they see themselves as the savior—the more evolved partner, whose role is to uplift their lover. "I am further along the road of integration than you," a Social Seven confessed cheerfully to his partner, "but I know you'll catch-up when the time is right." [31]

It can be difficult to be in a relationship with someone who assumes a well-intended guru status—the only role left is to be the admiring pupil. The Social Seven's idealized self wants to be recognized (in fact, gluttonously so) and acknowledged for all they do.

They like to rationalize, using whatever religion or belief system they're currently working with. If something fails, they simply move on to the next belief system. They will justify any confusion and upset they leave in their wake as part of their "spiritual journey." As Social Sevens disintegrate, they become increasingly unable to commit and may cancel dates, "forget" appointments, or arrive late, ignoring or denying the inconvenience and hurt they may cause.

Sexual Sevens: Imagine that tingly, buzzy feeling you get when you're talking to a prospective new lover, when a simple brush of your arm has you weak at the knees and the attraction is almost tangible. That's the rush Sexual Sevens crave—bursting with potential pleasure: "Where will it lead?" They're in love with the idea of being in love.

John Lennon's song "Imagine" reflects this Seven subtype. They are idealistic dreamers, less interested in material gain or worldly success than the other subtypes, yet often more self-involved. They can feel different to anyone you've ever met. As they have dreams, they want to know yours. Within minutes of meeting you're planning a great experience where both your dreams meet: "There's this tiny taverna in Spello where they serve the most amazing *antipasto misto*. Let's go!"

They can resemble Fours in their self-indulgence, vivid imaginations, idealism, ability to dream of a better world, and desire for the extraordinary, yet they are too enthusiastic, excessively happy, and optimistic to be Fours. They remind me of the "Fool" tarot card, where a young man accompanied by a small dog is about to gaily step off a precipice.

The Fool represents new beginnings, a belief in the universe, faith in the future, naivety, gullibility, improvisation, and spontaneity, which aptly applies to this carefree Sexual Seven, who walks through life with rose-tinted glasses. They long for the idealized world of their fantasies. [32]

When asked to respond to the words "sex and love," this Sexual Seven responded with:

> *Too much love and (too) little passion turns things platonic,*
> *people get bored and want out. Too much sex and too*
> *little love leaves one feeling used and replaceable as sex is*
> *so readily available. If you are in a relationship and there*
> *is an imbalance between the two, you will leave there*
> *disillusioned.* [33]

There may be frustration because the fantasy lover they spend hours dreaming about seldom materializes. Because Sevens can move towards aspects of a critical Type One, their real partner may not stack up against the fantasy. Sexual Sevens can develop a wandering eye because the perfect lover may be just about to enter the room.

More than the other types they can move from relationship to relationship searching for a love "high," only to be disappointed and disillusioned. They can approach anyone they're attracted to with ease, casting them under their bewitching spell [34]—but less integrated Sevens will find another muse just as their partner is starting to relax into the relationship. Many do remain monogamous though, because it's more about a juiced-up buzz than sex itself—it's the thrill of connection that excites them. (In fact, partners often complain that their Sevens don't have as much interest in sex as they'd like.) They may become entranced and infatuated with a person they see as exotic, even if it's not a sexual attraction. For a Seven, being celibate can be more bearable than having routine vanilla sex.

The Wings

Seven with a Six-wing (*Erotic with Paternal love*): In this subtype, the Six's anxiety meets with anticipation of the Seven. The Six aspect allows these Sevens to be more committed, compassionate, accountable, and loyal in relationships. Engaging, hard-working, and funny, they don't like being alone, yet can find fault when their existing partner doesn't meet their idealistic needs. What to do when the doubting Six arises? Moving on in the hope of finding the ideal mate comes at the cost of losing the security they have with a current partner. As they become needier of being in a relationship, Sevens open themselves up to potential co-dependence and even abuse.

They can be more vulnerable and insecure than the other wing type, and have a greater ability to be empathetic. They can also feel more guilt at hurting others or straying from the marital bed. Like Peter Pan, they struggle to grow up and take responsibility, and may rely heavily on a partner to sort out the more mundane aspects of life. When disintegrated they can become more paranoiac, scattered and irresponsible.

Seven with an Eight-wing *(double Erotic love)*: In this subtype, the Seven's fear of commitment meets the Eight's desire not to be controlled. More opportunistic, materialistic, [35] and confident than the other wing type, these Sevens are often financially successful and work in leadership roles. They're generous and will happily indulge a partner.

Their earthiness and practicality mean that their choice of partner may be someone who can assist their corporate or entrepreneurial growth, rather than a romantic ideal. The Eight aspect makes them unafraid of being alone—as such they can be tough on their partner, to the point of being hurtful and blunt. [36] They can be impatient, angry, and demanding, seeing issues from their own perspective only. Partners may need to tread carefully when it comes to confronting issues—this Seven doesn't take criticism well.

They can be hypocrites and can attack a partner about a behavior that they themselves do: "How dare you have coffee with an old boyfriend!" they can yell, having done the same the previous week.

Moving to Sexual Presence

What Blocks Sevens from Sexual Fulfillment

Sevens, like Fives and Sixes, are in the Fear triad, projecting themselves into the future of what might happen. If you're having sex and your partner is already thinking about the next orgasm (with you or someone else), they aren't present, and this can make sex lonely for the partner of a Seven. For Sevens, this need to plan the next engagement translates as never feeling satisfied with what is. Even a mind-blowing orgasm may not be fulfilling enough to a Seven who always wants more...

The fixation of planning can mean Sevens plan a future sexual engagement down to the smallest detail, resulting in problems going with the flow in sex. Sex becomes a mental rather than an emotional or physical experience.

How Sevens Can become Sexually Present

Face your pain: When the going gets tough and the Seven doesn't get going, that's a big step towards healing. Sevens grow when they learn to stick out the tough times in a relationship, because they then confront not only their own pain, but also that of their partner.

Practice sobriety: Ichazo lists sobriety as the Seven's virtue. [37] Unlike with gluttony, when sober you take no more than you need in this moment. When Sevens reach this level, they find true inner joy. They become more discerning of their desires as opposed to wanting it all. They are not anxious about having made the wrong choice of partner, but relish the attributes of the one they love. Commitment becomes easier.

Be present: The title of the book *After the Ecstasy, the Laundry* by Jack Kornfield reminds me of a Seven's growth towards finding the extraordinary in the ordinary. Just spending relaxed time together can be more blissful than chasing down the next social event. Happiness is not a goal to be pursued, but an ability to appreciate what is. Impulsiveness then gives way to sober restraint. Transcendence and acceptance happens between the poles of "the exciting, free-spirited, entrepreneurial, happy partner" who lives in the moment with "the escaping, fearful, trapped, unfulfilled partner" who's always looking for the next best thing. They learn not so much to see the world through rose-tinted glasses, but to take time to smell the roses!

Find a healthy work-life balance: In finding a balance between work and their personal relationships, Sevens find genuine fulfillment, taking joy in what is happening in the present. They stop using work as an escape, and can show up in a relationship as real, caring, and responsive, not needing a partner to buy into their world of idealization.

Move to joy: After running from their pain and their fear of deprivation, Sevens need to stop, face, and embrace it. They have already survived the pain—it's passed. There is no need to avoid it. Running is blocking experiencing their exquisite gift of joy.

Listen deeply: Sevens need to learn to listen on a deep emotional level to their partner, rather than viewing the interaction as a problem to be quickly analyzed and solved, or turning the conversation to themselves. Confronting your own emotional pain opens you up to experiencing others on a deeper level, where feelings are explored and shared.

Find intimacy: Sevens need to learn that when it comes to sex, they're not supposed to be instant experts. Taking time to discover their partner's subtle desires will bring intimacy, fulfillment, and enjoyment.

Questions to Journal

NOTE: It's useful to answer these questions no matter what your type.

- Does planning and anticipating future sex make the sex you are having less enjoyable?
- Does wanting it all mean you sometimes end up feeling empty after sex?
- Can you feel how moving ahead of yourself, is a way of avoiding truly being with your partner?
- How might that feel for them?

9

Type Eight:
The Lusty Lover

Eight's motto: "Life is rough but I'm tougher. Come here and let me show you how." "Let's do it now, my way!"

Eight as lover: Lust, the Eight's Passion, demands gratification, so Eights cut to the chase. Fights and making-up stimulates them. No doesn't work—if they want you, they'll find a way to have you. They demand control in the bedroom. Control and the desire to dominate can lead to S&M sex. Sex is passionate and plentiful, but hours of gentle foreplay could be missing.

Eights advance themselves: by moving lustily towards others, creating intrigue or intensity. "Step into the fire with me," they seem to say. They move against others to be in charge, take over, or dominate, wanting things to be done according to their needs. They seek autonomy and will not enjoy being restricted sexually.

You may relate to aspects of an Eight even if it's not your type: if you are a Seven or Nine (the wings), or if you are a Two or Five (the points of release and stretch).

Love type: Erotic (countertype). Sex is about self-fulfillment—an earthy, physical urge.

Relationship beliefs: "I have a strong sexual drive. I'm tough and self-sufficient. Relationships are good, but I don't need to be in one to survive. No one controls me. I need to be strong, or lovers will take advantage of me. Sex is good, more sex is better. I work hard, which earns me the right to play hard."

Sexual frustration: "I want more sex than my partner does. When I allow myself to reveal my softer side, my partner takes advantage of me." "Partners don't match my strength."

Understanding Eights' Sexuality

Brief Overview

Irrespective of their actual sex, Type Eights are the most archetypically masculine of the Enneagram types in terms of behavior, displaying the least emotional sensitivity (although Sexual Eights tend to be more emotional). [1] They are aligned with the *animus* of Jungian terminology. Their opposite type on the symbol is the extremely sensitive Four, arguably the most archetypically feminine type, along with Type Two. [2]

Together with Nines and Ones, Type Eights are one of the three Body/Gut types in the Enneagram, and are focused on the present. Because they are Body types, they enjoy the sheer physicality of sex. The Passion of Lust is appropriate for them: associated with sin and primal urges, it indicates forcefulness and physical desire.

With Lust as Eight's Passion, it's not surprising that the volume is turned up loud when it comes to sex! Eights go after life (and sex) with more urgency and boldness than any of the other types: "I see it. If I'm turned on, I want it *now!*" Eights desire intensity and passion, yet their very demanding approach to sex can have lovers retreating. [3] Enough is never enough.

Lust calls for immediate action—our initial attraction to someone is often fueled by lust, and our primal urge to procreate demands that our desire be fulfilled without delay. Lust does not understand the future. It doesn't dilly dally, nor is it bothered by the sweet murmurings of the poet, whose desire is softened by the heart. An Eight I knew would walk up to women at parties and say: "Hey, do you want go out back and have wild sex?" Incredibly, this blatant bravado seemed to work—he'd normally get at least one woman to oblige.

The color red and the emotion of anger are associated with Eights. Sexually, Eights will seek instant gratification, intense stimulation, and activities that enhance and enlarge the present experience. There is a grasping for the fullness of life, as Eights' larger-than-life emotions grab what is real: "If you're angry, be angry. If you lust, get naked!"

Eights want hot, steamy sex, making a partner's knees tremble as they gasp for breath, pushed up against the restaurant's restroom door. For Eights, sex is going to be the focus of the relationship. They want to be good at being "bad," and they may forget their partner's needs in their urgency. A headache may be of little concern if they feel the urge: "If she's had a hard day, give her a hard night!" They feel entitled to sex simply because they are in relationship: "I take care of you, so you need to take care of me."

Eights feel the need to protect and control a partner. Palmer notes that Mexican marriages are predominately Eight men and Four women: Eights feel uncultured in comparison to the elegant and arty Fours and so they respect them, and Fours are drawn to the Eight's ability to take care of them (rescue them) and their dismissive attitude to society and norms in general. [4]

Eights need to appear big and strong. "Don't mess with me," their body language reveals. Moving against the world, Eights can be amoral and antisocial.

The Arising of Type Eight

At some point in the Eight's childhood, the issue of powerlessness arose. Growing up in a world that feels unsafe in some way (be it conflict at home or an unsafe environment), young Eights felt the need to assume charge to survive, or to protect themselves or others in the family who may have been subject to abuse. They may have witnessed the abuse of power, either directed towards themselves or someone they cared about, who they felt powerless to protect. A common childhood experience is having to miss out on their childhoods, to assume responsibility for dysfunctional adults or look after younger siblings. To survive meant to display toughness—"It's me against you"—because they believed only the fittest and strongest would survive intact.

Not wanting to experience the feeling of impotence, Eights stand against the world to look intimidating, and they will protect the weak and challenging those they see as a threat. Horney writes about a personality that needs to create emotional hardness to avoid feeling vulnerable [5] because showing softness equates to feeling like a vulnerable child.

Eights in Love

Integrated Eights: Integrated Type Eights are warm, dynamic, and embracing. Being passionate, they will pursue the object of their affections with ardor. They love to step into someone's life and be the hero. Battling to pay your bills? Need help with your laptop? Don't stress—the Eight in your life will fix it. Eights work hard to make life better for those they love. At their healthiest, Eights will combine the very best aspects of a Two's love and nurturing with their own strength and power. For potential partners, particularly Self-preservation types who secretly want someone to take care of their survival needs (money, security, food), this can be a strong aphrodisiac. This quote from Marie Robinson[6] beautifully describes an integrated Eight:

> *Love means, in its very deepest sense union; union between individuals... It is the most basic and profound urge we have and its power for good is illimitable... the lover partner becomes as important as oneself... This fact is why real love never leads to domination or to a struggle for power.*

If you've been victimized in previous relationships, healthy Type Eights will work to build and empower you (because they know what it's like to feel victimized). If you're both dominant types, then the struggle for control can be exciting and bring sexual thrills. It's this intensity that juices Eights up—it makes them feel more alive. They want the volume turned up *loud!* Few people will engage with a healthy Eight and not remember the experience as positive.

Compassionate and loving, they can be very generous to the people they care about. When integrated, they drop their defenses and the need to control, and allow themselves to be vulnerable. This means that they are open, trusting, and have a child-like sense of wonder. Sex is then not about control and domination, but the sweet pleasure of two people opening their hearts to each other.

Average Eights: Eights are turned on by the heat of confrontation, so an argument may well end up with a certain amount of bodice-ripping in the bedroom. Their desire for excess drives them to seek multiple orgasms, which can make them sexual athletes. They enjoy competing for the attentions of a partner, provided they win in the end.

They can, however, lose trust in even the closest people in their lives, and a lifelong partner may be under constant scrutiny for suspected (but unfounded) unfaithfulness: "Did she really go to the gym or is she meeting up with someone?"

Eights seek autonomy, so will not enjoy any attempt to control them. They want to initiate boundaries for their partner, but enjoy breaking the same boundaries or rules themselves. They may want to know all about their new lover's past sexual escapades but will reveal little of theirs. In the average levels, they'll feel it is an act of justice to wreak revenge on anyone they see as having broken their trust.[7]

The desire to control, dominate, and possess a lover can leave little room for self in a relationship. Eights want partners to support and stand behind them, and may see their own demands as being a display of care rather than control. As they become less healthy, Eights become increasingly excessive in their demands: "Yes, we already had sex tonight, but it was so good I want another round!"

Their law is the law. They can become increasingly impulsive and risk-taking—not using condoms on a first date, or having a fling with a friend's wife while they're in the friend's home. They'll never lose an argument, so even if it appears their lover has won, an Eight will be planning a comeback (normally when others least expect it.) Eights can lack understanding for the hurt their outbursts may cause.

Disintegrated Eights: As Eights disintegrate, they become megalomaniacs and tyrants who surround themselves with cronies to do their dark biddings and use violence, threats, and even sadism in their sexual expression. I'm reminded of a friend who worked for a very disintegrated but powerful and extremely wealthy Type Eight. In restaurants, the Eight would see a woman he wanted to sleep with, and would send his hapless employee to negotiate a fee. These women weren't prostitutes—they were ordinary women eating out. That didn't matter to the Eight—he wanted them, and would pay the price (sometimes millions) to get what he desired.

The Eight's need to control strengthens as they become less healthy, and they can start to spy on their partners, employing the services of professionals, keeping watch via hidden cameras, or using apps on cell phones to track their whereabouts or suspected sexual activities. I knew an Eight who, long after his divorce, installed cameras and sophisticated spyware in his estranged wife's home so he could check on her and her lover's movements.

Bullying may take the form of actual physical abuse and they may feel omnipotent in their power. They may walk into the house, yell about something inconsequential like a wet towel on the floor or a dog turd on the lawn, be brooding and dismissive during dinner or even get violent—and still expect sex that night. The feeling is "I call the shots around here."

Partners may feel afraid to speak up or retaliate, and getting help may be too scary given the likely reprisal. As a result, Eights can start seeing themselves as being beyond the arm of the law.

It's interesting that high self-esteem is associated with rape and violence; shy, introverted, self-deprecating, and insecure people are less likely to commit violent crimes. Rapists in particular displayed a very high level of ego and confidence, believing they are "multitalented superheroes." [8]

Their lust and lack of restraint, together with the view that they are supermen/-women creates a dangerous combination. It's understandable that at the lowest levels of disintegration, Type Eights can become trauma-induced sociopaths or be psychopaths (innate condition). Feeling invincible, they hold power over everyone else, including their sexual rights.

When they are healthy, Eights are loving, faithful, truly strong, caring, and courageous partners, who are happy to take the lead in the bedroom or allow a lover to do so.

What Eight Dating Adverts May Look Like

Dan the Man! 32
Hey, babe, I'm your man!
Want to experience life with a guy who'll take you places you've never been before? I like making a woman feel like a woman. I'm a big man with a big heart (who's really bad at writing dating adverts)!

Me: Straight-talking, hunting, fishing, outdoor guy who can pack away a mean steak.

What I'm looking for: Sexy, voluptuous, warm, friendly woman who likes a man's man.

What I'm not looking for: Theatrics, bullshitters, money-grabbers.

So, if I want you to be my gal, I'll wine and dine you in a style you could just get accustomed to, and I promise I'll treat you almost as well as my Lamborghini.

Ava, 28

I enjoy life to the full! I dream big and live the same way.
Friends and family are hugely important in my life. I'm
fun and love entertaining. I am a very passionate person,
although some people find my energy and enthusiasm
overpowering.

I'm fascinated with human interaction and computer-
mediated communication and why people do the things
they do. I enjoy people who say what they mean and mean
what they say. I have my own car dealership (I can sell
up a storm!). I love travel and I love fast cars. I believe in
working hard and playing even harder. If I see something I
want (and this could be you), I'm not afraid to go after it.

The Passion of Lust and the Fixation of Vengeance

Lusty Eights go after what they want with urgency and passion—and
nothing can stop them. They can break all the rules if the result is winning their prize. They abhor the tentative and the timid: "The way you
slam your body against mine makes me feel alive." If they feel wronged or
slighted in love or life, they seek condolence in vengeance and retribution.
No one messes with them and survives intact!

This lust can see them aiming way above their societal fighting weight
for lovers that are more attractive, better stationed, wealthier, or are married to someone else. Nothing will stand in lust's way.

A Peek into an Eight's Bedroom

Even if they haven't got a lot of cash, Eights spend happily and draw on
credit if needs be. They are large and lavish, so expect King-sized beds,
satin sheets, a whole lot of the color red, a large-screen TV, and every
possible comfort. As in the rest of their lives, big really is better! They may
enjoy creating a sexual haven that fulfils their lover's every need.

Fantasies and Erotica

It's often in our fantasy world that we allow ourselves to explore our
shadow sides. For powerful Eights this could involve fantasies about being
submissive and weak, such as being tied up, not in control, or humiliated.

Unable to express their dominant aspect in a male-dominated society,
Eight women may have fantasies about being sexually aggressive. Dominant

women are viewed as being unfeminine, but there are no such rules in an Eights' imagination—they can take what they want with no repercussions. Eight men may enjoy fantasies in which they are the ruler of a threesome—this strokes their ego and appeals to their desire for excess (because if one partner is good, two is even better!). Fantasies could include maintaining endless erections, sleeping with lots of women, or being a sultan with a horny harem. Macho male Eights may find that any homosexual yearnings they've denied can be safely expressed in same-sex fantasies. Or men may enjoy submissive roles in their porn viewing and fantasies.

Eights enjoy exploring their sexuality and are prepared to try most things once. Sex toys, bondage, and role play can all be explored in cyberspace or with a partner, as this Eight suggests:

I enjoy looking for new things to explore sexually on the internet. But it gets boring. So recently I moved to scenes involving restraints, cuffs and ball gags. I tried this in reality and did sex in more taboo situations such as public places. I also tried switching between dominating and being submissive—I constantly want to explore my sexuality more. Watching porn in my fantasies and in reality.

Eight women also tend to be more liberated than some of the other types. Good self-esteem means they have the confidence to try the unexplored:

I'm practical about meeting my sexual needs. As a result, I don't accept sexist thinking and can be quite dominant, even aggressive maybe, which is probably why I'm bisexual. This openness gives me the permission to watch porn when desire arises.

It's also interesting that when Eights release to Type Five, they connect with the Five's enjoyment and exploration of taboo—the darker, forbidden aspects of sex. As such, they become more secretive and withdrawing, compartmentalizing their lives. Like less healthy Fives, they can hold extreme antisocial views, with increasing contempt for people they see as needy and weak. Sadism becomes a way of seeking revenge.

Naturally, this doesn't mean that every Eight you meet is eyeing your wrought-iron bedposts and wondering what size handcuffs to bring along.

In fact, far more people, particularly men, fantasize about BDSM rather than partaking in reality.[9]

Eights of Different Genders

Female Eights: In our hypocritical society, when an Eight woman enters a room, her boldness may be read as brazenness or pushiness, and her confidence as arrogance—characteristics that would be admired in a man. Her strong, sensual sexuality may have her being described as a "maneater" or "ball-breaker." Society often doesn't accept Eight women for who they are, and so they may not be able to express their true strong selves.[10] Female Eights are tough, bold, brash, confrontational warrior women. Interestingly, Female Eights may rate the power of their sexuality higher than the actual physical experience of sex.[11]

If an Eight Type woman wants a certain guy, she'll pursue him with vigor. (If you've watched the series *Good Behavior*, Ann Dowd as FBI agent Rhonda Lashever portrays an Eight woman pursuing a Nine man, Christian Woodhill as the parole officer.) This may be why Eight women often do marry Nine men, who are in the Withdrawing group (while Eight men are not nearly as likely to marry Nine women). At home they can rule the roost (and rooster), even if they don't at work.[12]

Although obviously any type can be gay, it's important to note the different societal experiences for Eights. In certain groups, gay female Eights may have found ways to express themselves: Dykes on Bikes, for example, a lesbian motorcycle club with 22 chapters, has subverted the use of the traditionally negative term "dyke" and celebrate a tough masculine "diesel-dyke" image. By expressing a strong/dominant female image, they are challenging conventional norms and finding a new avenue of expression that might appeal particularly to Eight women.

Male Eights: Watch a bulky, older, less attractive man ushering a beautiful blonde woman into a party, and the chances are you're looking at an Eight man with a Six or a Four woman. Their power, cash and charisma compensate for much. Male Eights are brash and macho, deriding men who don't display the same degree of sexual swagger. They want to keep the fights clean and the sex dirty. Sex is intense and stormy. Arguments can fly around the room together with clothing, and a female partner can be treated like a Madonna one moment, a whore the next[13] (watch the video of Riana and Eminem's song "Love the way you lie").

They can adopt a "love me or leave me" approach and may have no qualms about using women to bolster their egos and erections (discarding lovers when they no longer excite). For male Eights, maintaining an erection can be the focus, rather than having an orgasm.[14]

Eight men can typify the classic hero archetype: the gladiators of the world, presenting an image that says, "Don't mess with me." Part of their healing is rooted in the ability to acknowledge the innocent, vulnerable child within. With the balancing of these energies, emotional health is achieved and true love from their Type Two aspect can be expressed. Love then is power, and power is expressed through love.

In being the "tough" partner, gay, bisexual, transgender, or pansexual Eight men may secure a role in their relationships as the sexually dominant partner. Yet emotional vulnerability hides behind this exterior, making it especially difficult in some societies for them to express their sexuality. They may as a result feel they have to keep up their guard, remaining in the closet rather than risking exposure and the feeling of vulnerability.

Disintegrated male Eights may challenge their homosexual fears by gay-bashing and displaying homophobic behavior.

Love Type: Erotic (Countertype)

Eights are one of the three Erotic subtypes, along with Sevens and Threes, where sex is about action, physical urges, and the self.

A child may love its parents, but will focus primarily on their own needs.[15] The other two child-like Erotic types demand admiration, but Eights are the countertype because they are self-admiring and self-referencing—as a result, they don't crave praise and admiration the way the other two types do.

Sex and Self-confidence

Eights are invested in pushing their ego-selves out into the world, creating a bravado and strength that translates as confidence, giving the message that no one will get the better of them. It's not rocket science to discover that self-confident people are likely to have more sex—and Eights' self-focus and power lends them a strong sense of self-confidence. Irrespective of their looks, their charisma and charm will have people falling easily into their hearts and beds. While less confident people will be licking their wounds after a rejected pickup, those with strong self-confidence bounce back more easily. More confidence also equates to a greater willingness to explore.

Eights want partners who stand up to them and they enjoy verbal sparring. Doormats are meant to be walked over, so unless you give back as good as you get, they'll quickly get bored and frustrated. As one woman married to an Eight put it, "If I give him an inch, he'll take a number of feet. To keep the dynamic going in our relationship, I've had to stand up to him. If I hadn't, he would have walked all over me years ago."

It's All About Me!

Less healthy Eights can appear selfish and may be totally focused on their own sexual enjoyment rather than their partner's pleasure: "I saw. I conquered. I came!" Submissive types may find it intimidating to express their needs to an Eight.

Independence is important, so they will flagrantly ignore attempts to reign them in, while keeping tight reigns on a partner. They may work hard to afford special indulgences for a partner. They demand faithfulness, yet think little of having affairs themselves: "It meant nothing, really."

Gently Doesn't Do It

Eights dislike neediness, yet they attract those are in need of their strength. In a "cowboys don't cry" way, Eights can mistake feeling any genuine emotion as a weakness—if you ask an Eight to connect with their feelings," you've basically asked them to lie down and be beaten with a stick. Because Eights feel they need to dominate to avoid being dominated, being gentle equals being vulnerable, which equals a loss of their survival skill of autonomy. As a result, sex might not be about intimacy, love, or tenderness, but wham-bam-thank-you-ma'am!

Objectifying a Partner

You're racing to catch a train and people are blocking your way. As you push past them, bumping and shoving, the people are merely obstacles in your way. This is the way disintegrated Eights can view others.

Type Eights' tendency to objectify people makes disintegrated Eights the most insensitive of the Enneagram types.[16] Without love, sex is purely a release, conquest, or exercise. This can be a dangerous place to be if the Eight desires sexual practices that you're not comfortable with.

Power and Sadomasochism

It is always by way of pain one arrives at pleasure.
— *MARQUIS DE SADE*

Sexual deviation is defined as "a sexual practice that is biologically atypical, considered morally wrong, or legally prohibited." [17] It is possible that what one person considers deviant, another may consider "a bit of fun"—mutual consent is the key.

Eights' craving to feel more—more alive, more stimulated, more intense—can sometimes translate into pushing through expected sexual norms, and they can become addicted to sex that gives them power over others. Prostitutes can be instructed in various acts, or a partner might be made to act and dress according to the demands of the Eight. The extremely unhealthy levels descend into the darker world of rape, and the lower self's need for dominance, forcefulness, and sadism. [18]

Eights need to dominate—to literally be on top. Those Eights who choose to express their desire for control and be both tough and demanding find that being the "top" in BDSM (bondage, discipline, submission, and dominance) provides an outlet. Research reveals that people who engage in BDSM have lower levels of agreeableness than those who do not, and are less sensitive to rejection, less neurotic, and more extravert—all of which fits with the Type Eight's personality. [19]

BDSM "dom" enthusiasts were "tough rather than tender minded, willing to make hard decisions, and tend to be bossy and demanding in the way they relate to others, [20] while submissives or "bottoms" were found to be predictably more agreeable. Scott McGreal says this "suggests that doms have found a way to express their disagreeableness in a way that is actually welcomed and appreciated by their submissive partners. This contrasts with more ordinary disagreeableness in everyday life, which is usually seen as annoying and rude." [21] Another study found that compared to "bottoms" or the population as a whole, "tops" have higher self-esteem, satisfaction with life, and openness to experience; lower levels of agreeableness; and a greater desire for control. Although research varies, only a small percentage (between four and eight per cent) of women enjoy being "tops."

In sex, Eights may also feel the need to explore that shadow, vulnerable aspect of themselves by being the "bottom." Many high-powered business people report enjoying being "bottoms," often in paid sex—no doubt a relief and release of the stress of always being on top in business.

An interesting bit of research with 14,306 men and women examined the link between social power and sexual arousal in consensual sadomasochism, finding that power did increase the desire to perform S&M. The effect of power on arousal of sadistic thoughts (inflicting pain on others—more typical of Type Eight behavior) is stronger among women, while the effect of power on arousal by masochistic thoughts (inflicting pain on one's self) is stronger among men. The survey's findings saw power leading to a disregard of social conventions and sexual norms.[22]

Phallic Narcissism

Phallic Narcissists as defined by Willem Reich are described as being arrogant, charismatic, energetic, action-orientated, "impressive in bearing," and "ill-suited to subordinate positions among the rank and file."[23] They can be both men and women, although the latter is less common.

In describing Phallic Narcissism, Reich is for the most part describing less healthy Eights. Like Eights, they attempt to hide their vulnerability and feelings of inferiority. He describes Phallic Narcissists as standing against the object of their affections and having "concealed sadistic characteristics" to a greater or lesser degree, noting that "relationships with women are disturbed by a derogatory attitude towards the female sex." At this disintegrated level, Eights use their sexual conquests to humiliate and show complete disregard for their partner's feelings.[24]

Phallic Narcissists believe themselves to be sexual athletes, with attractive, submissive "trophy" partners. They love to work out, creating strong, attractive physiques to woo lovers, and may be unexpectedly aggressive in situations that don't call for it. They can charm, disarm, and just as quickly become hard and cold, leaving partners confused and self-recriminating: "It must be me." Like Type Eights, they typically have thick necks and large chests, as if they have puffed themselves up against the world. It's understandable that when they start losing power in the world (physically, financially, or in terms of status), they experience rage, anxiety, alienation, and depression. Like deflated balloons, all their bolster is gone.

For women, Phallic Narcissism develops after the age of four, when they may have experienced rejection from the mother or maternal figure and a greater degree of acceptance from the father. To receive their father's affection, they were obliged to dismiss their feminine side. They intimidate their male partners, diminishing their achievements. One case I witnessed involved an extremely wealthy woman who was on the board of numerous international companies. Her husband had noteworthy achievements in his own right, yet she delighted in belittling him and inflating herself, and gave him an affectionate but derogatory nickname.

In his description of Phallic Narcissism, Reich includes some aspects that fit more closely with the description of a Type Four—such as the need to be seen as special, inability to accept criticism, and tendency towards depression. With the Type Four sitting opposite Type Eight, this could be seen as an indication of the shadow aspects of the Eight.

Sexual Problems

Because of their high energy levels, Eights are often able to engage in sex more frequently than other types, and as a result see themselves as being superior. What Eight men seldom reveal is that they can experience premature ejaculation more than the other types. Limited discharge can mean that sexual energy remains awakened, leaving a level of arousal even after sex—in other words, there's more to be released. It can also mean that sexual gratification is more egoic than physical, and that partners can be blamed and then driven to find greater satisfaction.[25] Even if they don't experience premature ejaculation, there can be an emotional experience of feeling unfulfilled and a deeper desire for intimacy, though Eights may interpret it simply as a need for more sex. Eights can also be obsessed with the size of their manhood, because "real men have big penises." This can of course be a problem if they're not well-endowed.

Revenge

Eights test other people's sexual boundaries. If they don't get a direct "No," they can see it as an invitation to push harder, but it only works one way: do the same to an Eight's strong boundaries and the chances are they'll seek revenge under the guise of justice.

While Type Fours may commit crimes of passion that are driven by envy and jealousy, Eights are more likely to commit crimes of revenge. Like disintegrated Fives, they will withdraw and plot—especially if they feel someone hasn't obeyed their rules, or has hurt them.[26] Because they also enjoy confrontation, they may well take on someone for looking at their partner incorrectly.

Interestingly, in cases of infidelity, male Eights are more likely to take revenge on their partner's lover than their partner, who they see as being a victim—too fragile to possibly be responsible.

The Instinctual Drives

Self-preservation Eights: These Eights are preoccupied with getting their physical needs met, doing so with directness, immediacy, and force. What they want, they get—people, companies, sales, cars, positions, and (naturally) sex. They know how to survive in the world and aren't concerned with who or what they need to destroy to fulfil their goals—everyone is a potential competitor. Eights will contravene social norms to meet their needs (fulfil their lust), irrespective of marriage, religious dictates, or what the neighbors think.

Social Eights *(counterphobic)*: Chestnut refers to Social Eights as being the counterphobic Eight because they're less confrontational and aggressive than the other instinctual drives. [27] They're also more concerned with fulfilling others' needs than their own, and tend to be gentler. Being overly concerned about the ailments of those close to them, they may not care for themselves, so or will ignore their own physical ailments. A Social Eight remarked that he was OK with his wife's lack of interest in sex and was happy to be with her, even if sex was infrequent—a perfect example of the self-less Social Eight. [28] They can fear getting too close to a partner because they don't want to experience the pain of rejection. Because they appear more laid-back and less self-absorbed, they're often not seen as being Eights. According to Chestnut, Social Eight men can resemble Nines and Social Eight women can resemble Twos. [29]

Sexual Eights: These Eights tend to be the bad boys or gals of the Enneagram, the most likely to stray from the marital bed. They don't give a damn about going against society. The most charismatic of the three types, they demand attention and love sexual intrigue. Heady, seductive pleasure-seekers, they go after life with lust and passion. They control others by creating needs that only they can meet, like less integrated Twos.

They tend to be more emotional than the other two types. When asked to respond to the words "love and sex," an Eight replied:

> *[They] are extremely important to me. If it's missing in my life, I feel incomplete. It's caused me immeasurable pain. I've been broken and bruised, but somehow, I still manage to put my faith in it; that it's worth it.* [30]

Lovers can be seen as loyal subjects, rather than people with their own wants and desires. [31] They'll be crooning "I did it my way" (sung most notably by Frank Sinatra, with lyrics by Paul Anka), while drinking red wine and leaning seductively and protectively towards their partner.

The Wings

Type Eight with a Seven-wing *(Erotic love doubled)*: In this subtype, the Eight's power meets the Seven's hedonism. Type Eights are not the blushing brides of the Enneagram and will likely only compete with Sevens as the most sexually proactive of the types (although the energy levels of an Eight is real, while a Type Seven is more about creating hype). This subtype will, like Sevens, have an increased hedonistic expression, and will be more inclined to take sexual risks: "Sure my wife's out front in the bar, but you and I are here in the toilet cubicle!" "Condom? What the hell—let's risk it!" When hedonism, risk-taking, and aggression meet the Passions of Lust (Eight) and Gluttony (Seven), there's potential for whoopee with a mega wow factor.

Eights with a Seven-wing are more likely to seek their sexual thrills away from home, in clubs, on vacation or on work trips. Action-orientated types, they're most likely to take the initiative when it comes to sex, which may suit more submissive types, but will create fireworks with similar Advancing types (Threes and Sevens).

With both Sevens and Eights being double Advancing types, they're not going to wait for sex—the first date is just fine, the car on the way there even better. They'll dominate partners and manipulate them to get the action they desire. Should the partner not comply, they can expect a tirade, or a hostile withdrawal if they go to their Type Five aspect. At less integrated levels, it won't be hugely concerning to this Eight if their partner doesn't enjoy lovemaking.

Type Eight with a Nine-wing *(Erotic love with Maternal love)*: Here, the power of the Eight meets the desire for peace of the Nine. The peace-loving Type Nine brings a softer aspect to the Eight, although this subtype combines two Gut (anger) types as opposed to the combination of Gut and Head of the Eight with a Seven-wing.

While the Eight aspect will look to dominate and demand sex, the Nine aspect will be more submissive and want to be sexed. They'll be less aggressive and show a quiet strength, and are less likely to seek sex outside the marital bed. There's more of a protective feeling to them, particularly when it comes to close family and friends.

Interestingly, the Enneagram Institute refer to this wing type as "The Bear,"[32] which is the name given in the gay community to a large hairy man who projects the image of tough masculinity. Eight men of all sexual orientations often share this resemblance.

This wing type's behavior may be less consistent than the other subtype though—one moment they can be showering their partner with affection and gifts, the next they can be openly threatening and hostile. They can be tyrants in the workplace, but warm and accessible at home—or the other way around. When disappointed or jilted they may become reclusive, whereas the Eight with a Seven-wing becomes more reckless.

Moving to Sexual Presence

What Blocks Eights from Sexual Fulfillment

Thrusting against the world, Eights can be experienced by others as taking away their free will. As Eights push forward, their partners pull back, creating frustration for an Eight who feels less in control as a result. Eights can sometimes (often unwittingly) use their strong, energetic presence to make a partner feel small and less significant.

The need to be powerful decreases their ability to connect with the vulnerability of others. Eights deepen their sexual experience when they find the courage to open themselves to their own vulnerability and meet their partner on an equal footing.[33]

How Eights Can become Sexually Present

Let go of control: Eights become integrated lovers, moving from self-centered egotism to the full expression of compassion, when they stop making rules for their partners. When Eights relax the need to control, and when they see a partner's needs as being equal to their own, they start to heal.

Be equal as opposed to superior: Being fully present with a partner requires neither pushing forward or pulling backwards. It's important to stand with a partner, rather than against them. Dominating creates resistance and withdrawal in a partner—the opposite of what Eights deeply desire.

Connect with your vulnerability: Real healing is about allowing vulnerability and openness before, during, and after sex, rather than making others feel vulnerable. Allowing themselves to be held by a partner rather than needing to have a hold over a partner shifts Eights into experiencing sex with awe and wonder. Eights are then able to resolve the paradox of themselves as a courageous warrior and as a vulnerable child.

Let go of the need for excess: Life balance is a popular term, but it's very relevant for Eights, Sevens, and Threes, who can be excessive in all they do. Learning to balance action with thinking and feeling is an important step in integration.

Get in touch with feeling: A more integrated Eight takes time to feel emotions, rather than being reactive and responding in anger to an undesired emotion.

Life isn't a battle: Eights integrate when they realize that they are not at war with their partners, and sex is not a battle of wills. Healing is not about coming out on top, but about intimate co-operation, compromise, and engagement.

Questions to Journal

NOTE: It's useful to answer these questions no matter what your type.

- What impact does your need to dominate your partner have on them and you?
- In not accessing your own vulnerability during lovemaking, are you enforcing a belief that you are strong and your partner is weak?
- Does your fear of being controlled or violated affect the way you show up in the bedroom? In what way?

Exploring the Sexual Types:
The Retreating Group

Types Four, Five, and Nine

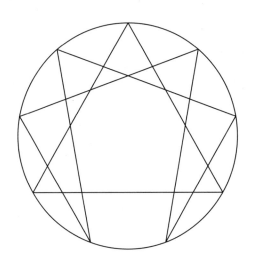

10

Type Four:
The Romantic Romeo (or Juliet)

Four's motto: "Somewhere, out there, my true soul-mate is waiting."

Four as lover: Fours are romantic, intense, self-aware, moody, passionate types who put a huge emphasis on their relationships. They long for a lover who "gets" them and with whom they can be deeply and authentically intimate. When less integrated, their relationship can be an emotional roller coaster.

Fours' retreat: by using fantasies, imagination, and the emotions attached to them in an attempt to heighten sexual intensity. They need to feel a deep, juicy connection with a partner, a buzz that is often more important than sex itself. They often feel like outsiders, and live through their idealized, fantasy self: "Me as the famous eccentric artist."

You may relate to aspects of a Four even if it's not your type: if you are a Three or Five (the wings), or a One or Two (the points of release and stretch).

Love type: Maternal countertype. Fours seek partners who will take care of them, yet they can also be caring.

Relationship belief: "I am unique—you won't find anyone like me out there."

Sexual frustration: "Everyone else seems so happy and in love. Why can't I find the relationship of my dreams?"

Understanding Type Four's Sexuality

Brief overview

Fours long for what they don't have: everyone else's grass is greener. This creates huge suffering and so Fours delve into the past, hoping that doing so may change the future. Fours often report feeling that they have experienced harder lives than others. Because of this perception, they feel a sense of entitlement—life owes them compensation for their suffering. [1] Fours are drawn to those who "get" them, who'll support them, who'll connect deeply with them and warm their gentle souls. Love, or the pursuit of it, becomes an all-embracing focus.

The need for emotional spark explains why Fours can enjoy same-type relationships (Four with a Four), although their favorite choice and the most common relationship type in the Enneagram is a Four woman with a Nine man. [2] Yet, instead of fulfilling their longing, when they do find a lover (and an improved identity), doubt is sparked again, and they may reject the partner to maintain the subconscious belief that they are lost (and therefore flawed). What they have never satiates. This creates an arising melancholy for what isn't and what could be.

Fours long for rescuers who they believe embody the aspects they feel they lack. Relationships get constructed on these expectations being met, which may mean partners have to deny certain aspects of themselves. For example, a Four who feels weak and incompetent may look for a strong, capable partner, but to maintain the relationship, the softer aspects of the lover cannot be expressed. When less integrated, Fours can get furious with a partner who doesn't live up to the expectations the Four has imposed on them.

They can become arrogant and elitist, raising themselves above others, who they believe aren't capable of understanding them (while still feeling inadequate themselves): "You just don't get it, do you?" "His taste is so plebeian." They can treat a partner with contempt only to rush back when the partner heads for the hills. This creates an uneasy tension between moving towards and moving away: which at the extreme, becomes simultaneous love and hate. Because they depend heavily on love, Fours fear rejection—it enforces their feeling of self-lack. Feeling unworthy yet not wanting to face this fear means they may withdraw from others.

When less integrated, Four lovers tend to be intense and moody—one moment deeply passionate and broody the next. They create relationships on their terms: "I've decided that until he behaves in the way he should, there'll be no sex."

Longing to be unique, particularly Sexual Fours experiment with their external image by assuming different roles or styles of dress. Someone with a purple streak in their hair, wearing vintage clothing, adorned with tattoos ("my body as art"), or sporting a beret with a red star is very likely a Four.

Fours are archetypal romantics and artists, dreamers who need to express themselves creatively but also suffer for their cause—the starving or unrecognized artist.

The Arising of Type Four

When we experience being One with God, we have true union—an awesome sense of connection with all that is, a wholeness of spirit that transcends the flesh. This is the connection longed for by Fours (and all of us, because we all have aspects of Fours within us). The word "tantric" means "the weaving and expansion of energy." This is what Fours desire: "By being woven together, we become more."

When we feel one with Being—with the wholeness (holiness) of life—we feel centered. As we move away, we experience a separation or split. Disconnection creates a fear of abandonment and a longing for reconnection. As we disintegrate, this desire for connection with Being morphs into longing for connection with another person: "When I find my soulmate, I will feel connected and whole again."

In childhood, Fours search for approval and love from their parents or the parents they would like to have. Like the Lost Boys in *Peter Pan*'s Neverland, Fours grow up seeking the missing part of themselves. In not finding that connection, Fours feel different from others—the black sheep of the family, feeling like they don't belong. Instead, they feel flawed and shamed into the belief that what they are is not enough. To counteract this, they create a belief that they are different from others, "special" in some way.

Fours in Love

Integrated Fours: Fours are kind, unique, self-aware and genuinely romantic. It's not possible to know what Enneagram type the Sufi poet Rumi was, but his sensitive words and devotion to searching for love reminds me of an integrated Four.

You will find the integrated Four involved in some form of creative expression, or possibly in the field of psychology. Integrated Fours are authentic and honest with themselves, and they desire the same openness from a partner. They want you to show up in your truth and need you to totally accept them in turn. They'll enjoy tantric sex or yoga workshops, and may be drawn to the work of an author like David Deida, who writes about sexual and spiritual relationships.

Fours tend to be reserved and intense, and don't enjoy superficial chit-chat. They want to delve into the deeper parts of themselves and the person they're in a relationship with. They make for passionate and aware lovers, often expressing their unique creativity sexually.

As a result, they may write you poems and will remember the special treat you enjoy and the way you like your hair stroked—intuitively tuning in to your body's needs. At this level, their relationship to suffering translates as having deep compassion for the suffering of others as well as themselves. They truly feel for their lover's problems and, in listening with an open heart, can be transformative healers.

Average Fours: These Fours will delve into their history and live current experiences through the lens of the past. Feeling they are lacking something, they project the feeling that something is always lacking in the world: the relationship that held so much promise will now feel empty; the partner is missing something the Four desires. Fours start to retreat into their fantasies, intensifying their feelings but not realizing that doing so inhibits real connection: "I want something more than just sex; I get deeper satisfaction from emotional intimacy. Sex is just an expression of intimacy. When someone gets my body, they also get my soul."

Focusing so deeply on their moods can make less integrated Fours become self-absorbed. They may use their image of being original and eccentric to attract a partner. They like things to be done their way and may dislike sharing,[3] particularly if they have a Five-wing. A new relationship may feel doomed even before it's begun: "This won't end well." Yet there's a sense of satisfaction in this unhappy end,[4] as if feeling victimized brings some reward or comfort from pain. They worry that prospective partners won't appreciate their special gifts or uniqueness and that they'll never be rescued into the life they desire.

Disintegrated Fours: Life and love have become a disappointment. Their idealized self has moved far beyond their actual self. They gaze lovingly towards Venus and find only warring Mars. They are disdainful of their partners, finding fault in all they do, becoming angry and self-sabotaging, yet hugely envious: "No one understands me!" "How can she achieve recognition so easily?"

Hypersensitive to their own needs yet insensitive to the needs of their partner, they feel as if they are surrounded by unsophisticated, crass morons who have no idea of style, true emotions, beauty, love... "The insensitive idiots!"

Fours feel misunderstood and may brood malevolently on how bad their lives are, while dreaming that a knight in shining armor will come to rescue them. They seek not so much a partner but an enabler, who will support them both financially and emotionally. Life feels tragic, and they are the unsung hero/heroine. They appear to enjoy each new drama, failure, or rejection, as it fulfils their belief that life has been especially hard for them. A vanity arises regarding their suffering. They want to be a famous musician but seem to have pessimistically given up the quest before they have begun: "No one has the intelligence to understand my work."

Feeling hugely let down by life itself, depression can arise. They feel victims and envy turns to a deep and bitter resentment. Everyone else is to blame, their partners particularly. "Life is so easy for you," they may scream and rage, spitefully hurting those who are trying to help them. Sexually they may immerse themselves in perverse practices and swing from being sadistic to masochistic with equal intensity—Romeo has become rancid.

Fours at their best are the loving poets, musicians and artists of the Enneagram, who instill beauty into our drab world. Through their heightened sensitivity and awareness, they allow us to be inspired to delve further into the meanings of our own lives – to see the beauty that is life.

What Four Dating Adverts May Look Like

Pierre, 32
So, here I am, this is me...
1. *I'm a romantic at heart (I once met a girl online and then flew halfway across the world to meet her, sure she was my soulmate. OK, so I was only 18...).*
2. *I feel like the family I grew up in wasn't my real family—bit of a black sheep, I guess.*
3. *I'm the guy who dropped out of school and opened a decorating business—no boss and loads of free time (and beautiful things).*
4. *Music. Oh yeah. I play some acoustic guitar and write songs. Music carries us back to emotions we felt in the past. Feelings are addictive to me.*

5. *I love to dance salsa and am learning the tango. Just waiting for that night in the Asia Bar in Bariloche with you...*
6. *I do Body Stress Release therapy for a few clients (just so as you know I like to massage...)*
7. *Definitely decaf and vegan.*
8. *Waffle addict.*
9. *Extrovert 16%, introvert 74%, undecided 10%*
10. *Limelight—no way*
11. *Favorite artist: Frida Kahlo*
12. *Travel—to weird and totally wonderful places*
13. *Road-tripping, meditating, auras, yoga and thoughts as energy—yes to all*

If you could be my real soulmate, contact me.

Fatima, 43

All profiles seem the same. Everyone is crying out to say how good they are, how cool they are or how much fun they are. But how real are you? I'm tired of the lies, the excuses, the fakes... I'm looking for my best friend. I don't know if the world is going to last forever, but I know I'm going to be with you forever!

I don't know when I'll finally meet you to warm my heart and join me for a better, happier life journey, but I know I can't stop looking for you, and can't stop calling you in my heart...

I also don't know what life holds for me tomorrow, but I do know that we only get older, and I'd feel safer getting old with you.

Maybe it's about the right time, the right place, the right person... Can online dating be any good? We'll see! :)

The Passion of Envy and the Fixation of Melancholy

I worked with a couple who were both Fours: he was an artist and she was an art critic. Their relationship had started as an intense, fiery meeting of minds and bodies. Then his art had been repeatedly rejected and he'd refused to sculpt again. She had supported them but took on a string of lovers who were drawn to her elegance and power in the art world. She envied his free time and lack of responsibility. He envied her fame and glamourous lifestyle. The celibate war between them continued for more than 30 years. They couldn't leave each other, yet they couldn't really love each other either.

Seeing everyone else as having it better than they do creates envy in Fours. Some may not be aware of their envy, but it can emerge in arrogance and aloofness, or in unconscious "accidents" that affect others: "Oops, I just spilled coffee on your painting." "Sorry I broke your favorite vase—I didn't mean to." Acknowledging their envy creates further shame. [5]

To the Four, others appear fulfilled and happy, but there's an incompleteness in their own lives, [6] leading them to question, "Am I flawed?" Envy is an intense feeling—Naranjo refers to it as "the most passionate of passions." [7] This feeling of lack creates sadness, yet is also the space where Fours report they feel most deeply and create their best work.

Think of Frida Khalo, overshadowed in her art career by her more famous (at the time) artist husband Diego Rivera. She suffered through polio and a traffic accident, while Diego claimed the artistic fame during their marriage. She had her first solo exhibition a year before she died in 1954, and only really started being recognized in the late 1970s. This is the story of many a talented Four.

When Fours move from envy to acceptance, and from fantasy to making their dreams materialize in realty, they attain a sense of self-worth.

Shame

Heart types (Twos, Threes, and Fours) have issues with shame and guilt, so they work to present an "improved" image of themselves. Seeking affirmation and approval, Twos do for others, Threes achieve, and Fours desire love: "If someone can love me, then I have worth."

Fours who have idealized their partner in the beginning of a relationship ("You saved me") unconsciously project their lack of self-worth on to their partner and begin to find fault in the lover.

A Peek into a Four's Bedroom

Fours often enjoy the quiet sanctum of their homes or apartments. They're lovers of beauty, so their bedrooms often reflect this in a stylish, minimalistic way. Cool colors, a beautiful pottery piece picked up on one of their travels, a particular tone of grey, soft lighting, and plenty of textures, comfort, and great art—or whatever best shows taste and reveals their mood.

The more hippie-like Four with a Five-wing may opt for handwoven throws, wooden floors, candles, incense, and trippy music, and will be less tidy. The Four with a Three-wing may want to impress with art by trendy artists, and have a more refined, elegant taste in furnishings or a minimalistic approach. Generally (depending on the influence of their partner), the room will be artistically decorated, stylish, and unusual—a place to truly relax and escape the harsh world.

Fantasies, Fetishes, and Erotica

Because a Four's inner world is often more in focus than their outer world, they have a greater tendency towards fantasy [8]—but this interior engagement has them feeling an external lack even more intensely. Fantasy masquerades as fulfillment and can become a way to cope.

Fours' shadow sides emerge in their fantasies, so they may want to switch their usual style and assume a dominant role. Alternatively, the need for masochistic sex can mean that Fours may enjoy being spanked or flogged. Interestingly, some animals only ovulate after being bitten—a biological example from nature for pleasurable pain. Spanking can also originate from guilt for enjoying sex—being punished for pleasure.

One-night stands offer excitement though seldom the emotional intensity Fours desire. Incense, a glass of wine, candles, a book, and their own fantasies can seem a better option. Some Fours report fantasizing having sex in public places—the beaches, boardrooms, or bathrooms they would normally avoid—which makes the thought of leaving their sanctuary more inviting!

Women who only have fantasies of the bodice-ripping variety may find it difficult to separate sex from love. [9] Some Fours may find themselves spending hours creating fantasies where they are rescued into a world of wealth, power, and fame.

Fours may find that their loneliness leads them into addictive sexual behavior. The artist who can't paint, the writer who can't repeat the brilliance of his first novel, the fashion designer whose clothes remain on the rail may look to random hook-ups, watching series, drink a bottle of whisky per night, or take drugs as a way to ease their emotional pain and avoid taking concerted action to improve the situation. [10]

Fours who feel lonely, detached, or ignored by a partner may enjoy pornography to fill the day and their intense sexual longings. It can feel like revenge against a partner who they feel is unavailable—allowing them to be safely unfaithful. Pornography may also provide a solution to the feeling that their needs aren't being met—on screen, the actors appear to meet the Four's every sexual desire.

Fetishist behavior is possible as Fours start acting on sexual impulses. [11] The most popular fetish is feet, and things associated with the feet such as stockings, shoes, and socks. [12] Feet are followed by hands and hair—and shoes, gloves, and underwear by extension. But fetishes can be as bizarre as getting turned on watching beetles being crushed, looking at statues, or the thought of katoptronophylia (having sex in front of a mirror). [13]

According to Drs. Mark Laaser and Tim Clinton, sexual fetishes can result from the brain's attempt to work through wounding or trauma from childhood [14]—the early sexual experience that led to arousal becomes imprinted in the brain, laying the pathway for future excitement. If the fetish becomes compulsive, controlling the impulse may be a difficult.

More than any wild sexual gymnastics though, Fours are looking for connection. If a partners shows up for them in the bedroom, they won't mind indulging them in turn. (Lucky they kept that nurse's outfit!) They normally have great imaginations and abhor vanilla sex—if there is trust in the relationship, they'll be open to trying something new.

Fours of Different Genders

Female Fours: Fours are generally associated with more "feminine" traits—sensitivity, gentleness, intuition, and vulnerability—and it does appear that there are more Four women than men. There are also a higher proportion of gay people who are Fours than in any other type, according to Naranjo. [15]

As mentioned in the chapter on Eights, Eights represent the archetypal male and Twos and Fours share more feminine traits. Roles get assigned to these types in same-sex relationships that relate to the male/female archetypes. So, a lesbian Eight woman may be described as "butch" and a Four woman as "femme." [16]

Because of the way society has been traditionally structured, it may be easier for female Fours to find someone who will support and take care of their needs. The powerful and wealthy Eight businessman whose Four wife expresses herself through sculpture may be able to enjoy his wife's creativity (because it reflects a socially "acceptable" structure)—but the wife of a wildly creative male Four musician may get resentful when he practices endlessly but does little to bring home the bacon.

Romantic Fours particularly with a Three wing, enjoy the finer things in life—design, fashion, travel, exotic lovers—and prefer not to have to worry about mundane issues. While a luxury yacht is a better sexual lubricant than a rowing boat, enough is seldom enough for a Four woman. They can appear to "have it all," yet even as they realize their dreams, there's a part of them that is already wistfully fantasizing about a different reality.

While Four women with a Three-wing may enjoy being hit on, the other wing type might find it offensive:

> *I detest getting attention based on my looks. It's shallow and meaningless, even though I'm supposed to enjoy the compliment. If he were to say, "You have beautiful auburn hair and I love the way it cascades over your shoulders," as opposed to, "You're great-looking,"—something more personal—it would be better, because he'd have really noticed something special about me.*

Four women are most likely to be attracted to steady types whose sense of humor allows them to withstand the emotional fallouts and melancholic moods of their partners. For the Four, having someone who affirms their uniqueness and builds up their self-worth goes a long way to navigate rocky times in a relationship.

Male Fours: Melancholy allows Fours to feel with more intensity. As such, happiness is not as much of a goal as connection is. They don't need emotional depth from everyone, just their partner. They enjoy the connection that is sparked in fighting rather than a civil cerebral discussion. Like Eights, fighting is intense—real, passionate—and on the other side of war lies love and delicious makeup sex…

Four men, particularly Sexual Fours, want 100 percent of their partner's attention, so even their own children may prove to be an irritant at times. If a longed-for relationship becomes a disappointment, less integrated Fours will believe that their partner is to blame.

Looking for love so intently while being driven by loneliness and the desire for connection can lead to Fours to find love in the wrong places—with abusive lovers and risky sexual habits. While sexual addiction can occur in less integrated Fours, for others, sex is about the all-encompassing emotional connection, which goes way beyond mere orgasm:

I want my sex life to be meaningful, not simply physical. I can't relate to the hook-up culture. I'm much too self-aware, so I can't imagine myself comfortably having sex with a stranger. I want and expect something more from sex than "just sex"—real connection—yet I can't seem to find it. Something is always missing.

This comment sums up what Four men are looking for in sex: "I masturbate alone to fill a physical need, but for me sex is about sharing myself emotionally—head, heart, and body. Then it's heaven."

Love Type: Maternal (Countertype)

In the Maternal Love triad, the other two types (Two and Nine) are outwardly focused in nurturing others. While Fours are understanding and self-sacrificing, and can be empathetic in the role of social worker or psychologist, for example, they are more commonly self-focused, particularly when less integrated. They seek carers or people they can be dependent on rather than the other way around, which makes them the Maternal Love countertype.

Sex and Depression

Oxytocin is released when we touch or hug humans or animals. This hormone promotes feelings of well-being and happiness, and a positive outlook, and assists us in feeling more compassionate towards others. It's also been found to increase dopamine and serotonin, which relieve stress and anxiety, and lower blood pressure. Fours who drift into melancholy need physical touch (as all people do) to move towards greater happiness and well-being. It's understandable that being deprived of touch can have the opposite effect.

Fours create an idealized version of themselves. While Threes believe they are already their idealized selves, Fours feel as if they are unable to be their fantasized self [17]—it's the man trying to capture the moon. While a Three may honestly believe themselves to be superior in the bedroom, Fours may feel that they miss the mark—and their never reaching their ideal creates feelings of shame and guilt. It is this cycle that makes Fours one of the types more prone to depression.

Fours desire intimacy and authenticity—"sensual gratification," to quote Naranjo.[18] He suggests that Fours need the soothing effect and release of regular sex to avoid possible depression. For Fours, craving validation through love translates into a hunger for sex. Sex in turn reinforces Fours, making them feel worthy of love. In the moment of orgasm, they experience (if fleetingly) the longed-for experience of being whole—one with the other.

Dependence as Sexual Fuel

If sex, money, and power lubricate the wheels of love, this is especially true of the Four. Disintegrated Fours have an exaggerated sense of entitlement; at less integrated levels they often seem incapable of supporting themselves.[19] Offit defines four types of dependencies:

- *Social dependence—where loneliness, which is often felt by Fours, drives people into relationships.*
- *Economic dependence—where the power of the purse determines who we have sex with. (Naranjo found that the need for financial support arises from the desire to be cared for.)* [20]
- *Parental dependence—where someone takes care of us too much like a parent. (A good example of this is George Bernard Shaw's Pygmalion, where Professor Henry Higgins undertakes the instruction of flower-seller Eliza Doolittle. An attraction develops during her elocution lessons.) Fours desire a parental archetype to protect them; it's as if the world is too tough for their sensitive selves.*
- *Pain dependence—when the desire to receive pain, either emotional or physical, becomes a need.* [21]

All these dependency characteristics have the potential to create relationships where sex is stimulated by loneliness, cash, being cared for, or masochistic needs. In Fours, it can translate as falling into relationships and sexual experiences where they may consent to sex even if they don't desire it: "Every day my husband expects sex, whether I want to or not. I just lie there and let him get on with it. Doing so ensures he'll be tolerable to be with and I get the lifestyle I desire."

Disintegrated Fours can feel hopelessly ill-equipped to deal with life, and their dependencies can eat away at their self-esteem. They may mope around at home, accusing a partner of neglect simply because the partner is working to support them. To get the attention they feel is waning, they may act self-destructively, self-harm, throw hissy fits, behave cruelly, or blame others for problems in their lives. Partners can suffer because disintegrated Fours may not see the person on whom they depend as having needs and desires of their own.

"Love" appears to offer the solution to the Four's dilemma of self-hatred. It holds the promise of providing understanding, company, and enhanced self-worth, sexual enjoyment, and financial security, as well as the end of the need to fend or be responsible for oneself and of envying those who appear to have love. Love becomes a way to complete oneself, because less integrated Fours feel incapable of finding wholeness within themselves.[22]

Masochism: Tied-up Freedom

You're an artist, but creating your art is a painful process. Fears of being mediocre or, worse still, plain boring, keep you awake at night. You love the art, but it's hard to produce. Pleasure and pain mingle in your studio and in the bedroom. The torture you experience in your fantasies mirrors the torture you feel in real life, satisfying you in a way that vanilla sex doesn't. The way you beat yourself up emotionally makes it seem natural to be beaten physically.

Leopold von Sacher-Masoch (from whom the word "masochism" derives) was born in the Ukraine in 1836. A writer, he had an inclination for fantasies and fetishes involving dominant women (preferably wearing fur). His best-known work was a novella titled *Venus in Furs*, in which we gather he wrote about his own desires—but he went further in real life by having his mistress (the aptly named Baroness Fanny Pistor) sign a six-month contract making him her slave, adding the condition that she wear furs whenever possible. The two traveled to Italy: Leopold disguised as her servant in third class while she traveled in first. His private life would have remained just that had it not been for his wife of ten years, Aurora Rümelin (later Wanda von Dunajew), spilling the beans in a memoir called *Meine Lebensbeichte (My Life Confession)*.

This desire to seek pleasure from pain or humiliation is not uncommon in Fours. Harold Kelman—neurologist, psychiatrist, psychoanalyst, teacher, author and close associate of Karen Horney—wrote that masochism is a way that we cope in life by being "dependent and self-minimizing." He saw it showing up mostly in the sexual arena, but it also arises in the way people avoid responsibility and criticism while accusing others. It's a world where suffering is elevated to a noble status or virtue, and as such demands both love and acceptance.[23]

The American Psychiatric Association removed sadomasochism from the *Diagnostic and Statistical Manual of Mental Disorders* in the 1980s, which is just as well—with one in ten people having experimented with S&M, a whole lot of the population would be considered mentally unstable! S&M allows people to lose their normal identities as well as relax, with no expectations placed on them to perform. If you feel yourself to be inadequate, ugly, ashamed, or "bad," then being hurt can turn the emotional pain into a physical experience followed by temporary relief and even euphoria. For a brief time, anxieties that occur in ordinary life from mortgages, taxes, deadlines, and financial problems all dissolve with a flick of the whip; the masochist is only aware of what is happening in the moment.

When disintegrated, the self-effacing, self-disliking, dependent Type Four is arguably the unhappiest of the Enneagram types. Life centers around suffering; they suffered for love. In marriage it's understandable why Fours' top choices for partners are the accommodating Nine followed by the strong Eight.[24] From a psychological perspective, the desire for pain to be pleasured occurs when we are afraid to express our aggression outwardly, and so internalize the anger in the form of pain. While Eights provide the security Fours desire, zoned-out Nines offer none of the intensity Fours crave. Fours create drama, but Nines want peace.

When Love Gets Tainted

As they move to more average levels and loneliness creeps in, Fours may start compulsively looking for love: "I do occasionally have one-night hook-ups, but even though the connection isn't long, it's still intimate." As disappointment replaces connection, the desire to find "the one" is amplified, making the search more desperate and hook-ups less discerning. Shame increases, stimulating the desire for a "parent" who will be their savior, until there are simply random encounters with self-debasing sex masquerading as love. Tainted love replaces authentic love.

The Instinctual Drives

Self-preservation Fours *(counterphobic)*: Being the counterphobic type, this Four may be difficult to identify. Instead of taking their pain, sadness, and suffering into the world, it is internalized to the point that they may even appear upbeat in comparison to the other two subtypes. Whereas the others believe that expressing their hardships to the world will bring the attention they crave, this subtype believes that they are more likely to get their needs (sexual and other) met by *not* displaying their pain.[25] Self-preservation Fours describe love and sex in the following ways: "as sweet as it can get," and "when love and sex do go together, magic, beauty and all kind of gorgeousness happen," and "love is being able to put sex aside, because it's not always about sex. Love is two people being there for each other when shit gets real."[26]

These Fours are more proactive and, if lonely, more likely to actively look for a partner in order to replace their feeling of longing. Rather than being a victim, they may seek out victims to uplift—by becoming a psychologist, doctor, or philanthropist of sorts. They may look after others to their own detriment, such as living with an elderly parent or incapacitated partner, or being a single parent who won't get involved in a relationship because of the children. Naranjo refers to this as "self-enslavement."[27]

They see their pain in others' pain, which can result in them rescuing a partner while hiding their own need to be rescued. Even a wounded animal or pet can resonate very strongly with their own woundedness.[28] I recall a Self-preservation Four who found an injured baby bird, which she nursed for two days. Weeks after the bird had died, she was still mourning its loss deeply.

Despite their connection to the pain of others, these Fours are stoic like Ones. They persevere where other Fours would abdicate, holding in their emotions rather than expressing them. Envy can arise, however, regarding things of the physical world such as homes, wealth, art collections, health, sexual stamina, or the beauty of other people's bodies.

Social Fours: Chestnut refers to this type as "Shame"[29]—the type that feels most inadequate, suffers more openly and becomes attached to their pain as a result. Suffering creates an identity, as if they will achieve enlightenment by martyring themselves: "I feel things deeply. The world to me feels uncaring and fractured. Everything within me connects—spirit, head, heart. I feel what others can't. And yet I can't find the romance I desire. I wonder what's wrong with me."

These Fours enjoy social interaction more than the other two subtypes, yet may feel socially inadequate,[30] as expressed by this Social Four:

> *I love social interactions yet can avoid them feeling somewhat shy. But sex is a lure and my desire to connect to the other person is huge. So, like a wounded tortoise I*

*stick my head out into the social arena. I like the physical
pleasure and the subtleties. For example, watching a drop
of sweat roll down his chest, the way he watches me undress,
the sound of his breathing... I enjoy feeling possessed by a
man—protected—desired. I'm very passionate, though often
the connections aren't long lasting. Then I'm alone again.*

They may appear soft and sweet, but behind closed doors they vent
their repressed anger. Being Social, they are more likely to choose a mate
who is also a Four (with other types it's unusual to choose someone of
your own type) or who shares the same social values.

They are more aware of their pain and may be confused as to its source.
Their lives from others' perspectives often don't appear too bad—certainly
no worse than most—yet these Fours believe their lives have been tough:
"I had it much harder than my siblings."

Social Fours may long for the social-status needs such as talent, money,
fame, or power that their partners appear to have. They may compare
themselves unfavorably to a partner's previous lover:[31] "Why would you
want me after your ex?" Envy can also arise in relation to another person's
fame, status, popularity, ability to woo a crowd, get sexual conquests, or
ability to mingle with the rich and famous.

When they marry, they may conjure the idea that a partner's friends
and family don't like them and then create that reality through their
behavior. As they navigate society, they may feel like misfits and may
align themselves with gangs, punk rockers, hipsters, or "glitch hoppers"
(a music genre centered around aesthetic failure and glitch-based audio
recordings)—anything that speaks to being different or unique. When
disintegrated, they can give up completely, becoming totally reliant on
others for support.[32]

Sexual Fours: This is the most competitive[33] of the Four subtypes, with
the added spice of envy, as if the Sexual Four is saying:

*I desire who and what you are, so rather than just going
after what I desire [like Self-preservation Fours] or feeling
ashamed for what I am not [like Social Fours], I choose
to compete with and beat you—even destroy you [like the
vindictive achievement of a Type Three].*

Competition is the natural progression from envy: "If I can't have what I want, then I'll make sure you can't either, by ruining your hopes and dreams." This can be devastating to a partner, particularly one who is less able to defend themselves.

This Four also wants to compete for the attention of significant others and may not respond well to being upstaged. They want to be better than others and don't care if they offend along the way. They envy others' relationships or, if in a relationship themselves, they envy those who seem carefree or whose partner they believe is better in some way. They can cast a green eye over others who have more success in sex or who are more attractive—and resent them for it. Fours could be madly attracted to those who don't show an interest in them, while rejecting those who do.[34]

Chestnut sees this subtype as making others suffer rather than suffering themselves, as is the case with the Social type.[35] To get a partner to support them, they may belittle or humiliate them, so the partner feels that no one else would want them. They would rather their partner suffered the pain they don't want to feel. It stands to reason that this type may be more inclined to sadism than masochism.

Shameless rather than shameful, Sexual Fours are also more likely to act on impulse and have spontaneous illicit sex, becoming arrogant and uncompromising if confronted. Their desires take priority over a partner's, and this would include the sexual rules of engagement.

They may initially show up more like a Social type (in the form of the brilliant but wounded artist) but revert to their main Instinctual Subtype once the relationship has developed.[36] As a partner might say:

> I'm in a relationship with a Sexual Four and I was surprised
> to find that he was a Four, because there was none of the
> romance I'd been led to understand that Fours are good
> at. I've come to understand that he believes any display of
> romance (candles, poetry) would be tacky and inauthentic.

Angriest of all the Enneagram types,[37] the more they express their dislike of others, the more their own self-hatred arises. In their relationships, they desire more intensity than the other subtypes—they don't care if you argue with them as long as you show up with them.

Interestingly, when they wrote what came to their minds regarding "sex and love," Sexual Fours seemed the least able to express their emotional views, choosing to respond with abstract answers such as: "he," and "what makes the world go around." [38]

They can work harder than the other two instinctual types on their appearance and are the most sensual of the three Fours. Riso and Hudson refer to this type as "Infatuation," [39] as they swing from love to hatred and back again with ease, which creates the potential for a stormy relationship.

The Wings

Four with a Three-wing *(Maternal countertype and Erotic love)*: In this subtype, the envy of the Four meets the ambition of the Three. This type feels themselves to be more refined than the other wing type does. They have a need to climb the social ladder and may portray themselves as being higher up than they are. I recall one Four man who set off to England determined to let go of his middle-class background. Within a few years he'd met the Queen, been to Lords on several occasions, owned a sumptuous house in Surrey, and acted more British than the British— yet was always envious of the "true" British gentleman.

Their Three-wing makes them more active, ambitious, and able to accomplish things than the other wing type, [40] but their desire for refinement often has them experiencing those around them as unintelligent, boring, insensitive, or loutish.

Four with a Five-wing *(Maternal countertype with Paternal love)*: Here, the envy of the Four meets the avarice of the Five. While Fours reach out for what they desire, their Five-wing tells them their quest is pointless—there's not enough love for them in the world. They need to hold on to what little they have, rather than risk losing it. This attitude can result in them staying in unloving relationships.

This type has a cooler personality and may find it difficult to connect with the source of their pain. They also tend to be more melancholic. They are like the hippies of the Sixties—anti-establishment, creative in an idiosyncratic way, lovers of love, yet there's a torturous expression in their lives which is often expressed through their artistic creations.

Unlike the other wing subtype, they have no desire to mingle with the rich and famous, but, like hippies, choose a simpler lifestyle outside the restrictions of society. This also goes for their sexual attitudes, which may be different from the norm—like "free love," or open relationships.

Moving to Sexual Presence

What Blocks Fours from Sexual Fulfillment

If Ones look for what needs to be corrected before they can relax and enjoy sex, Fours look for what is missing or "wrong" in the relationship: [41] You're madly in love, standing holding hands on a romantic tropical beach watching the sun set over a brilliant turquoise sea… yet the faint smell of rotting seaweed pervades the air and becomes the focus.

Fours can become oversensitive and react in anger to things that were never meant, remaining withdrawn and moody for days while their partner remains confused. They also like to dwell on the past, and may be lamenting an ex-lover while ignoring the one in their bed.

The feeling of being loved one moment and rejected the next can be confusing for a partner, who begins to feel that there's something wrong with them and may withdraw: "Maybe they don't really love me? I can't seem to please—nothing I do is not enough."

Appreciating the half-full cup rather than bemoaning it being half empty can help Fours enjoy better relationships and sex: "I came to realize all my wife meant to me. There's so much about her that I love, yet for years I only saw what she wasn't. Becoming aware and appreciating what she is changed our lives."

How Fours Can become Sexually Present

Find the missing piece: You've just made love, and it was great, but something stopped it from being amazing. You can't quite get what it was. Maybe the way your partner touched you could have been gentler? Maybe the orgasm could have been more intense and longer? It was there, but not there…

Imagine a puzzle where there are always pieces missing. The picture is never whole. To the degree they are integrated, Fours feel there are fewer missing pieces—to heal is to realize that all the pieces are already there, you just need to see them.

Let go of shame: For so long Fours have projected their own feelings of shame onto a partner (or switched from over-glorifying to the opposite), creating a push-pull relationship: "I love you! Oh, wait I don't." When they realize their self-worth, Fours see the self-worth in others. When they can stand steady and authentically see what is, without the need to enhance or detract, their cups become truly full and in holding all that is with what they perceive is not, they transcend the need for the duality.

Let go of the need to be special: If Fours accept that at times they can be boring or not unique, while sill acknowledging their special gifts, they no longer lose energy resisting one and trying to enhance the other. Both states of being are OK.

Move from envy to having your own identity: If Fours can see that what they envy in a partner is really an aspect of themselves that they have yet to acknowledge, they will no longer envy what they perceive someone else has or is.

Embrace reality over fantasy: When Fours stop fantasizing about what a relationship might be and enjoy the one they're in, they engage with life and their current reality. They also let go of being overly sensitive (brooding over a partner's perceived slight) and rather look for the positive qualities a partner brings to their life.

Questions to Journal

NOTE: It's useful to answer these questions no matter what your type.

- Do you truly love and accept all aspects of yourself?
- Does your fear of being a bedroom bore affect the way you have sex?
- How would a tendency to focus inward affect yourself and your partner when having sex?
- How does sexual fantasy affect your ability to engage with the world and reality?

11

Type Five:
The Lonely Lover

Five's motto: "Distance binds us closer right?" "I enjoy observing sex; it fascinates me."

Five as lover: As lovers they can be emotionally detached, fearing that involvement will be draining, yet when they do make love, they can bring their fervency into the bedroom.

Fives' retreat: by shifting into their thoughts and being intensely head-focused. They don't enjoy superficial chit-chat. They need to withdraw from others to connect with their feelings.

You may relate to aspects of a Five even if it's not your type: if you are a Four or Six (the wings), or if you are a Seven or an Eight (the points of stretch and release).

Love type: Paternal. Fives keep their distance and have a cooler, more cerebral approach to love. They don't want to feel too reliant on another person, desiring connection yet fearing it.

Relationship belief: "Being detached emotionally and physically is how I feel safe, and even superior—I'm not a slave to my emotions and desires."

Sexual frustration: "Every time I sleep with someone, they start making demands on me and my time—why can't we have sex and then get back to work?"

Understanding Type Five's Sexuality

Brief overview

Although Fives can be tender at times, their partners more often complain that they are distant, either physically, emotionally, or both. Relationships can make Fives feel dependent or depended upon. As a result, they may find taking care of their own sexual needs less complicated than engaging in human interaction. They tend to have a numbed exterior yet are usually sensitive if you get close to them. They're loners who don't appear to mind being lonely—in fact, most prefer it.

Fives want to believe they have mastered the mechanics of sex (and life)—sex becomes cerebral, rather than emotional or intuitive. If the choice was attending a lecture on "Understanding the Mathematical Mechanics of Sex" or having actual sex, many Fives would carefully weigh up the choice.

Because they feel inferior, they collect knowledge as a way to enhance their capabilities—knowledge becomes the way to power. In relationships they will try to attract a mate not through flashy dressing, but by impressing them with information, often on obscure subjects. One Five looking for love posted a complex mathematical equation on Facebook, suggesting that any woman who could supply the correct answer would clearly be a good match. (He remained single!)

They are likely to start discussing intellectual concepts after sex, rather than whispering sweet nothings in their lover's ear. Fives also tend to withhold information regarding past liaisons and sexual secrets. Their chat-up lines can be awkward, but they are typically intelligent and kind.

Fives hide from the world under a veil of nihilistic (but knowledgeable) disinterest: "None of this concerns me." Feeling separate, it's difficult to relate to love, which seems to demand the opposite. Sexually they may desire a mate but negotiating love with intellect and knowledge creates a paradox: cupid holding an encyclopedia. It is often easier to withdraw and deny that they have a need for love.

You'll find Fives hanging out as professors, academics, IT professionals, or writers—anywhere there is knowledge to be gained in a specific field. They seek a quiet work environment and don't enjoy bosses breathing down their necks.

The Arising of Type Five

Fives are one of the three Head and Fear types, along with Six and Seven. Their Passion is avarice, which translates as feeling that there is not enough—not enough love, time, money… While Ones tend to be frugal, Fives fear that their limited resources will be depleted, so can withhold them.

Fives developed this fear from childhood, when they may have felt there wasn't enough nurturing. Enneagram author Sandra Maitri uses the analogy of a being marooned on a desert island, holding on to what few resources there are,[1] or sucking from an empty breast.[2] The loss of connectedness with the prime nurturer is experienced as a deeper loss of connection to Being.

Paradoxically, some Fives report having felt smothered by their prime nurturer, where their boundaries were not respected, and love was experienced as consuming, even invasive.[3] In this event, fear arose in feeling that they must hold on to what little autonomy they had.

As children, Fives didn't feel truly seen or understood. The parent would not have intended this, but rather would have lacked the ability to attune to the child's needs. So, the little Five retreated from the family into their own world and headspace, where things felt safer and less threatening, and where thinking ruled over feeling.

Fives feel isolated, observing rather than engaging, and minimizing their needs so they don't have to rely on anyone or anything else. In relationships, this creates the fear that a partner will repeat their childhood experience of depleting their resources or making demands on them.

Fives in Love

Integrated Fives: Integrated Fives are fascinated and curious about their partners, and can have penetrating insight into them. They want to understand their lovers. In relationships they feel confident and competent and are appreciative of their partners, displaying a deep level of compassion.

They are independent, yet prepared to share their world and its secrets. Instead of removing themselves to quietly connect with their emotions alone, they now trust a partner and can as a result share their inner emotive worlds. The selfishness of their less integrated selves transforms into selflessness. They are outgoing and cheerful companions with a wry sense of humor.

In the bedroom they are explorative and uncensored in their desires. They also become more persistent in the pursuit of a partner, rather than giving up at the slightest hint of rejection. "Sharing is caring" becomes their way of interacting as they develop a rich emotional (as well as intellectual) life.

Average Fives: Fives become increasingly detached from the world and those in it. Caring for themselves (and others) becomes irrelevant, and close relationships are harder to contend with. They may be attracted to someone, but not feel confident enough to follow up and so may ridicule that person: "She's just a blonde bimbo." "He's not the sharpest pencil in the box."

As a result, Average Fives may find themselves single (apart from Sexual types), or in brief and emotional rollercoaster-type relationships. Coping with loved ones becomes just too much: "I need space," they yell.

Work or the latest project becomes a way of avoiding relationships. Fives may claim that they are too busy to engage in any form of social activity with their partner (should they still have one), yet time is often wasted on completely random tasks, such as creating a detailed database of birds they've spotted, compiling lists of their favorite music, or researching an obscure movie genre. They can become increasingly secretive, yet jealous of any attention their partner may receive.

Fives start amputating their relationships as they feel more incapable in them. They'll tell themselves, "I never really loved her," or "Men are problematic—I dated a guy five years ago and it was a disaster, so I'm not going there again." They can become frustrated with themselves for feeling sexual urges: they don't want to feel as if they need or rely on anything or anyone.

Fives' boundaries become increasingly rigid. They'll be pernickety about sharing a suitcase, or will see their partner's spoon dipping into their dessert as an act of hostility.

Disintegrated Fives: Isolated, helpless, depressed, Fives slip into a world where life and its potential beauty is pointless. They become cynical and just want to be left alone.

Like Origen of Alexandria, an early Church Father (born in 165 AD), who castrated himself to stop his sexual desires, disintegrated Fives castrate themselves emotionally. Their interactions become increasingly argumentative and provocative as they try to undermine others' pleasure: "Do you know how many sexually transmitted diseases there are out there?" "Sex is just an expression of our animal instincts." At this level, they can provoke outrage with their sexual beliefs such as: "It's unhealthy to remain in a monogamous relationship." "Sex is a purely physical function; intimacy is a deranged illusion to compensate for our inadequacies…"

They want others to reject them to confirm their nihilistic view of the world. They are selfish and self-absorbed, ending relationships irrespective of the pain they cause others. They can further alienate others through a lack of hygiene, which starts to be seen as a waste of time.

They become more outlandish in their ideas and more eccentric in their behavior. Like Dr. Finch, the psychiatrist in the film and memoir by Augusten Burroughs, *Running with Scissors*, who believes that God is speaking to him through the shape of his feces. The outlandish Dr. Finch attempts to raise children in a house that is filthy, falling apart, and open to the elements, where anything goes—including sex in any form.

Another extremely disintegrated Five is Frederick Clegg in the thriller *The Collector* by John Fowles. Clegg starts off collecting butterflies and ends up abducting and imprisoning a young woman called Miranda. He desires her, but his social ineptitude means he's unable to form a normal relationship with her—instead, he adds Miranda to his collection of petrified, pretty objects.

Life at this level becomes meaningless and disintegrated Fives can become nihilistic, schizoid, psychotic, or develop schizophrenia.

Because integration is a choice, Fives can form caring and loving relationships when they learn to explore their emotions, express the compassion they feel, become less serious and more playful, and find a partner who accepts and appreciates their brilliant mind and their idiosyncrasies.

What Five Dating Adverts May Look Like

Ferdinand, 43

I'm always interested in learning new things, whether it's history, politics, or the guitar. (I started teaching myself piano last year and am loving the challenge.) I've lived alone for most of my life, but now want to share it with someone. I don't need a huge amount, but having my own space will sometimes be appreciated. I love interesting conversations, so if you'd like to debate Tolstoy versus Flaubert, I'm your man.

In return, I can make a mean pizza or chat about most things. I guess I'm a creature of contradictions—a night owl who's an early riser (I battle to sleep), an athletic bookworm, and I can be funny and serious at the same time. Swipe me and let's see if our minds can meet!

Stephanie, 32

OK, I'll be honest… I'm not great at socializing. Don't get me wrong, I like going out for drinks and having fun occasionally, but I really enjoying finding out about stuff (currently my interest is in Latin American black-and-white music). I love the beach, and photographing birds, and also movies, writing, and reading. I enjoy the outdoors and learning about all the things I thought I knew, but now realize I had no idea about. It's a crazy world—let's be crazy together.

The Passion of Avarice and the Fixation of Stinginess

Fives view the world as being low on resources, and feel that in limiting their own needs, they limit their dependence on the world and others. Best then to remain alone and limit one's sexual needs: "If I can get by with less, I'll have less to buy."

The commonly understood meaning of the word "avarice" as extreme greed for wealth or material gain does not reflect the true essence of a Five's wounding. It's in the adjective "avaricious" and the older fourteenth-century meaning of "stingy"[4] that we find a better understanding of why this word has become synonymous with Fives. It's not the lust of an Eight (going after), but rather a holding on. Even their feelings and thoughts can be drained by a partner.[5]

A Peek into a Five's Bedroom

Walk into the bedroom of a Five, and you're likely to find it messy with books, papers, or other signs of the Five's interests. Their habitat is merely a place to sleep, have sex, and work, so it's unlikely that any significant cash will be spent beautifying it. Furnishings may be minimal and sparse. The room may be dark (you can see the computer screen better that way). Expect thick blinds and closed shutters or curtains to shut out inquisitive neighbors.

Self-preservation Fives are frequently hoarders, so the room could be crammed with their collections. Piles of dirty laundry, grimy plates from snacks, and empty food cartons are a possibility. The bed may not have been made (unless someone else has made it). Those with a strong Four-wing may display a minimalistic, but aesthetic approach to bedroom décor.

Fantasies and Erotica

Fives are very comfortable with being in their mental sanctuaries. Their introverted natures make them feel awkward around people. Their low sense of self makes them self-critical. As a result, many would rather daydream or fantasize about having sex.

Fives lose control when they submit to the wishes of others, so in their fantasy world they may switch to situations in which they're in control. This, together with their interest in all things dark and often socially unacceptable, may have them fantasizing about the weird and (at least in their eyes) wonderful.

Fives may also fantasize about remote sex toys, such as the vibrator that is operated from a cell phone, so they can bring their partner to orgasm from across the room (or even on another continent). "I fantasize," a Five revealed, "of a naked woman strapped into a dentist's chair, where I control the leavers and various other gadgets. I can then observe what pleasure she may be getting from what and how I control the machine, but am not involved physically or emotionally myself." Another Five described his approach to fantasies: "I have categories of fantasies and further subcategories. In some instances those are categorized even further."

Having spent so much time conceiving sex means that when Fives do get sexual with a partner, there can be tremendous energy and drive—their intense nature can have them wound up with desire like a spring.[6]

Fives may also explore intense and intimate fantasy situations where they do share their secrets with a significant other, which in real life they may not do. Research by Israeli psychologist Gurit E. Birnbaum and collaborators, who studied the fantasies of 48 couples over a three-week period, showed that for "avoidance attachment" types (like most Five's), most fantasies involved acts of aggression and alienation (emotional distancing), either with themselves as the aggressor or their partner, as well as the desire to escape from reality. Problems in their relationship led to an increase in these fantasies. The report also suggested that using fantasies was a way of avoiding emotional closeness.[7]

Most people view porn for sexual release (a pleasure-seeking strategy to elevate uncomfortable moods or emotions caused by anxiety, depression, loneliness, fear, or boredom, or simply a way to relax), but there are those who use porn as a maladaptive coping strategy.[8] Internet porn watching is widespread across the Enneagram types,[9] so, Fives are far from alone in their interest.[10]

According to Covenant Eyes, a software company offering online services that help people overcome porn addiction, pornography addicts (like all addicts) often feel they have little control in their lives. For a Five, their long-suppressed need for love results in them feeling unlovable and powerless, but watching others have sex brings an attractive feeling of power. For once, they're in charge—by changing websites, or delving at will into the deep, dark web, where society's taboos can be explored. Women or men who would normally ignore them are there for their entertainment and to fulfil their needs. Internet sex is secretive, and Fives enjoy being secretive.

Porn may alleviate some of their sexual tension, but beneath this drive is the intense but denied desire for connection. Despite their urges, they may be virgins for longer than most other types.

Fives of Different Genders

Female Fives: How do the sexes show up in Fives? It's believed that there are more male than female Fives. In presenting themselves to the world, Five women will likely choose a sensible haircut (not spending time and cash at the hairdresser is a bonus) and wear nondescript, muted colors. Unless they have a strong Four-wing, makeup and fashion are of little interest, and they may be confused by other women's interest in such things, even viewing them with contempt: "I guess if you don't have brains, you have to cultivate beauty."

Five women may be more emotional than their male counterparts and be able to share their thoughts and feelings to a greater degree. They will however need a partner they can mentally spar with—perhaps more so than male Fives, who may view a less intelligent partner as less challenging and more likely to elevate their own status.

For female Fives, avarice in relationships can be experienced in many forms: "He'll drain my time/be after my money/want me to attend his business functions/demand I cook for him…" When it all becomes too much, Fives start telling themselves that the best way forward is to limit their need for a relationship. Being single becomes a preferred lifestyle and telling yourself you don't need a man (or woman), becomes the way to cope with the innate desire for a mate.[11]

Male Fives: Male Fives spend little time on their appearance: typically they'll have ruffled hair and be wearing crumpled shirts and their well-worn favorite trousers. Five men need much enticing to emerge from their "man caves."

Relationships come with demands: "I'll have to take her out for supper, then there's the cab cost, the wine… And I might not even get laid. Better to stay home."

They may enjoy researching kinks, fetishes, or the way a vagina works and then introduce these ideas into the bedroom. Sex can become like a fascinating research study—or a problem to be solved, like the formula MSN mathematicians developed to work out how long love will last, which, incidentally, for heterosexual couples is: $L = 8 + .5Y - .2P + .9Hm + .3Mf + J - .3G - .5(Sm - Sf)2 + I + 1.5C$. And for same sex couples: $L = 8 + .5Y - .2P + 2J - .3G - .5(S1 - S2)2 - I + 1.5C$. [12]

Keeping everything in the head is another way to avoid intimacy. As one Five put it: "Sex provides a great release for me and I see it as such, no more. It's a problem to be solved for which I enjoy thinking up new solutions and creating new techniques to better solve it."

For Fives, entering a relationship comes at considerable cost to themselves. Life is a battle between following their own thoughts and projects, versus having to feed into the needs of the relationship. A tough task.

Love Type: Paternal

Paternal love is experienced as a cool, more reserved approval rather than an intense emotional experience. It's a guiding light to follow.

Fives enjoy being specialists or authorities in certain fields (particularly Social types). In relationships they want to be someone who feels competent enough to inspire love from a partner, who they see as lacking their insight and expertise: "I'll be the North star for you to follow."

Detached Love

In 1987, psychologists Cindy Hazan and Phil Shaver ran a "Love Quiz" in the Denver local newspaper, the *Rocky Mountain News*. They classified the respondents according to the three infant attachment types—Secure, Anxious-resistant, and Anxious-avoidant—that had been identified by Mary Ainsworth, a developmental psychologist known for her work in attachment theory. Hazan and Shaver were looking to match these early forms of childhood attachment to adult relationships. The first part of the quiz consisted of a checklist of adjectives relating to childhood experiences with parents, and the second part consisted of three descriptions of how one could experience love. The description of the Anxious-avoidant type fits nearly perfectly with a Five's experience of relationship in that they:

- Don't allow themselves to depend on others
- Feel uncomfortable and even nervous with closeness
- Don't enjoy partners wanting them to be more intimate than they feel comfortable being.[13]

It's not that Fives don't have attachment needs, rather that they have learned to suppress them. Doing so makes them feel both superior to others and safer.

In *Attached*, their book on attachment therapy, Dr Amir Levine and Rachel Heller talk about security in a relationship. Being assured of having a partner we can depend on gives us the confidence to take risks, be creative, and go after our dreams. Goals supported by partners are more likely to be reached. Ironically, it's been found that attachment allows for greater independence.[14]

Fives often don't reach their potential, possibly because their focus is on a project rather than a career, or they are too stingy to give extra time to work. Is it possible that not having a reliable relationship adds to the chances of failing? The Fives I know who have succeeded in their professions have all had a secure relationship. There is a possibility that when Fives integrate and reach out to another, they gain not only a relationship, but also a greater chance of being successful.[15]

Pan or Bisexual

From a survey of over 1,552 participants who knew both their Myers-Briggs and Enneagram types, most Fives appeared as INTP, ISTP, and INTJ. Author Heidi Priebe asked each of the survey's respondents to reveal their sexuality as heterosexual, bisexual, pansexual, homosexual, or "other." Fives rated third highest in pan- or bisexuality after Fours and Nines—suggesting that Retreating types are more open to sexual exploration across genders.[16] Comments by and about Fives support these findings:

> *I enjoy researching the degree of homophobia and EQ of each person I date. I want to analyze them to see if they*

have become stuck in heteronormative roles.
My Five male friend was surprisingly open about his
exploration into homosexual sex. He's straight but wanted to
explore it. He still prefers women but says he will go with a
guy again if he feels so inclined.

Perhaps in viewing sexuality in terms of research, Fives are able to move beyond normative gender roles.

Love from Afar

Fives often appreciate their partners more when they are absent so they may choose long-distance relationships or partners who are emotionally absent, complying or undemanding. When Fives feel that a partner is becoming too dependent on them, or if they feel they are becoming too attached to a partner, they may force themselves to distance themselves, to find out how much the person they have left behind really means to them. It's as if being apart makes love clearer—more defined. There is a mental struggle between attachment and detachment. A Five may announce that they're setting off to walk the Camino, taking themselves on a research trip to a remote area of Alaska, sailing solo around the world, or choosing a job that involves constant travel—whatever will allow them to regain a sense of independence.[17]

It's not that all Fives will have lovers across town or across continents, but Fives will see the attraction of a relationship that is there, but not there—it offers brief, intense sexual release with no further demands, which suits most Fives perfectly.

I was told the story about a Five in a long-distance relationship. The object (word intentional) of his affections arrived for a visit, and once in bed, he fondly leaned over to kiss a photograph of his lover before going to sleep—while she was lying next to him! It was easier to kiss an inanimate object, than engage with a real live woman.

Don't Expect Flowers!

Rather than having the rebelliousness of a Six or the standing against others like an Eight, Fives are cynical about that which society holds dear. They can forget birthdays or anniversaries (and even if they do remember, they might not respond) and they ridicule events like Valentine's Day as being "too commercial" or seeing religion as "the opiate of the masses."

Many Fives don't want to be distant from others, but just don't know how to go about connecting with them. Fives often seem to have missed out on understanding the norms of basic interaction and may feel ill at ease and unsure how to navigate social functions. Sometimes Fives' behavior can appear eccentric and they can be very impractical, so partners may find themselves sorting out resultant issues.

Peeping Toms

What happens when you have a strong sexual desire, but find human interaction awkward, even threatening? When you like to observe rather than participate in sex? How do you chat up a potential partner when you feel self-conscious? When the darker side of life both intrigues and excites you? When you don't feel confident forming a relationship and fear the demands it would make on you? When you prefer being a witness—a detached observer of life?[18] Put this potpourri of behaviors together and there is the potential for a less integrated Five to enjoy a bit of voyeurism. It's not for nothing that some Enneagram traditions name Type Five the "Observer."[19]

It's not always the sexual act itself that voyeurs enjoy; sometimes it's simply a glimpse of naked flesh or seeing their unknowing victims undressing that turns them on. Recording these thrills is also common Five behavior. I recall an old chap who would wander around at board-sailing competitions, a handkerchief around his mouth highwayman-style (supposedly for the wind and sand) and an old video camera—he'd be filming any bikinied body he could find. This kind of behavior is obviously extremely abusive to the person being watched and is a criminal act if you're over 18. The strong urge to watch people in compromising positions coupled with a knowledge and fear of the consequences can be excruciating for Five voyeurs.

Voyeurism can also take the form of watching other people engage in sex in sex shops, or watching a partner in bed with a stranger. Getting turned on by listening to private erotic phone calls or watching someone defecate or urinate are other forms of voyeurism: "I was a kid of about 12, climbing in a barn on the family farm, when I saw a hole in the floor below me. I peeped through and found one of the workers urinating. I was fascinated. It triggered something in me and from then on I was drawn to voyeuristic behavior." This experience confirms that the disorder can stem from an accidental sighting, leading to a habitual form of release that becomes pathological.[20]

One could argue that all Internet porn requires a form of voyeurism, in which case 19% of North Americans could be classified as voyeurs.[21] This is the percentage of frequent visitors to adult-content sites, while 79% of 18- to 30-year-old American men watch Internet porn at least once per month.[22] Most voyeurs tend to be men, but the number of female watchers is on the increase. As part of the definition, voyeurs prefer watching someone more than having sex with a partner themselves.[23]

Voyeurs in Japan are known to take cell phone photos up women's skirts in tubes and other crowded places. The problem became so widespread that cell phones have been designed to make a noise when taking a photo, even if they are set to silent.[24]

Famous Sexologists

Remember American sexologist Alfred Kinsey? In 1947 he founded the Institute for Sex Research at Indiana University (now known as the Kinsey Institute for Research in Sex, Gender, and Reproduction). He is best known for writing *Sexual Behavior in the Human Male* (1948) and *Sexual Behavior in the Human Female* (1953).

As can be expected, Kinsey's research on human sexuality was highly controversial at the time. His research went way beyond theory, to observing and participating in sexual activity, occasionally with co-workers, pushing the boundaries for his studies, and exploring sexual taboos.[25] He displayed many attributes of a Type Five.

Kinsey's work was furthered by William Masters and Virginia Johnson in their book, *Human Sexual Response*. Amongst their findings was the sexual response cycle, a four-stage model of arousal involving excitement, plateau, orgasm, and resolution.

The couple also explored women's orgasm—in particular, the ability to have repeated orgasms—at a time when many still did not believe women had orgasms! They started treating sexual problems such as impotence and reported successes in this and other areas of sexual dysfunction. They also brought to light the sexuality of older couples, including post-menopausal women.

From available data it appears that Masters could very likely have been a Type Five too—happy to research and observe sex, and occasionally taking part. In describing himself in an interview with the *New York Times*, Masters agreed he was not sociable. His ex-wife and colleague, Johnson concurred, referring to his workaholism and agreeing that he was not people-minded.[26] It is interesting that two significant early explorers of Western sexuality were very possibly Fives.

The Study of Sex

The detached, intellectual, or cerebral approach to sex can take many forms. Like in the cases of Kinsey and Masters, it can become a science. I knew a man who attended a workshop to learn about a vagina where they used a demonstration plastic replica. I'm not saying this isn't worthy of study, but the disembodied focus indicates a Five's slide towards disintegration.

A Five's line of release[27] is to an Eight—a connection that implies the potential for Fives to see partners as objects devoid of their own needs and feelings, as in less healthy Eights.

Divulging Sexual History

Fives' need for secrecy can play out in many ways, such as covert sexual viewing, using prostitutes for acts they may feel uncomfortable asking their partners to perform, or wild flings. An extreme situation involved a grieving wife I knew who, at her husband's funeral, found another family at the graveside. It turned out that the Five had had two wives on different continents. He'd traveled widely for work (not uncommon in a Five), and had created two outlets for the brief sexual intensity he desired, and a whole lot of alone time while traveling between. Neither wife nor their children had ever known about the others.

Sexual intensity with secrecy added to the emotional mix becomes an antidote to the Fives' intellectualism. It's not as invasive to reveal yourself sexually as it is emotionally, and intimacy is created by a secret shared. A word of warning on secrecy and a Five's need for privacy: opening a letter addressed to them, or reading a message on their phone (even if it's just from the plumber) is going to drive them wild with anger and stir up all those childhood feelings of having their space invaded. Best avoid.

While Fives enjoy honesty, when it comes to revealing details of past relationships or sexual habits, they can become very closed, leaving a partner feeling excluded and frustrated. As one Five put it: "There are simply some parts of my life that I would not feel comfortable revealing. Some may see this as being emotionally withholding, but for me it's about protecting my privacy."

Problems in Relationships

Because in their childhood Fives typically experienced either a lack of a deep bond , or an overwhelming and invasive experience with their maternal figure, they will invariably subconsciously replicate this in adulthood. If the Five is an only child, this adds to the feeling of disconnection. As adults, Fives can either attract "mothers" (or men assuming that role) as partners, or alternatively go it alone.

Disassociation from the body can mean not only that Fives find relationships threatening, but that they find it hard to connect with their own and their partner's physical and emotional needs, which can feel overwhelming. Engaging the services of a prostitute who places no demands other than payment may feel safer than a long-term relationship.

Partners of Fives will have to understand that their attitude of "I don't need you—I can do perfectly well on my own" is simply a fear of being too depended upon—it is not a rejection of the partner. Having their Five say, "Sex is just a physical act, like going to the toilet," is not exactly going to have partners flinging off their clothes in wanton lust, so they'll have to find ways of understanding their Five's signals. Fives will try to bond through engaging in activities with their partner: one partner may enjoy bird-watching while the other has an interest in photographing birds, or they may both enjoy writing (but in different parts of the house, if possible!). [28]

Anxiety

If they are not at ease with their partner or surroundings during sex, Fives will be uncomfortable and anxious—so a massage given by a Five to their partner may be anything but relaxing. Likewise, foreplay can feel nervous. The partner may have the feeling that they need the Five to breathe deeply, relax, and slow down.

Their anxiety means Fives often suffer from insomnia. A partner may wake up at 4am to find them behind a computer watching porn, playing "World of Warcraft" or reading. They build up tension and nervous energy, which at times makes their sleeping erratic or impossible. Sex can help relax them.

Sex is Submissive

Having someone else take the sexual lead (provided it's not sprung unexpectedly upon them), can smooth the way to orgasmic bliss. But it's a fine line: too much touch, feeling invaded by an unexpected visit, or being cornered at the bar will likely have Fives retreating, telling themselves that they never really wanted sex, even if the desire is there. Once in the bedroom, they will likely respond well to having a partner taking an active role or showing them what would please.

Because sex is a relaxing mechanism for Fives, they may enjoy intense but slow sex, where they don't have to think and can experience a sensual, more meditative approach. It's also where they can allow their repressed feelings to emerge to a trusted partner. Disconnected from others for most of the time, they are liberated by feeling super-connected.

Open to Experience

The lust of Type Eight (their line of release) encourages Fives to engage with the world, but avarice holds them back. Here, the Five's potential for being asexual meets the Eight's strong sexuality. Add the planning and spontaneity of the Seven, which Fives access through their line of stretch, and this can lead to intense one-night stands or brief, illicit, and risky encounters—perfect for a Five who can then retreat, with no strings attached.

In sex, because Fives enjoy moving outside social norms and are often fascinated with the dark, esoteric aspects of life,[29] they're not afraid to explore. If a partner's deep desire is for an unconventional experience, then of all the Enneagram types, Fives will be most likely to enter it alongside. Five should remember however that their partners may not share their openness or enthusiasm for exploring unusual sexual practices.

The Instinctual Drives

Self-preservation Fives: This subtype is the most typical Five.[30] Being the most withdrawn of the three subtypes, self-preservation Fives may hoard objects behind safe and very private walls. (I've known two Self-preservation Fives who didn't have doorbells!) At its core, hoarding reveals a need to not need others: "I am my own castle, where I cannot be touched." These Fives may become hermits, for whom the outside world represents all that is demanding; their walls provide a safe haven.

These Fives are also the least able to effectively communicate their feelings.[31] This comment from a Self-preservation Five regarding sex and love is typical: "Love and sex are intimate concepts that I find hard to talk about. I am still figuring out my freedom of expression around these." Another uses clever wit to deflect from feeling: "Both go together = I love sex." And perhaps the saddest response about love and sex: "Are irrelevant." [32]

Social Fives: Fives tend to express their avarice through an intense desire to know more, make some sense of it all, and retain knowledge. In the search to become experts in their chosen field, they can sometimes become "heavenly, but no earthly good," meaning they lose connection with the daily norms of life: the idealistic dreamers and seekers who forget to pay the bills. I asked a Five why he'd spent so many years learning to astral travel while avoiding relationship responsibility. The answer: "Daily life is boring. People are like sheep. They haven't learned to think for themselves. I'm searching for something beyond the ordinary."

These Fives want to be recognized in a chosen field and admire the knowledge of those who know more than they do: "I've made a list of the most intelligent people I know in the world," a Five confessed. Interacting with those who share their interests (in various societies or groups), Social Fives give the illusion of connection with others, though this is an intellectual, rather than intimate or emotional connection.

In answer to thoughts that arose around the concept of sex and love, Social Fives replied: "Are things I could do with more of." "Are lots of fun, mainly sex though." "We are born in flesh and blood and we might as well enjoy love and sex. This is who we are, let's explore it."

Sexual Fives *(counterphobic)*: These Fives are more like Fours in that they display avarice in their need to hold on to the ideal of a perfect relationship or person—a lover they will allow to share their inner world, rather than rejecting like the other two subtypes. With their Eight connection, Sexual Fives want someone to stand in the fire with them: "us down the rabbit-hole together." [33]

These two Sexual Fives described sex and love:

> *[They] are amazing. To find a special person that you share a special connection with on an emotional and physical level, is the greatest feeling any person can have.*

> *As a society we should build sex and love more. Love for the importance it plays in our emotional wellbeing, and sex as a beautiful natural thing shared by individuals.* [34]

If they find a significant relationship, they can be romantic and more emotionally open than the other Fives. But they have high expectations, which others might find hard to meet or maintain. This is why a Five responded that sex and love are "Overrated," and another that they are "awesome, but painful." [35] Unlike the other two instinctual drives, Sexual Fives are counterphobic in not wanting secrets in their relationships. The 1989 classic movie *Sex, Lies, and Videotape* is about a drifter, Graham (played by James Spader), who is impotent and creates a video library of interviews with women about their lives, sexuality, and sexual fantasies. This sharing of their mutual secrets is typical of a Sexual Five in relationships.

The chances are strong that billionaire Paul Getty was a Sexual Five. He had an insatiable sex drive (well over 100 lovers) and was reported to take H3, the so-called "sex-drug" to maintain his potency well into his 80s. Like a typical Five, he recorded his sexual conquests meticulously in a book. He married five times before realizing that casual sex offered better value for money than expensive divorces, but ever fearful of his resources being plundered, he had women sign a document absolving him from any responsibility should they fall pregnant. Although he could not be drawn into divulging anything about his private life, he did once confess to the media that he kept woman at a controlled distance to avoid getting hurt. [36]

With the emotional intensity of Fours and the mental focus of Fives, Sexual Fives are the most focused on sexual fantasies in which they can explore the dark and the deep. Physical sex becomes the way to release the noise in their heads. They inhabit these dark worlds more frequently as they disintegrate and shift towards the seedier side of sex.

The Wings

Five with a Four-wing *(Paternal and Maternal countertype love)*: In this subtype, the Five's knowledge meets the Four's creativity. The "Iconoclast" in the Riso/Hudson Enneagram tradition, [37] these Fives ridicule romantic niceties: "I'm not prepared to be part of some commercial propaganda to extract cash from the blindly led public." They can be quite impractical when it comes to daily living, for example paying $4,500 for a bill instead of $450 and not noticing the difference. Four's emotion combines with Five's detached emotion, creating confusion, but imagination and conceptualization can result in new ways of creating and thinking.

In addition, the Four's creativity and introspection along with a Fives' need to withdraw into cerebral space makes this subtype one of the most reclusive and independent of the Enneagram types (along with a Four with a Five-wing). Forming relationships may then be problematic—these Fives may prefer being modern-day hermits.

Five with a Six-wing *(double Paternal love)*: Here, the knowledge of a Five meets the loyalty of a Six. In this double Thinking-Fear type, the trust issues of a Six also combine with intellectual reclusive needs of a Five: relationships can't be trusted, but knowledge can. These are talking heads who find connecting with their hearts and bodies difficult, making relationships secondary (or lower still) on their list of priorities. They can be the person in the office who tries to engage, but laughs too loudly or who makes inappropriate (even hurtful) comments without realizing it. They may enjoy observing others rather than interacting with them.[38]

Sexually they may also be awkward and may frustrate their partners with the need to turn everything into an intellectual observation: they may be physically present, but emotionally they have never even entered the room, as expressed by this Five:

> *Even if I'm having sex, my thoughts can be miles away on some other sexual fantasy. Partners often pick this up and it doesn't go down well. I have real trouble getting out of my head during sex and being in the moment, because my thoughts are always racing with this or that idea. Even when I'm really attracted to someone, I'm not sure what approach to take, so I usually try to be smartass.*

If challenged, they can become reactive and dismissive, insensitively deriding all who disagree with their sometimes outlandish ideas.

Moving to Sexual Presence

What Blocks Fives from Sexual Fulfillment

When Fives fear that a partner may ask more than they can or want to give of themselves, they hold back from truly being present, studying their way through sex as opposed to engaging from the heart: "Hmm, she seems to enjoy it when I do that. I wonder why?"

This can result in a diminished capacity to really enjoy the pleasures of life, including sex, as these two Fives suggest: [39]

> *My type probably dampens both having sex and my sex drive. It takes a lot for me to feel safe, even with a long-term partner. In bed, I'm so busy analyzing and trying to process the what's happening, that I can't just let go or be present.*

> *Problem solving can give me as much of a high as having sex. Maybe even more. Sex itself is a problem I want to solve. I spend a lot of time thinking up solutions to the problems I experience in sex or exploring new techniques in my mind and wondering if they would work.*

Fives need time alone to process their feelings. If, however, they do share their feelings with a partner in the moment, and connect with their bodies, it opens up all three centers: head, heart and body, allowing for a deeper sexual experience.

How Fives Can become Sexually Present

Engage with the world and others: Achieving the intimacy we all desire means taking the risk of moving into the world and becoming part of it. Fives move towards genuine presence and nonattachment when they find the courage to be in a relationship, and when they can connect with their feelings and express them in the moment.

See abundance: Fives should use their great imaginations to visualize the world as an abundant place, where there are enough resources for themselves and others. Think about the abundance of semen in each ejaculation: 600- to 3,000-million sperm cells per fluid ounce! Limitations reside only in their beliefs.

Know that knowledge is not power: The mind is only an aspect of one's being—it is not the whole of it. Moving into an intellectual space as protection is to miss out on exploring your potential. Fives need to be aware when they do this, and look for the underlying reasons or feelings they are avoiding. They need to acknowledge that although they have done loads of research and know a lot about sex, they don't know everything.

Connect with your body and emotions: Fives need to observe their body's needs and their feelings, which will open them up to being aware of their partner's sexual needs. They need to be aware of their emotions and physical sensations: "Am I hungry? Does this touch feel good?" Sex is not a problem to be figured out—it's about touch, sensation, and shared emotion. That is how true presence will arise.

Questions to Journal

NOTE: It's useful to answer these questions no matter what your type.

- Does your desire to focus on researching and exploring potentials cerebrally, affect your ability to show up emotionally and physically for your partner?
- Do you see sexuality as a resource that can easily be depleted?
- Does sexual imagining, observation (in whatever form) and conceptualizing, replace the ability to truly engage with another person?

12

Type Nine:
The Sensual Sweetheart

Nine's motto: "That was great for you, wasn't it?"

Nine as lover: Nine lovers are generally relaxed and accepting—happy to please (if that makes you happy). They are sensuous and uncomplicated lovers, but fussing about inconsequential issues can mean they forget their own arousal in the process. They can have a wonderful healing quality about them that makes a tough day seem so much better, and their vivid imaginations can add extra spice to sex.

Nines' retreat: through daydreaming or losing their sense of self. Merging with a partner is another way of retreating, to the point that they may not even know what their sexual desires and needs are. Some may use sex to retreat—losing themselves in the physicality of sex but avoiding showing up emotionally or mentally.

You may relate to aspects of a Nine even if it's not your type: if you are a One or Eight (the wings), or a Three or Six (the points of release and stretch).

Love type: Maternal. Nines are very nurturing of others, but when not integrated they lack the ability to nurture themselves.

Relationship belief: "Whatever pleases you works for me." "I don't see a problem."

Sexual frustration: "I'm happy with the way things are. Why do you keep pressurizing me to change the way we have sex?" "Don't keep asking me what position I like during sex—I don't have the answers."

Understanding Type Nine's Sexuality

Brief Overview

The word "sloth" derives from the Portuguese word *preguiça*, meaning "slowness" or "laziness." Nines aren't necessarily lazy—I've known Nine marathon runners and gym bunnies—but sloth can manifest as a laziness of spirit, an unwillingness to show up for themselves, and a sluggish resistance to change. Indifference and indolence are masked by tolerance and a good-natured cheerfulness. To others Nines seem to have found the keys to contentment: "I can't believe you ever get stressed," a partner will say to a Nine.

Nines blunder happily through life, seemingly unaffected by the world around them. Easily taking on the opinions and beliefs of their partners or social groups, they are congenial fence-sitters. The good news is that this can make them excellent lovers because they'll happily go along with a partner's suggestions. The bad news is that making love to a Nine can sometimes feel like making love to an inanimate object: they're there in body, but their minds are somewhere else.

Nines are essentially kind and don't want to cause hurt or pain to others. They are people-pleasers. To be liked, they become great listeners who are good-natured and supportive. To a Nine, it's better to be indecisive than to make a displeasing choice, so they'll leave that to someone who isn't afraid of confrontation. (If things go pear-shaped, then they won't be to blame.) They're happy to apologize (even if they're not in the wrong) to smooth troubled waters, and typically accept responsibility for their own actions. As partners, they go with the flow and are loyal. They can explode in anger occasionally, but peace is quickly restored, albeit in a passive-aggressive way.

Nines are the peacemakers and mediators of the Enneagram, and often find themselves in this role with warring family members or friends. They may find it hard to identify themselves as Nines because they have merged with another person, and so may identify another person's type as being their own, or they may find themselves in parts of many other types.

Nines sit at the top of the Enneagram symbol, moving from the Divine realm above to the earthly realm below, with its conflicts, pain, and aggression. Here they have fallen asleep to the true nature of their divine soul: they have forgotten themselves. Small comforts make it easier to bear; keeping the peace becomes a way to still a troubled world. To maintain this comfort and illusion of peace, Nines must deny or avoid all that threatens it, such as their own anger, difficult changes, painful emotions, making decisions, conflict, and strong opinions. But without these, they become mere shells: the lights may be on, but no one's home. Nines become lost in the trivia of the world and avoid more important issues: the sacred is replaced with sudoku, cross words with crossword puzzles.

The Arising of Type Nine

Chat to a Nine and they'll likely report having had a happy childhood. This is a type in need of everything being "nice"—only after much self-work are Nines able to admit that all might not have been blissful.

Typically they felt overlooked as children—lost in the family system. Middle-child syndrome is common, but not always the case. Mum was preoccupied with work, her own interests, or taking care of a large family. Little Nines learned to not make a fuss and to deny their needs so as not to anger others. Complaining served no purpose or fell on deaf ears. To be demanding meant to alienate one's parent, so the young Nine learned to sublimate their desires for the sake of being "loved."

As a result, Nines may not drink water when thirsty, eat when hungry, know when they are full, allow themselves the luxury of a massage, or connect with a sexual urge. Everything else is more important: "I just need to do this [insert trivial task]."

Naranjo notes that many Nines report having Type Four mothers, while Nine and One parents are also common.[1] As this Nine notes:

> My mother was a Type One. She made the decisions, so
> I never really knew what I wanted. If I ever did express
> a need, such as an outfit I'd prefer to wear, she had very
> articulate reasons as to why my choice was wrong. In the
> end, to keep the peace, it was easier not to have an opinion.
> It was less painful because if you didn't have an opinion,
> then you didn't feel bad if it was ignored or over-ridden.

Nines stand at the door of life, letting others through and desperately hoping someone will notice them and say, "After you."

Nines in Love

Integrated Nines: Integrated Nines have hopped off the fence and are able to make decisions that are based on their own feelings, thoughts, and desires as well as the greater good—they have merged with themselves and are independent. They are genuinely content, embody peace and harmony, and as such create a sense of relaxed ease with others. Anger (theirs or others') no longer scares them. They can show up in relationships and be fully present, receptive, and engaging. They view themselves as neither inferior nor superior, but equal.[2] Sexually they can surrender to others or take a more dominant role, yet not lose touch with their inner essence. They have a relaxed, receptive approach to sex and are emotionally aware and truthful in conveying their needs and desires. Sex is spontaneous and natural—part of the way of things.

The need for idealizing a partner at the expense of their own self-worth has gone, and they can be powerful and serene mystics. They bring a calm, grounded, and laid-back presence to a relationship, which is soothing for the more uptight Enneagram types. These undemanding Nines are truly present for their partners—a haven from the world, communicating through touch and intuition as much as or more so than with words.

Average Nines: Nines start idealizing others and seeing themselves and their own needs, opinions, and desires as being less important: "I don't mind what we do in bed—you choose what you enjoy." Even if sex is the last thing they feel like, they'd rather peel off their clothes than cause a dispute: "No, I'm not feeling great, but if you want sex tonight that's fine, honey."

They don't want to show their light to the world, as this has the potential to upset others, so Nines start living vicariously through a partner, seeing a partner's achievements as their own (while downplaying their own successes): "I'm no one special." They can start to become doormats for their (often unwitting) partner to wipe (project) their dirt on.

These Nines will become the role that their religion, family, or community sees as most normal or appropriate. Sex can be conservative,[3] with little exploration, despite the Nine's sensuality. They become submissive—sex happens to them (at least in the preliminary stages of desire). They start unplugging from their world, drifting away on a sugar-coated cloud. A Nine will appear to be listening to their partner discussing a problem in their sex life, but will lose themselves in a lengthy explanation or steer the conversation to a less emotive topic, oblivious to their partner's frustration. The very peace they seek provokes anger.

Pets start becoming substitutes for authentic human interaction: "At least Rover understands, don't you, boy?" Alcohol can be used to dampen anger—the world is a happier place after a few drinks.

In a Nine's mind, the idealized version of their partner moves further away from the person. Partners feel unheard, because their Nine is focusing on something irrelevant. Life starts to feel for the Nine like walking through a swamp. It's hard to move, be it out of an unhappy relationship, situation, or job. Nothing gets resolved because Nines refuse to see or deal with the problem. They've put on blinkers: "Things will get better for sure," they say as they sink deeper into the mud.

Disintegrated Nines: Avoidance of relationship issues is replaced with an impenetrable wall of resistance as the Nine becomes more passive-aggressive. Resentment gets repressed, only to explode before the next emotional shutdown. The illusion of a happy relationship is light years away, but Nines refuse to see reality—they'd rather be abused than abandoned.

Repressed aggression becomes depression. The independence of their integrated selves has deteriorated to chronic dependence. They are stubborn and refuse other people's help, numbed to everything and everyone and in complete denial. I recall talking to a woman who I discovered had been divorced for many years, yet who was in complete denial that her ex-husband had remarried. To her it was a temporary absence, and he'd soon be returning to their marital bed.

Disintegrated Nines become neglectful of their bodies, taking little care with clothes or their appearance. Resentment has encroached on sex, which under these circumstances is unlikely to be happening.

Their peaceful, naturally happy, nurturing energy draws people to them. They accept and forgive as easily as they laugh. They can also be extremely accomplished in a variety of fields. All told, they are wonderful, loving people to be with.

What Nine Dating Adverts May Look Like

Sunshine Sue, 34

You could say I'm an amateur everything. I surf, cook, hike, read (loads), paint for pleasure, blog sometimes, love crossword puzzles and animals, and hate filing things. So, I do a lot, but haven't won prizes for anything yet! I belong to several clubs—a book club, a writers' circle, Save the Coastline. I get on well with pretty much anyone, which doesn't really help when you work from home! (I'm a freelance editor.) I've been told I'm easy-going (true because I hate arguments), so if you love a good fight, move on!

I love my life and the people in it. I'm a cat person, although I don't dislike dogs. Cats are just so independent and furry.

A great night is spent on the couch with a good movie, but I do like eating out too. Sushi, Italian, steakhouse, Indian, or Mexican are all fine with me—it's the company I'm after. Likewise in men—I really don't have a "type." If you have something interesting to say, I want to hear it. Let's meet at my favorite bar. On second thoughts, what's your favorite bar?

Jake, 34

I'm 34 years old and work as a scrum master in IT. I work night shifts and I can honestly say that I love my job because it gives me the opportunity to connect with people—and who else can go shopping at 11am on a Monday and visit the park afterwards? I have a dog called Fred (yes, a basset) who's the current love of my life, but there is room for another.

Family is very important to me and I have fun with mine at least once a week (I love board games). It's always been a dream of mine to have a large family of my own one day—the more kids, the merrier. I'm pretty much into the experience of life rather than the trappings, so I try make the best of each day. On weekends I'll be hiking, just chilling reading a book, or watching a series.

Above all else, I value honesty and kindness in a partner, so if you're a genuine person who doesn't sweat the small stuff, send me a message!

Anger

Nines are one of the three Gut types, meaning they have issues with anger. Because they rarely express that anger (it would disrupt the peace), it becomes so repressed that many Nines have no idea how angry they are—through their stubbornness, emotional absence, or passive-aggressive behavior, their anger slips through the cracks in their psyches. Other Nines may suddenly burst into a rage, only to quickly back down.

Nines express anger unconsciously by "forgetting" appointments, showing up late, "accidently" breaking things, misplacing important information, or finding themselves unable to have sex. For a partner, fighting with an inanimate Nine can prove to be very frustrating, and so they may erupt in anger, only to have the Nine respond "I don't get why you're so angry." [4]

The Passion of Sloth and the Fixation of Indolence

Sexually, Nines may be happy to spend their entire lives on the first position of the *Kama Sutra*: "If it ain't broke, why fix it?" They enjoy what's familiar and what their community regards as "the norm"—Naranjo refers to this as "robotization." [5] As such they can be sexually conservative.

Sloth manifests as an inability or laziness to connect with their own thoughts, opinions, and feelings, which Nines will in many cases deny rather than express. Partners and family's needs are viewed as more important than theirs: "Home is where *your* heart is, my dear."

During love-making, some Nine's thoughts may be distracted and wander away on irrelevant thoughts: "Did I put the dog out?" "Is the washing machine still on?" They seem more interested in what is on the periphery than the action in bed. They can be slow to take action even when aroused or to deviate from set routines: "We have sex Monday, Wednesday, and Friday, after the kids are in bed, missionary position, lasting approximately 10 minutes." "We have sex at bedtime. It's not bedtime now so we shouldn't really be having sex… or do you think we should?"

A Peek into a Nine's Bedroom

With Nines, bedrooms are about comfort rather than style. Although at times they may shake off their lethargy and attempt a revamp, for the most part they'll think about it and then consider the mess and decide it would cause too much of a disruption.

Nines usually love pets (pets are unconditionally loving and don't create uncomfortable vibes). Expect a few cats or a dog lazing on the bed as if they own the space (they probably do).

Clutter may also be an issue: piles of books, magazines, and unfinished projects. They may enjoy TV in the bedroom and often leave it on to block having to listen to their true self. Although they appear to spend time tidying, most of the time nothing much changes (unless they have a strong One-wing): the bedroom they tidied this morning will be littered by this afternoon. The décor may have faded with time, but this won't worry a Nine too much. Generally, their favorite room will be a warm, comfortable space.

Fantasies and Erotica

Sensual Nines have spent so much of their lives submitting to the wishes of others that fantasizing about having others submitting to their own desires can be thrilling. As this Nine says: "I'm an attentive lover. I can easily move between taking the lead or letting my partner do so, if that's what they enjoy—I'm pretty flexible and accepting in that way."

Being easy-going and the most forgiving of the types, Nines may accept a partner's quirks and kinks without judgement: "Sure, he watches a lot of online porn," a Nine confessed, "but it relaxes him and makes him happy, so I'm okay with it."

Used to being in the background, in fantasies Nines may allow themselves to be the star of the show. Alternatively, while fantasies of being overpowered are common in many types, Nines may find this appealing because it absolves them of choice or responsibility, as well as any feelings of guilt. They will submit to sex:[6] "He did this to me!"

Like Type Fives, Nines may enjoy observing rather than partaking in sex. If a partner is too demanding (sexually or otherwise), Nines may fear merging with them—this is disconnection taken to another extreme.

Erotica is something that can be enjoyed with no disruption: you can have sex (albeit alone), from your peaceful fantasy place while drinking a beer or slugging a glass of wine in-between.

Nines of Different Genders

Female Nines: Routine is how Nines view a healthy sexual relationship. Conservatism is less likely to cause problems, because it doesn't stop willing and enthusiastic participation. While a partner may enjoy a few kinks, however, anything too off-the-wall becomes uncomfortable for a Nine. This inflexibility can be perceived as Nines being unexciting lovers—steady, but lacking fire. They're often solid rather than sylph-like in form. Their appearance is mostly not of huge concern to them, so they may not make the best of what they have in terms of physical appearance.

To the extent that a partner is explorative, Nines will follow. Sex is an opportunity to create peace in the home and reconcile any differences. It may sometimes feel like something of a chore, but if it makes their partner happy, then that makes them happy. As these Nines said:

> I rarely initiate anything different in our relationship. I leave
> that for Bob. It's not that I don't like the idea of something

*different and am usually up for it, if he wants to go there. But
if I were to initiate something and it turned out badly, it could
be awkward or maybe even create conflict. I haven't experienced
that, but still wouldn't want to risk it.*

In one piece of research done on 457 couples, Nine women commonly
paired with Six men, followed by Fives and Eights.[7] Nines in relationship
with Sixes create dependability, loyalty, stability, safety, and predictability
with a degree of freedom.[8] This potential for flexibility is suggested by
these two Nine woman:

> *I'm pretty conservative. My most exploratory sexual act was
> when I fell in head-over-heels love with another woman. I
> was too restrictive though to go there. I predictably went back
> to heterosexual relationships, but I do wonder if in a different
> environment I could be bisexual. I guess if I met someone who
> took the lead, then I would go there.*

> *Open marriages or polyamorous relationships do seem
> interesting, but would I ever engage in them? No ways! There
> is way too much potential for conflict. If I'm honest with myself
> though, I do sometimes think I could be pansexual.*

Male Nines: Nine men often marry Four women (in the wonderful
paradox that flows through the Enneagram, the most self-denying type
with the most entitled type). In fact, a Nine male with a Four female is
the second most common pairing (male Eight and female Two being the
most common).[9]

Another common partner for a Nine man is a strong Eight woman.
Being less assertive themselves, the Nine may be attracted to a more
assertive partner. The woman may use that role to boss her partner,
resulting in a hen-pecked husband—a Nine who is unable to move to
the point of release (Type Three), where Nines develop self-confidence,
are more directive, and less procrastinating, and the point of stretch
(Type Six), where Nines find their courage and ability to assert themselves.[10] Unless the Nine man is well integrated, his Eight partner may
get frustrated when he doesn't stand up to her, while he may withdraw
in silence.

Often not as outwardly ambitious as some other types, and lacking in self-worth, some Nines may feel they have little to offer a prospective partner. A partner may want to take them out of their comfort zone (playing World of Warcraft with a pizza and a beer on Friday after work), but stubborn Nines may dig in their heels. Some Nines may find it stressful to initiate a relationship, so would rather stay home and avoid the risk of rejection. Nine men in relationships want to be the "good guy"—the family man who doesn't upset things:

> *The idea of doing something different (in or out of the bedroom) appeals, but I'll seldom initiate it. I'm happy to go along with my wife if she does. I make sure she orgasms before I do. If she's not happy, then I'm not. I enjoy spending ages in foreplay, even if it's just cuddling or stroking her hair.*

Love Type: Maternal

Type Nines are nurturing, hence their association with unconditional maternal love. They spend most of their lives minimizing their needs while focusing on the needs of others and are typically passive and submissive—although the stronger their Eight-wing, the more resistance there can be and the fiercer protectors they'll be of their children.

For most Nines, their experience of sex will feel like: "When's it going to be my turn?" "When is this going to be about me?" "When is my partner going to figure out what works amazingly for me?"

Low Libido and Sexual War

Unable to disturb the peace by expressing their anger means, Nines can passive-aggressively withdraw from sex if they feel rejected by a partner, or if they feel a partner has taken advantage of their kindness. The bedroom can become a silent battleground, where nothing is said and all appears to be well—only it's not. On an unconscious level, this can manifest as "forgetfulness:" "We can't have sex. I forgot to take my pill." A Nine may find many reasons to avoid sex: "The loop is too uncomfortable." With men it can take the form of premature ejaculation—because no one can be blamed, it bears no obvious malice.[11] In some circumstances, even illnesses such as thrush or herpes can be a manifestation of protest against a sterile love life.

For lethargic Nines, the bedroom can be more about sleeping than sex. They might mean to have sex, but sleep beckons sweetly once they're lying down. Nines see themselves as good people, certainly not people who would want to consciously harm others, yet the "bad" person manifests covertly in their shadow. In their emptiness, silence, lack of opinion or emotional display, or ignorance of an issue, they haven't done any wrong: "How can you accuse me?" Yet a silent, miserable war can continue below the surface.

Couples may seek help about this loss of libido, confused as to why they're still happy to be with their mate but are no longer attracted to them. What a Nine often won't realize is that it's their own aggression turned inward that has them turned off. [12]

In contrast, some Nines can use sex as a form of disengagement. Having lots of sex and/or a sexual daydreams may be a way for Nines to lose themselves. In sex, the essence of the Nine is somehow missing as they drift away into their own sex space.

The Inability to Connect with One's Own Sexual Needs

It's fitting that the Nine is the last of the Enneagram types, for much of their lives is about waiting for others to go first. It's as if they've been overlooked, and are part of the furniture. Nines feel that being great will make them vulnerable—if they shine their light too brightly, it will swiftly be snuffed out. Flying below the radar is safer, and even if they are very successful, they'll tend to downplay their achievements, like this Nine:

> It took me three years of therapy to finally own the fact that I was a successful artist. It seemed like such a grand and desirous thing to be. When I started telling people that I painted, I think most of them thought it was houses.

Nines may be hard-pressed to share their fantasies or sexual desires with a partner: they may be obtuse, beating around the bush, avoiding eye contact, or being long-winded. The more honest may simply say, "I don't know what I enjoy or what turns me on." Not knowing or being able to convey what you want makes the sexual experience less intense. Partners may start to feel as if sex is a one-sided affair, or that what they are doing is not pleasing to the Nine. Being unable to fan the wild fires of passion, partners may feel ineffective as lovers. More integrated Nines, particularly

Nines with an Eight-wing, can be naturally very sensual, yet are often unaware of the erotic effect this has on others.

It's important for a Nine's lover to realize they are not being rejected—it's more that they need to gently bring a Nine's awareness to sex and create the desire for sex through romance. Then the dirty dishes and unfinished work lose their importance and pleasure can become the focus.

Everyone Else's Needs Are More Important

While Nines are great at putting other types at ease with their accepting, laid-back, and forgiving attitude, the flip side of the coin is that they can numb out to reality. Riso and Hudson refer to Nines as being "nobody special,"[13] as if they exist only for others: "Your wish is my command." While this may seem like a selfless buddha role, their emotional unavailability can be frustrating for a partner.

It can also make Nines feel they lack personality, especially the more subdued Social and Sexual types. If they have desires, they either aren't aware of them or seem unable to communicate them. Confront the issue and try to get them to discuss the lack of fire in the bedroom and they'll withdraw without explanation. They dislike anything negative or painful; no amount of threatening or provocation will get them to respond.

Because Nines can be disconnected from their bodies, they may not connect to their own arousal. Even if aroused, a Nine's natural inclination to prioritize chores and trivia over their sex needs can have them happily continue with the crossword. If a partner is not aware of this trait, they may think their Nine is not into sex—they may need to express their own need for their Nine to respond.

Living through Another

Although its most true of Sexual Nine types, merging Nines may mimic the postures and gestures of a lover.[14] They tend to create an idealized version of a partner, social group, family member, or friend and then live through these images, rather than create an idealized version of themselves.[15] Most often these people or groups will appear in the Nine's eyes as having strong opinion—this energizes the Nine, and helps them feel more awake and alive to the world.

Nines can assume the role of caretaker or enabler in a relationship. They can also become totally dominated, losing all sense of self, becoming very frustratingly insipid, and even boring to some types, as described by this Nine:

> *The weird thing was, I was supporting the family and*
> *doing the bulk share of parenting, yet we ate out where*
> *he wanted to eat out, went where he wanted to go on*
> *vacation, had meals at times that suited him... The list*
> *of compliances is endless, but I never really saw it any way*
> *other than that's how things worked. Inside, though,*
> *I burned with resentment. Even that was hidden to me*
> *for years. Me, angry? You're kidding, right?*

This is a recipe for disaster, because Nines can have their compliant natures taken advantage of (financially or otherwise). When you think of yourself as being less than, others will treat you accordingly. When they finally do start factoring themselves in, Nines may find that their voice is still not heard, or that they go too much the other way and become oddly outspoken.

Perhaps more sobering is that integration necessitates looking inside ourselves for clues to development, not outwards towards others. When you are not being yourself, integration becomes impossible. If a Nine merges with an integrated partner, whose growth is it really?

Making Decisions (Or Not)

Ask a Nine to make a decision, even a small one such as, "What would turn you on most right now?" and chances are you'll get a blank look. A Nine's partner may be forced to make the decision on their behalf. Nines can take a long time to act, and could stay in an unhappy marriage for 50 years before making the decision to leave.

It is difficult to discern what they want. They may say yes when under pressure, but it'll turn out later that they meant no. If a decision is around changing something you've got used to ("Hey, how would you feel about using a vibrator this time?") the answer will seldom be direct. If it is, it may only be the answer they think their partner wants to hear, not how they really feel about the issue.

If a Nine's partner is themselves indecisive, immense frustration can result when both parties wait for the other to make the first move. Nines may have a habitual way of initiating sex, such as:

1. Is it Tuesday?
3. Have drink with partner.
3. Reach over and fondle knee.

This approach can feel comfortable for a Nine, but uninspiring for a more adventurous partner.

The Instinctual Drives

Self-Preservation Nines: In answer to a question about love and sex, a Nine's response was "My sex life is good, [I've] got no problem."[16] I'd like to ask their partner if they agreed.

Nines find themselves seeking ways to switch off whatever is uncomfortable in their world and to blend with whatever is of comfort. Disconnected but appearing content, a Nine will use distraction as a pleasant escape. Home becomes the focus for comfort-loving Self-preservation Nines.

Work, if it's interesting and not stressful, can also be a respite from a fully engaged life. These Nines are "salt of the earth" types, grounded in the now. Sex may be a good idea, but reading a book or watching TV may take preference because it's easier (unless not having sex threatens to make a partner angry, in which case Nines may comply).

Their earthiness makes Self-preservation Nines more like Eights, and they often have the sensuality of an Eight, but without the assertiveness and desire for action. Food also provides easy comfort: when cupid doesn't play ball, a burger and fries can soothe a lonely heart. Nines may be kind and loving to a partner yet live with very little reciprocated love in return—Chestnut writes that Nines of this type can substitute fun for love.[17]

As physical appearance doesn't overly concern them, these Nines can be inclined to let themselves go. As addictions[18] creep in to dull life, Self-preservation Nines may opt out of sex: they don't love themselves, so why would anyone else?

Social Nines *(counterphobic)*: These Nines merge with groups. The desire to belong (most often they never quite feel that they do) means they can be over-accommodating and generous to a fault. Feeling somewhat isolated, they work hard to be accepted, denying their own needs and feelings so as not to burden the group.

They are counterphobic because they go against sloth to be more outgoing and active—Social Nines are extroverts who are unselfish and will make huge sacrifices to belong. [19]

They are extremely hardworking, and can be quite active in groups and communities, being generous, fun, and funny, like clowns who mask their inner sadness and deny their own suffering. "Do you ever get down?" a friend or partner may ask such a Nine. This Social Nine's response to the question of love and sex is typically upbeat and fun: "[They] are filled with all kinds of adventure, complications, and wonderful connections." [20]

Social Nines may find it difficult to say no to a sexual advance, even if they are not in the mood. They fear being alone and can be unconditional about their sacrifice to a partner, becoming a target for abuse rather than leaving. They may work hard to support a family or spouse, having little time or money left for themselves. They supposedly lead full lives, yet might find that their inner self remains neglected and empty.

Sexual Nines: When I think about Sexual Nines, I'm reminded of the poem "On Marriage" by Kahil Gibran.

> *Fill each other's cup*
> *but drink not from one cup.*
> *Give one another of your bread*
> *but eat not from the same loaf.*
> *Sing and dance together and be joyous,*
> *but let each one of you be alone,*
> *Even as the strings of a lute are alone*
> *though they quiver with the same music.*

Nines could learn much from the words of this wise sage, because Sexual Nines would happily drink from the same cup, eat from the same loaf, and dance to the tune of a single-stringed lute while joined to their partner at the hip. They need to learn that true union requires two separate beings, not one being the other.

If Self-Preservation Nines merge with comfort and Social Nines with groups, Sexual Nines merge with a partner (or a significant other like a parent, child, or friend). If sex is the merging of body and mind, then Sexual Nines represent its essence: they lose their sense of self in another. They can't be, unless they are with another: "You are, therefore

I am." A partner who is devoted to their work (who puts work above them) will be difficult for them to deal with, because just as they make a partner their reason for living, they desire the same back. Life's purpose becomes "us."

As a result, personal boundaries may blur. They'll sacrifice their own desires to feed a partner's, as connection and intimacy become the foremost concern. To maintain it, they'll be good listeners, alter their schedules to accommodate yours, be easily swayed to follow your decisions and the lifestyle you want, all without realizing this is what they are doing. With their focus on relationships, their lack of assertion and the joviality of the other two subtypes, they can resemble Fours. Partners will feel nurtured, loved, and understood, while Nines claim to share their opinions, feelings, and beliefs. [21]

Whatever looks upsetting will be avoided, even if at great personal cost to the Nine. Over time, this can become the accepted way the relationship runs, and Nines may start feeling taken for granted. Rather than expressing their anger, they start to retreat, often not realizing the root cause of their anger. Partners used to being nurtured can feel abandoned when a Sexual Nine withdraws to smolder. It remains difficult for Nines to leave a relationship: "Better the devil you know," they'll tell themselves.

Searching for a special bond, Sexual Nines want to drop their barriers and feel a deep connection, but the very thing they desire will be illusive if they don't have a sense of self. This can be a frustrating experience—they can have the orgasm but still feel alone.

This type is more likely to be sexually explorative than the other two subtypes. Yet anger dampens their desire, and so Sexual Nines can be frigid or impotent (passive-aggressive behavior). Alternatively, in trying to maintain or attract a relationship, they may be overly sexually engaging, even promiscuous.

The Wings

Nine with and an Eight-wing *(Maternal and Erotic love)*: In this subtype, the peace of the Nine meets the strength of the Eight. Nines with an Eight-wing make excellent leaders, having the strength and action of an Eight, and the kindness and inclusiveness of a Nine. You'll often find them as CEOs or corporate leaders. In relationships they're less likely to be dominated, having a firmer, stronger Eight stance. The Eight's need for action and confrontation can create a paradox for the peacemaking, slothful Nine: "Don't mess with me," though these Nines will retreat fast if confronted.

Nines with a One-wing *(Maternal and Paternal love)*: Here, the Nine's peace meets the One's perfection. More merging than the other wing type, these Nines can get stuck in relationships that don't feed them. They are less outgoing, and more inclined to be judgmental and moralistic. They do the right thing in relationships (even if they covertly push a partner into being the villain). Given that the mind is the largest sex organ, they can bring creativity and vivid imagination into the bedroom, although the One's need for respectability may make them less inclined to explore sexually.

Moving to Sexual Presence

What Blocks Nines from Sexual Fulfillment

A partner may be waiting in the bedroom all fired up for some hot sex, but their Nine is noticeably absent. Disgruntled, they get up and find them feeding the cat, doing the dishes, answering an email, or cleaning out a cupboard. These seemingly unrelated and trivial chores that Nines find important may get in the way of their partner's desire for intimacy: [22] "I'll be there in a moment..."

Growing up, work came before pleasure, or homework came before play—particularly if they had a One parent. This translates later into housework/professional work before sex, or that their needs (including sex) aren't important, but cleaning up is. (And by the time the chores are done, Nines may be too tired for sex.) All this can have a partner feeling that their Nine is making excuses, that they don't want sex, that their Nine has no libido, or that they themselves aren't appealing enough—all of which can hurt a partner who doesn't understand the Nine dynamic. [23]

On the surface a Nine may seem like the perfect lover: they make their partner's needs more important than theirs, don't value their own feelings and emotions, and can negate their sexual urges. At its self-negating extreme, they feel they aren't important enough to worry about, and there's too much else to do.

Sandra Maitri writes about Nines needing to feel, rather than simply occupy their bodies. [24] Great sex means being connected to all three aspects of self (mental, emotional, and physical). Partners may need to ignite the sexual fire within their Nine lover to help bring them into their bodies and as such create arousal.

How Nines Can become Sexually Present

Merge with yourself: Healing for Nines comes not through merging with a partner, group, or their various comforts, but rather through merging with themselves in acknowledging their own sexual needs, desires, and opinions. They need to maintain their own identity, even when being intimate with another. The path to integration lies with being authentic rather than living through an idealized version of their partner.

See your needs as equal: Nines become self-actualized when they view their needs as equal to their partners—neither greater nor lessor. It's a process of self-remembering and realizing that they do count (much more than they think).

Be open to change: Integrated Nines are open to exploration and doing things differently. If it doesn't work, then it's fine—you tried. Using their vivid imaginations can bring excitement into sex.

Become open to reality: Nines need to accept this universal paradox: by holding on to only the "good" parts of a relationship, they lose the potential for depth and balance. The happy times sometimes also require times that are less fulfilling, and that's OK.

Focus on your own desires: Acknowledging their right to experience pleasure brings them into Presence—and the world won't stop if the kitchen isn't clean. Nines deserve to enjoy their sexuality but need to connect to their bodies. Asking "Where am I feeling that emotional pain in my body?" is a great way to remember (and re-member) their body connection.

What do *you* want? Nines need to consider what it is they want from sex and verbalize that to a partner. Journaling may help them consolidate their thoughts and feelings.

Acknowledge and release anger: Anger creates a defensive wall that blocks intimacy. It is healing to become aware of their anger towards a partner and then work through it, rather than suppressing it.

Questions to Journal

NOTE: It's useful to answer these questions no matter what your type.

- How does your need to maintain peace affect your ability to be connected to your sexual desires and expression?
- What effect could this have on a partner? And on you?
- How does an inclination to merge with a partner affect you?
- Is sex a healing, intimate space for both you and your partner, or is it more about fulfilling their needs and in doing so, maintaining harmony?
- What are your sexual needs and desires?

The Type You Love

Why you'd be attracted to different types,
how to engage with them,
and what to expect when things go wrong.

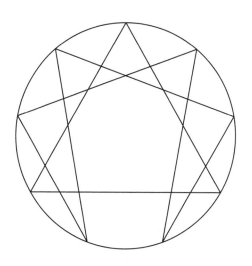

13

Why You'd Be Attracted to Different Types

What Type Makes the Best Lovers?

The answer is simple: The lover who is most integrated. The more integrated you and your partner are, the more open and present you'll be—and the more intimate sex you'll experience. If your lover is disintegrated, it doesn't matter what type they are—the ego is in the driver's seat.

There is however the issue of Retreating, Advancing and Conditional types. If two Retreating types are in a relationship, there may be mutual understanding of the need to retreat, but less of a spark. With two Advancing types, the constant need to confront may be overly explosive, albeit exciting at times. Two Conditional types may be so focused on meeting certain conditions that sex can get lost along the way.

If we run briefly through each type:

- A disintegrated One could be being critical (of your performance, body, the condition of your bedroom—hardly a turn-on. But an integrated One will be serene and accepting,
- A disintegrated Two could feel clinging and exhausting, making you feel guilty for "all I've done for you." But an integrated Two is nurturing, loving, and compassionate.
- An unhealthy Three may be busy waving flags about their prowess as a lover, leaving you as the supporting act. A healthy Three is authentic and will show a genuine interest in you.
- A Four in a disintegrated state may be so self-focused that you feel ignored or insignificant, while their melancholy is unlikely to be an aphrodisiac. An integrated Four will show up as romantic, sensitive to your needs, and emotionally strong.
- Having sex with a disintegrated Five may feel as if you're a sexual experiment being researched. But an integrated Five is an innovative, understanding, kind, and playful lover.

- A Six who is not emotionally healthy may exhaust you with their fears and concerns before you've even taken off your jeans. Sixes who are healthy will show compassion and affection, and will be well-grounded.
- A disintegrated Seven could be so caught up in their mind about a future possibility or what you're going to do later that sex could feel like it's being checked off a mental list. An integrated Seven will be enthusiastically appreciative of you, thoughtful, and genuinely content.
- A disintegrated Eight might come on to you so lustfully that you feel the need to back away. Integrated Eights are prepared to meet you as an equal, allowing their gentleness to be revealed while still being strong and honorable partners.
- An unhealthy Nine could zone out to the point that you could feel like you're making love to an inanimate object. But healthy Nines will be fully engaged, sensuous, sexually imaginative, and proactive.

Choosing a partner is also about personal preference and your own needs. Would a One's desire to do the right thing make you feel secure in a relationship? Would the care and thoughtfulness of a Two work for you? The drive and confidence of a Three lover? The romantic nature of a Four? The innovative and exploratory capabilities of a Five? The loyalty and compassion of a Six? Do you want the excitement of a Seven? An Eight to protect you and take charge? Maybe the gentle desire to please of a Nine?

Perhaps reading through the types will give you an idea of what type is most likely to inspire you. (And then, as life goes, you'll fall for someone completely different!)

Why You'd be Attracted to a One

When you meet a One, they'll most likely be conservatively well-dressed. You may be attracted to their ideal of creating a better world. They come across as wise, ethical, responsible and disciplined—if you've previously been involved with a cheating, irresponsible addict, the One's stability may prove very attractive. You may admire the One's willingness to fight on behalf of others, or for what they believe is right, and they can be inspiring in that regard.

In their desire to be "good" they can make wonderful marriage material, being dedicated providers or homemakers, and offering a stable, secure home life—the kind of guy or gal you'd want to bring home to meet the parents.

In the bedroom they can take charge, and when in love they can be passionate and even a bit romantic. They won't forget an anniversary or your birthday, and will do what's expected of them to celebrate. Ones are seldom overweight and often enjoy exercise, so they typically have trim physiques—they are great eye candy!

Why You'd Be Attracted to a Two

Twos are known as the seducers of the Enneagram. They know just what to do to please a partner: they've spent a lifetime hooking into people's needs so can easily morph into what you desire a partner to be. They don't do this for everyone, but rather for a specific person or group. When less integrated, they are the histrionic personalities[1] of the Enneagram, whose art is seduction.

They are the person who will offer you everything you ever wanted—the knight in shining armor or the loving, desirable damsel. Particularly if you've had a history of neglect or unhappy relationships, the Two may be a dream come true—they'll make sure your favorite brand of shampoo is in the bathroom, offer you freshly squeezed orange juice in the morning, give you a massage, and take you on that dream date: "At last," you may say, "I've met someone who is empathetic, emotionally supportive, and who gets my needs."

For a Two, the need for attachment and attention can mean even a night alone becomes daunting. Because finding a mate is so much top of their list, Twos work hard to make themselves attractive. They'll dress well, use expensive perfume or aftershave, and workout at the gym. When they feel the relationship is steady, some of these habits may fall by the wayside.

Why You'd Be Attracted to a Three

Threes are charming and ambitious. Phallic[2] types (cocky and self-assured), they exude confidence, and it's a great aphrodisiac. Someone who appears to have it all can have us wanting to be part of what we feel we're not—we'll be hoping some of the Three's gold dust will rub off on us. In addition to their natural charm, brand-conscious Threes generally take a lot of care in creating a desirable image: think designer sunglasses, La Prairie skin cream, Kate Spade handbag… They exude glitz, glamour, and style.

Threes look good on any arm and "scrub up well," often having an interest in fashion and knowing how to make the best of themselves. (Only an intimate few may see them slopping around in pajamas at midday after burnout has hit.) Consequently, walking into a room with a Three will have admiring heads turning in your direction. They're often also physically attractive, an attribute which they can take great pains to enhance (with the possible exception of the counterphobic type)—think tummy tucks, boob jobs, and other kinds of cosmetic surgery.

They draw lovers to them like moths to a flame—sex, power, success, and fame can enhance any shortfall in looks. They'll make you laugh, flatter you, offer help on the project you're working on, and wine and dine you in style. They want to be seen as fun, clever, witty, and pleasing, so will go out of their way to get you to enjoy their company. Interested in bettering themselves, they can usually carry a conversation on many different topics, even if it's only superficially.

They are skilled at marketing their desirability. Threes achieve their sexual demands by shining—being the star.

Why You'd Be Attracted to a Four

When you're at that elegant art opening and someone enters the room looking trendy yet "different," there is a reasonable chance you're admiring a Four. Fours often present themselves as intriguing and mysterious, and it's a tantalizing aphrodisiac. They can appear to be standing on the sidelines of the party, yet draw you to them like exotic jewels. When you're with them, they see only you in the room.

They are intense and alluring—electricity pervades their sensual touch. "This person beats to a different drum," you say to yourself, and are drawn to discover why. They may expound at excited length about their latest creation and in a world of robotic insensitivity, you love their passion. Their fragility and vulnerability make you want to save them.

Together, you'll read books while sprawled in front of log fires; travel the world in your minds; or curl up drinking wine and listening to poetry. You'll spend hours caressing, only to fight outrageously, then passionately make up. Your Four may write songs for you with hidden love messages, send flowers, or create art or a story about you—they'll be what every romance book ever promised.

Why You'd Be Attracted to a Five

Fives are smart. They know a lot about a lot of things, so it can be fascinating to engage with them. I recall a woman falling in love with a Five because:

> We'd have these long discussions into early hours of the
> night. His ideas were original and thought-provoking.
> While I wasn't attracted to him physically, he was funny
> and clever, and that was an enticing combination.

If they happen to be your professor, or a renowned scientist under whom you're doing your PhD research, you may be attracted to their wisdom and knowledge.

Fives see life differently, and as a result their observations can be both insightful and quirky. They have the depth that may be perceived to be lacking in some of the other types. If you understand them and their need for privacy, aren't demanding, and don't push them to reveal what they would rather not, they can be incredibly loyal and caring partners. Sometimes their awkwardness and intensity make them especially attractive and vulnerable.

Although often not athletic (unless it's a sport they do alone such as cycling), they are often ectomorphic,[3] having a slim, slightly muscular build—a trim and attractive litheness.

Why You'd be Attracted to a Six

Integrated Sixes love you for who you are—not because of your inheritance, your prestigious job, or your looks. They see the real you, and this can be very appealing.[4] In not wanting to feel threatened themselves, Sixes want to not be threatening to others, and are often friendly. They develop a self-deprecating sense of humor: "Look," they seem to say, "if I can make fun of myself, then I'm not someone to be feared." They often enjoy entertaining and are hospitable hosts.[5] They are responsible, taking charge of finances and paying the bills to ensure that things run smoothly. This is a big bonus to partners who don't enjoy this aspect of life!

Be prepared to watch horror movies on dates—Sixes sometimes attempt to counter their fears by watching worst-case scenarios. It's a safe way of being afraid! Despite their low sense of self (or maybe because of it), Sixes do enjoy taking charge, which can mean taking a more dominant role in the bedroom.

Sixes can be loyal supporters of a partner's cause and can sincerely enjoy their partner's achievements. To this end they are happy to take a back seat and make personal sacrifices in order for a partner to achieve a goal.

If a Six has accepted you as a serious partner, they view it as a lifelong commitment. Should you encounter problems along the road (as we all inevitably do) a Six will focus on the issue to be resolved, rather than the partner. If you're there for them, they'll be there for you.

Why You'd Be Attracted to a Seven

Sevens seduce with charm, excitement, banter, and brains. Their cheerful presence lightens even the most dour atmosphere. It's understandable that you'd be attracted to this intuitive, perceptive, quick-witted person who can make you feel so good about life.

Sevens are typically fun to be with—party animals who'll liven up the room. They can be Peter Pans in their refusal to grow old. They want to do it all and will happily take you along for the ride (provided you can keep up!). Hold them back or spoil their fun, and they'll move on fast. Sevens are also very independent, and while they may tolerate a certain amount of limitation, freedom is paramount to happiness. They won't enjoy it if you are constantly checking up on them, or if you're moody and miserable.

Confidence is the biggest aphrodisiac and Sevens usually have an abundance of it. They're "cool": they dress well, they know interesting people, and, like Threes, know all the best new places to hang out. They're entertaining conversationalists and enjoy a partner who can match their pace.

Life with a Seven is not boring. They're often worldly and have traveled widely already. Be prepared for a rollercoaster ride through life—your Seven wants to visit (yet more) foreign lands, trendy new restaurants, and inspiring natural wonders.

They're keen to make a difference in the world (particularly Social Sevens), so will appeal to those who share the same ideals.

Why You'd Be Attracted to an Eight

When an Eight walk into a room, you can almost smell the power. Charisma and confidence oozes from every pore. They can be inspiring—and there's no way you won't notice them. They often have a slight swagger, and their "I'll take care of it" attitude can promise safety and protection for a partner. Their generosity and big hearts will have you wanting to leap across the table saying, "Take me now!"

Eights are typically leaders or will be in management in their chosen field. Sex is often about power, and power can lead quickly to passion. They come across as assertive—a trait likely to attract an array of sexual conquests.[6]

Eights enjoy socializing. They love to be seated at the head of a large table of family or friends, or to hit the clubs in an all-night buddy binge. Eights are impulsive, so they may just as soon leave the club once they've hooked someone who's attracted them. Without further thought they'll forget previous plans and head across the room with a witty opening line.

If you break through an Eight's barriers you can find a surprisingly soft, compassionate, and sentimental person beneath the heavy armor.

Why You'd Be Attracted to a Nine

There are few people who don't like Nines. Their desire to please, and their warm, affectionate disposition, ability to sympathize and generally cheerful contentedness make them difficult people to dislike. In their company you feel held, calm, and relaxed—they will put any nervous suitor at easy with their happy banter.

Nines are unassuming and don't take themselves too seriously. Even if they've achieved much in their lives, they're reticent to wave flags about it. They love participating in family events or socializing with friends. They enjoy feeling part of a group, yet often say they never really feel included.

They're kind, generous to a fault, forgiving, and helpful. They want to please you. Nines, particularly those with an Eight-wing, are also sensuous lovers. Some Type Nines can go after a sexual partner with the ambition and drive of a Three, using sex to prove their autonomy, or to merge with a partner's strong desire.

What's not to like, right?

14

How to Engage with
Different Types

Chatting Up the Types

You've identified the person of your dreams. Now you need to engage with them. You suspect what type they are through your own and others' observations, but what approach should you take to best connect? The Enneagram can be hugely helpful here. Even if you're wrong about their type itself, your approach may well appeal to a type that is part of their overall make up (their wings or points of stretch and release). Give it a try and see if it makes a difference to the way you'd normally approach someone.

How to Engage with a One

Your priority? Be on time for the date! Ones hate poor punctuality. Ones will be attracted either to those they see as more fun-loving and relaxed than themselves, or alternatively to those they see as sharing their beliefs and principles. They are usually reasonably confident and garrulous, so you may not have to do too much talking. They'll enjoy it if you listen and agree with their point of view. Holding out on having sex will demonstrate that you too have morals and codes of conduct.

Reassuring your One that you appreciate all they do to make life better will go a long way to easing their self-imposed restrictions and recriminations. An offer to help will work wonders; sitting reading a magazine while they perform chores won't. If you've messed up by being late, they will forgive relatively easily, provided you make a formal apology.

How to Engage with a Two

Because of their tendency to define themselves through their partner, Twos are often attracted to the following types of people:

• The downtrodden: partners who have been abused or who feel like victims. Twos like to fulfil the role of rescuer or enabler.

- Those needing help: partners with a disability or physical limitation, who need help to overcome addiction, or help in some form (an introduction, a job, financial aid). Twos like to assist, anywhere where their benevolence can shine, and can love so well that they don't see the "flaw."
- Beautiful people: like the Four they move to, Twos enjoy eye candy, someone attractive to hang on their arm, which enhances their own sense of self. Twos are often themselves attractive in a soft, curvaceous way, so want a partner to match their looks.
- Successful people: Twos (particularly Social Instinctive Twos) enjoy partnering with people who have the potential to "make it" in life: the up-and-coming author, the start-up guy with ideas and ambition, the talk-show host who's getting noticed by larger stations, or the developer whose app holds great possibilities.[1] The Two can be there when the growth/success/fame happens and can claim at least part of the success as their own: "You could never have achieved this without my support." Or they might opt for a supportive role of someone who is already successful.

To win over a Two, create a romantic setting, make them feel needed and appreciated, boost them (particularly in company), and create fun and excitement in the relationship. Reciprocating their gestures can work wonders—the odd lunch, a small gift, or loving email—but not so they feel they need to give you something bigger in return. Deep down, they believe that to express their needs is a surefire way to be rejected. Occasionally having the focus on the Two rather than on the partner is a wonderful reminder to Twos that they do count. Physical touch is also important, as is constant reassurance that you adore them. They spend much of their lives listening and showing interest in you, so reciprocate by making them feel worth listening to. Let them know how much you care about them and how proud you are that they are in a relationship with you.

How to Engage with a Three

Threes "work" a room—particularly if well-connected people are involved. Once you've engaged with them, it's easy to let them do most of the talking: An occasional, "Oh, wow, really? That's amazing," will hold their interest. Tantalize them with name-dropping and a few hints about your important social connections; they'll also perk up if you appear worldly wise and having interesting (and inside) information or skills to share. It helps to be wise and witty.

Sex can be about performance, so let them know if the experience was enjoyable. Threes work hard to better themselves and need to feel that their efforts in and out of the bedroom are appreciated. Threes don't have loads of free time, so be prepared to have busy, active weekends where you find yourself playing second fiddle to a career or sport.

Initially, a new Three lover will want to appear to be the perfect partner,[2] but the façade will fall with familiarity. Look for ways to bring the sparkle back into the relationship.

Let your Three know that it's them that attracts you and not their achievements and outside image. Enjoy the cash they can bring, and the wining and dining that accompanies it, but let your Three know that you'd still be there for them, prince or pauper.

Threes are caught in a trap: feeling that they need to earn appreciation, they get confused when their hours at the office produce anger and resentment in a neglected partner. Allow them to see that it's OK just to be, not do. Realize that in this space they may feel vulnerable and will need your affirmation and support. They may appear to have not taken your critical comment to heart, but alone they may feel overwhelmed with sadness. Remember they feel that love is to be demanded, rather than received spontaneously.

They derive security through activity, which can be exhausting, so allow them to realize that not accompanying them to every event isn't rejection, it's just time for you to unwind. Accept that having them work late will be part of your life (except for the Sexual subtype). You may need to plan vacations together, or else they'll be "way too busy" at work. Find activities outside work that you both enjoy. Threes love to improve their skills, so go winetasting, on cooking courses, to sports clinics or art workshops, or whatever else inspires you both.

Let lovemaking be slow and smoldering, rather than something that can be ticked off a to-do list. Gently get them to understand that orgasm is not the aim, but part of the journey. If they can see that it's not essential to pleasurable lovemaking, it removes performance anxiety or the need to feel they always be at peak.

If you can manage to get them to slow down (good luck!), allow them space to connect with their deeper feelings—to feel, rather than think their feelings. This can be confusing for Threes and they may not be sure if what they're feeling is real.

Having a clingy partner seldom works for a Three—they'll enjoy you more if you're also independent. Praising them for successes works well; focusing on their failures doesn't.

How to Engage with a Four

You would be ill advised to introduce yourself to a Four and babble on about them being a Four (in fact, you'd be ill-advised to do that with any type)—particularly because Fours don't enjoy being viewed as anything other than unique. When teaching, I'm likely engaging with a Four if their first words at the workshop are: "I don't enjoy being put in a box."

Doing the opposite, however, works wonders. Try something like this: "Wow, the moment you walked into the room I sensed there was something different about you. Let's leave the crowds and head to an intimate place I know where this Mauritian serves the most incredible cocktails. I want to discover more about you."

Fours do not want to appear boring or ordinary, so acknowledge their exotic and unusual traits. Enjoy their smoldering sensitivity and ignite the creative intensity they thrive on: "Casual sex, or sex without a deep connection, is not what I'm after. I guess I'm an intimacy junkie. I want all of you—your naked body and your naked thoughts."

Allow them to express the depth of their feelings. Encourage their creativity (Fours need to feel creative to feel alive). Realize that they are seeking deep intimacy rather than fun and a good time. Don't allow their reminiscing about past lovers get to you—instead, gently bring them into the present with you.

Good taste is important to artistic Fours, so remember this when you get ready for a date. Other types may not enjoy your retro Audrey Hepburn look, or your take on James Dean, but a Four could find it seductive!

How to Engage with a Five

Fives do not enjoy feeling engulfed by someone, so pouncing on them and boring them with small talk is a sure way to have them running for the door (which, being Fives, they'll be standing close to for just that reason). They're unlikely to make the first move. A good way to spark an engagement would be to standing alongside them (not face to face, as that would be experienced as too invasive and confrontational), while asking them questions related to their current project or interest. Draw them out slowly. Fives are normally useless flirts, so don't mistake a lack of flirting for a lack of interest.

Fives feel largely socially inept—the whole dating game and subtle signals make no sense to them, and they'd rather keep conversation intellectual than embark on chit-chat or anything too emotional.

Fives find the preliminaries of a relationship difficult to navigate—they may want to connect but feel unsure as to how to approach the person they desire. Writing emails and SMSs could be a non-threatening way to engage, giving the Five the opportunity to demonstrate their intellect and wit. In person, they may try being intellectually arrogant in a "take it or leave it" manner, or they can become belittling to partners: "You wouldn't understand this concept…" They will likely attempt to impress you with their knowledge. If you don't force them into an emotional corner, Fives can display kindness and emotions that are insightful.

Feeling disconnected from the body, sex can become a way for them to feel more connection. Partners may be chosen not so much because of their pleasant dispositions than because they happened to be available at the time. If the Five is in a relationship, they may be active sexually, but the performance could become "mechanical" in time. [3]

You may also think that your Five has zoned out of feeling, but many Fives report going back to their "caves" to sit and reflect on a relationship. It's not a personal affront but a necessary recharge of their batteries. What you may feel is aloofness may just be awkwardness: being with people is draining (unless they're discussing an interesting topic with experts in the field), but being alone is energizing.

When you're lying in each other's arms, it's more likely that your Five will be discussing the theory of relativity than how much you mean to them. If you can accept that this is their way of connecting, you'll be fine.

Fives can be devoted life partners, but will always feel that being in a relationship comes at a personal cost. By giving up focus on what they want (and feeling deprived as a result), Fives demonstrate their commitment to the relationship.

Some Fives can become asexual for periods of time. Certain Five priests or spiritual seekers may tell themselves they have risen above their bodily desires (and indeed some may have), but for many it's simply a need to retreat to the safe place in their heads, rather than true liberation from lust.

Do not arrive unannounced on their doorstep—Fives hate intrusions. Do allow them time alone and don't force them into social interaction (cocktail parties and parties are the worst!). Try to listen to them—they hate repeating carefully-considered information. Fives will express emotions if and when they feel comfortable doing so. Putting them on the spot will only drive their feelings deeper.

How to Engage with a Six

According to Claudio Naranjo, Sixes want to approach potential love matches but are afraid to because they feel unsure of themselves. This differs from Fives, who are not conflicted but simply indifferent when it comes to making that initial move. [4] Sixes enjoy being approached (it relieves them from needing the courage to make the first move), but they may also be suspicious: "What does he *really* want from me? Why would *he* be attracted to *me?*"

Sixes may feel that your cleverly planned one-liner holds a hidden agenda: "What's really being said here? Do I need to be worried?" They are hugely sensitive to rejection and need to feel that they are totally accepted before they can relax into a relationship. They feel loneliness and alienation immensely and long to be part of the social scene, both for safety and acceptance. [5]

Sixes can also appear fickle, so you may feel as if they like you one day but not the next. Understand that this is due to their own uncertainty and fear: "Will this work? Do I really want a relationship right now? They've had more partners than I've had—does that mean they can't be trusted?" With so many "what if's," it's hard for them to progress with certainty.

Sixes' suspicion creates a world where few can be trusted, including themselves. Whose advice should they follow? [6] They may need affirmation from a partner, friend, or colleague to confirm their decisions, but by asking for this they invalidate themselves. It's for this reason that the word "ambivalence" has become associated with Sixes. [7] They will enjoy a partner who can talk through their fears and concerns with them and instill the confidence to trust their own decisions—someone who encourages them to step into the unknown, while holding their hand.

If your Six feels they can trust you, you'll have the start of a great relationship. Interestingly, if you try to control or manipulate a Six, you could well meet a rebel.

How to Engage with a Seven

Sevens are garrulous about their plans and exploits, and they can exaggerate: the fish they caught grows by several inches with each telling of the story. It's not done to boost themselves, but rather to make things more interesting. To get the juices flowing with a Seven, being a good listener helps, but so is meeting their enthusiasm with your own.

Remember that they are not as confident as they'd like you to believe, so when they are funny, impress you, or say something insightful, it can work wonders to acknowledge them. Sevens, like Fives, enjoy witty puns and so laughing or responding with one will earn their respect. Puns may also reveal a Seven's feelings—emotion disguised as wit.

Sevens can be shocking in their ideas and sexual desires, so you'll need to be comfortable with this. (If they suggest hot sex in a friend's kitchen pantry during a dinner party, you'll need to be happy to oblige.)

They'll be looking for the positive in a relationship by downplaying any negatives. Despite their slick, confident exterior, Sevens can be extremely sensitive to any form of rejection.

Sevens enjoy drifting in on a joyful tide of love only to flow somewhere else when the mood arises, and then happily return. If you try to pin them down on too many dates and times, you may find them canceling. They sometimes don't understand that their absence and energized reappearance doesn't work for a partner, who may feel abandoned and used. Allowing them space to move and maintaining your own interests is crucial: "I'm off to surf, honey. See you after your cycle."

How to Engage with an Eight

Eights love straight talk, so strolling over to them and saying something like: "What are the chances I get to see you naked tonight?" may be enjoyed by an Eight, as long as they feel in control of the outcome. They enjoy sassy speech and a partner's ability to meet their direct humor. Don't attempt to lay down rules, control, or dominate them—leave them to make the plans.

They thrive on being assertive. They also find it stimulating to fight, so they won't back down (unless it ends up in the bedroom). Eights find sugary niceness annoying, ditto with ingratiating behavior. They can see through it for what it is, so it's best to be 100 percent authentic.

They enjoy excitement, so suggesting a quiet night at home with Netflix (unless it involves raunchy sex) will be uninviting. Get them juiced up with banter. Massaging their egos won't go amiss either! Expect blunt honesty: "You're such a sexy woman, but those tights don't work for me."

Their passion can be misinterpreted as anger, so you'll need to learn how to discern between the two. Also, realize that they may be mad one moment, but the next it will have blown over completely. If you see the softer side in an Eight and allow them a safe space to express that side of themselves, you'll have won them over.

How to Engage with a Nine

Nines are self-neglecting. If you notice them and show interest in their lives or hobbies, you'll attract their attention. Nines often feel as if they don't quite belong. Getting them to feel part of your group is a good way to connect with them: "We're all going to watch the game on Saturday. Want to come with me?" Nines are convivial and although some can be shy, they enjoy being social (if they don't have to do all the work). They make friends with anyone with whom they identify, so they are easy to chat to. Invariably, though, you'll need to make the first move. It's usually easy to start a conversation with them (unless they're disintegrated and numbed out). Provided you don't get confrontational, they'll happily listen to you.

Be aware, though, that Nines can be indifferent, even dismissive of strangers at first. If they don't feel some connection with you, they'll need to warm up by learning that you can be trusted.[8] They won't want to reject you outright and risk offending.

They want you to relax and enjoy yourself, and their emphasis will be on pleasing you. They like feeling that they belong to a family group and are very much part of a partner's life. Nines can lack passion being more feminine/watery in their demeanor. Fire attracts them—being inspired, creative, expressive, and taking action is a turn-on for a Nine.

Remember that Nines are often going to tell you what you want to hear, rather than what they actually feel or want. If a Nine is keen, they'll be trying to second guess which you'd prefer: "Would you like to come out for dinner? Curry or Thai?" Your needs seem to be more important than their own. If you understand this, you can draw out their real desires by saying: "You mentioned that you love Thai food since your visit to Thailand. Should we try the new place up the road?" Simply being acknowledged for having needs is hugely endearing to a Nine.

15

What to Expect When
Things Go Wrong

When we get into the lower levels of integration, divorce for all types gets understandably messy. Divorce for anyone of any type is never a pleasant experience, and tends to push us into the less integrated aspects of ourselves. Hopefully the shift is temporary and once resolved we can move into healthier levels of being. Perhaps, with the insight in the following pages, it may be possible to maintain ourselves at a more integrated level and move between the polarities of "I'm right—you're wrong," into transcending the need to be either. I hope so.

Divorcing a One

Ones don't want to be seen to be "bad" person in a relationship. Divorce is not perceived as the "right" option, so it will be hard for them to move on. Ones will doubt themselves and secretly worry about their faults, all the while condemning their partner for leaving them or causing the relationship to fail.

"But you were miserable together," I said to a One whose husband had walked out of the marriage. "You were forever complaining about him and nothing he did was ever right, so surely his leaving is a good thing? A time to start afresh and find someone who's closer to your idea of a good partner?"

Her response? "But he should never have left me. It's not *right*. He should have stayed!"

Because Ones are on a mission to make the world a better place, they don't see themselves as being critical but as helping others become better. They also battle to accept criticism. As a result, they may fail to accept any responsibility for playing a part in the breakdown of a relationship. It's hugely healing if they can open themselves up to the idea that both parties may have caused the breakdown of communication in the relationship.

Divorcing a Two

Perhaps the Two's lover has stopped needing their attention. Perhaps, like King Henry VIII,[1] the Two has tired of the novelty of their current partner and is seeking new stimulation (Naranjo uses the word "capricious"[2]). Or perhaps the Two feels they are not receiving the praise and gratitude they desire. If a Two finds that their partner is no longer desirable, they can swiftly change affections and move on, making quick, even irrational decisions. The partner may be left wondering just how deep and connected the relationship really was.

Affection can rapidly move to indifference and less healthy Type Eight behavior, such as revenge and destruction. It can be most confusing to a partner that the loving, warm person they once knew has become hard and cold in the blink of an eye.

Once the exciting seduction of a new lover is over, Twos may find it frustrating to be constrained. They may long for the freedom of their single days, despite craving a relationship when they are single. A steady relationship may suddenly feel confining and the Two's eyes may wander to the cute new employee, wondering if this potential conquest will satiate their desire to be a savior. They enjoy independence in themselves, but not in their partners.

When Twos disintegrate, they can become needy and clingy.[3] This may make their partner tire of them, particularly the more detached cooler types, who may find the constant control and need for attention exhausting and invasive. Some may see through the Two's boastful attempts to make themselves out to be a better catch, and may regard them as being deceitful, particularly when they acknowledge that all the giving was simply a ploy to get.

If they have been taken to the cleaners in a divorce, a Two may complain in order to gain sympathy or, alternatively, gloss over their loss because they want to appear generous or in control to their next prospective partner.

Divorcing a Three

Divorce can push a Three's abandonment and shame buttons. A disintegrated Three's tendency to be competitive and enjoy winning combined with their potential for "Vindictive Triumph"[4] creates the potential for a nasty, drawn-out battle, where the focus is on winning at any cost.

Seeing themselves as victims, even if they have flagrantly flaunted their marriage vows, Threes will protest that no matter how reasonable the divorce settlement, they are the hapless losers. They are used to beating the odds and many have financial success behind them, meaning expensive and skilled legal teams. They can attempt to wear their partner down with endless accusations and delays, conveyed in court with their charismatic charm. Children can get caught in crossfire and become pawns in the process. The angry Three's needs and compulsion to win are central.

Partners will want to draw a line under the ensuing drama, but for disintegrated Threes, closure is less important than control and ultimate victory. The truth may become skewed to serve the Three's ends, and reaching a compromise is not an option. If legal fees escalate, the Three will believe they will win and won't have to pay the costs. A partner's exhaustion and damaged reputation may have them agreeing to an unfair settlement. If the Three ends the process with very little, they'll be confident in their ability to recreate wealth quickly.

With integrated Threes there may be no need for these tactics. They'll understand that it's not about "winning" but about getting the best result for all parties.

Divorcing a Four

Like Threes, Fours fear being abandoned—if they are not the instigator, divorce can be devasting. Having seen you once as their adored soulmate, they can become vindictive when you threaten to leave (even if their impossible behavior was the cause.)

They will feel hugely wronged—even if they've driven their partner to the depths of despair by refusing to do anything constructive with their lives, or been too self-absorbed to see their partner's own struggles, or have had affairs, or been highly temperamental… Because of the cycle they create of attraction, relationship, finding fault and then either being rejected or rejecting, Fours may have a number of relationships or even marriages in between periods of loneliness.

Fours may have initially idolized a partner; when the traits they projected onto the partner are found not to exist, they have no hesitation in pointing out their "faults," turning their disappointment into attack. Fours are left feeling like tragic victims. A deeper sense of shame arises for not being able to maintain a relationship, and then the search for a redeemer begins again. If someone does love them, there must be something wrong with that person for seeing them as remotely loveable. Being jilted escalates their feelings of worthlessness.

They may see themselves as saints ruined by a sinning partner: "You forced me into having an affair to find the love you weren't giving me!"

If the Four is not integrated, love soon becomes war. Divorce becomes a competition they need to win to beat the offending partner into the humiliation they feel. When it comes to a settlement, they may see their "suffering" as giving them the right to demand what is not theirs: they have suffered, now it's your turn.

Fours may drag up the trauma of a past relationship or the sordid intricacies of their divorce as if it happened last month. Should an ex find a new partner, the volume of aggression can be turned up. They may make false accusations, engage with different teams of lawyers, attempt to rally support from family members, or do whatever it takes to destroy the new relationship.

Self-preservation types might find their dependency buttons pushed and get angry as a result: "Who will look after me now?" Social Fours could view their divorce as a drop in status if they were married to someone rich or famous. Sexual Fours may feel as if they are an even greater failure than they already feel themselves to be.[5]

Divorcing a Five

Type Fives are the most likely of the types to be comfortable being single. They may stay married but opt for a long travel adventure or a series of them as a way to be alone. As one cyclist making his way across Africa told me: "If I'm home with my wife and son I long to be on the road, yet when I'm cycling, I miss them."

As with many things in their lives, Fives can abdicate rather than work through tough times.[6] Breaking off the relationship may seem the most obvious and safest route to go. A partner, on the other hand, may feel as if their Five doesn't really care and may as a result feel taken for granted.

Fives can become resigned: "She's probably better off with him anyway." Love for Fives can quickly become a burden, rather than a joyful expression. To a partner, the Five can seem cold, indifferent, aloof, and difficult to engage with intimately. Fives are concerned that by expressing their feelings, others will feel empowered to use this knowledge at their expense.

Although Fives can be very argumentative when it comes to attacking beliefs and theories, in personal relationships they're more likely to detach in a conflict situation. They can be dismissive, with an attitude of "This is really beneath me; I don't really care." Alternatively, they'll believe that it's easier to go along with people than to waste the effort of confronting them. As a result, they can be easily dominated or, like Eights, can smolder and seek revenge.

They may experience divorce as a release—an end to the pain of feeling so depleted by another. Sure they may be upset, but there's another part of them saying, "Yes! Now I get to focus on my own things!" without interruption or having to feel that their resources are being consumed.

Divorcing a Six

Marriage involves vows. Breaking these vows goes against the Six's belief in keeping their word.[7] The Six will have followed the relationship rules: they will have fulfilled their responsibilities and marital obligations. You, however, did not. Responsible Sixes are unlikely to leave their children in the lurch financially, and typically continue to view their parental roles seriously.

Throughout the divorce proceedings, Sixes may experience ambivalent feelings. One day they may feel the need to settle things amicably even if it means giving more than they'd like; the next day, they may angrily thwart all attempts at a civil break-up, becoming paranoid in the process. They can adopt a "fight or flight" approach—either fleeing from the trauma or counterphobically meeting the legal threat head-on. If feeling persecuted by lawyers, they may unpredictably lash out to show that they can't be messed with. You will have become the enemy.

Divorcing a Seven

Sevens run the risk of acting too fast at the first hint of relationship difficulty. They can also appear to move on from a divorce relatively swiftly, hiding their insecurity and feelings of inferiority under a seemingly contented mask. Using their future-focused thinking, they can already be envisioning a new relationship, which is disconcerting for the spouse so easily dropped.

If love and having a good time are viewed as one and the same, it's understandable why Sevens would see love as being lost when confronted with humdrum responsibility. A Seven I knew divorced her husband and made plans to travel abroad with a friend, but got cold feet at the airport and ended up remarrying her husband—her desire for security ultimately overriding her Sevenish desire for new experiences.

Sevens can be extremely verbally manipulative—you'd have to be astute not to come out of a divorce badly. Alternatively, to overcome the pain of the proceedings as quickly as possible, they may be overly generous in the package they agree to, throwing away all they've worked for with the confidence that they'll soon recoup their losses. As a Seven said: "I walked out of the door with the clothes I had on and my car keys. I never went back."

Sevens can react strongly to any implication that they have acted wrongly, because it taints their view of their idealized self.[8] Even if it was their rash behavior that led you to the divorce court, they'll proclaim their innocence (and judge you in return).

Because many Sevens believe that they are on a self-developmental mission (the so-called "New Age" movement was undoubtably a Seven concept), they see their relationship as part of that development: "Think of what we've learned from each other, and how we've grown." To them, a divorce indicates that it's time to move on to the next learning curve, with someone else. They don't always understand why this might be a problem, and why their ex might not accept the change with as much guiltless ease and enthusiasm as they do.

Divorcing an Eight

If an Eight divorces you because *they* have had an affair, you could get a fair settlement, particularly if children are involved. If divorce was instigated because *you* were unfaithful, or because you feel intimidated, or are tired of being controlled or undermined, then expect a messy process. Eights do not take well to being side-lined. The combination of Eights needing retribution, enjoying conflict and not allowing themselves to lose does not bode well in divorce. If you do emerge victorious, be prepared for acts of vengeance further down the road (which they'll frame as "justice").

Aggressive legal letters will do little to intimidate an Eight, and could ignite a desire for retaliation. They thrive in battle and must dominate— and may use intimidation, physical attack, and threats to ensure victory. Full of their own self-importance, they make promises to engage the services of those who can fulfil their plans: "If you win this divorce for me, I'll make sure you never look for work again."

A disintegrated Eight will see their (ex-)partner as an annoying object, and believe they have sole ownership of them. Losing a divorce or being taken advantage of would be considered a personal weakness and must be avoided—no matter what the cost or consequences.

Divorcing a Nine

Nines will seldom take it upon themselves to end a relationship. In fact, they'll often stay for years in relationships that are toxic or even abusive, rather than disrupt their lives by deciding to leave. Because they feel helpless or unhappy alone,[9] Nines may stick with the devil they know rather than risk facing their own demons. Their problems with initiating action may also make it difficult to instigate divorce proceedings, no matter how unhappy they are.

They'll tell themselves that things aren't as bad as others say, that it's better to sit out the tough times. They may engineer a breakup behind the scenes, hoping that their partner will make the decision to leave (and be seen to be the felon), rather than actively take a stance themselves.[10]

The entire divorce may take place without an angry word being spoken—everything could be frightfully civilized. During the silent war of the predivorce years, the Nine would have withdrawn from interaction using distractions such as the laptop (very popular), cell phone, newspapers, magazines, television, friends, work, crossword puzzles, board games, sport, housework, or looking after the children. Isolation or removal of their emotional and often physical presence could have left the partner feeling desperately alone, yet with little tangible to accuse their Nine of doing.

During a divorce, all the years of having agreed with or having gone along with the partner (against the Nine's own unexpressed desires) may come home to roost—repressed anger can be expressed. Not valuing themselves, they may feel that divorce was inevitable: "Who would want to stay with me?"

More integrated Nines cannot understand those who might take advantage of them or who lie about assets. They trust others implicitly, and can be confused when a partner is found wanting in this department.[11] Mediators and peacekeepers of the Enneagram themselves, a trusted mediator may work well to avoid lengthy and costly legal fees.

Q & A with Ann

What types are more likely to be pansexual, gay/lesbian, or bisexual?

Research from various sources does differ, but drawing on Myers-Briggs research and correlating those types to the Enneagram Types, it would appear that Fours and Nines have a higher percentage of gay women and Twos, Threes, and Fours of gay men. Bisexual females were most commonly found in Fours and Fives and in men, in Fours and Sevens.[1] Pansexual types tend to be Fours, Fives, and particularly Nines. In many types, however, the percentage difference is small and further research would need to be done to be conclusive.

Interestingly, Myers-Briggs INFPs (225) and INFJs (280) scored highest when it came to viewing themselves as bi- or pansexual (24% and 19%).[2] These two types are seen to correspond most closely to Enneagram Fours and Nines respectively, according to a study of 4 703 people who knew both their Briggs-Myers and Enneagram types in the Enneagram and MBTI Correlation done in 2015.[3]

A survey by OkCupid, an online dating site, found that 33.03% of INTP females (predominately Type Fives), were bisexual. In males the percentage was far lower at 4.63%, yet it rated the third highest. This then corresponds with Priebe's findings.[4]

Why include divorce as a topic in the book?

Roughly 40–50% of marriages in the USA end in divorce[5]—a statistic that is hard to ignore in a book about sex and relationships. Clearly something is going wrong (or relationships are changing). Understanding why you or your partner reacted to a divorce the way you may have in the past may help you avoid going down that road again and help heal issues that have caused conflict.

Why did you include fantasies in the book?

I was at a dinner party with friends when my husband brought up the subject of sexual fantasies. There was a stunned silence at the table as most guests went into denial of ever having had fantasies. Really? Clearly, he'd touched on a raw nerve. People were not open to further discussion.

Brett Kahr, a psychologist based in the UK, surveyed 18,000 people in Britain and America, asking them about the frequency and content of their fantasies. He found that 9 out of 10 people have sexual fantasies and proposed that in fact everyone did, the other 10% being too inhibited to admit to it.[6]

Viewing porn could be seen as a way to bring our fantasies closer to reality. If we fantasize about two blondes in bed with us, the Internet can bring the fantasy to a visual reality. It appears that most of us can happily chat about sex, but fantasies are still, for the most part, taboo. Yet we all do have sexual fantasies.

Freud believed that the motivation for sexual fantasies was unsatisfied desires. But others disagree, saying that fantasies are a normal part of everyday sexuality. (Studies have since shown that Freud's assumptions were incorrect.)[7] People who have sexual difficulties apparently seldom fantasize while masturbating or having sex. Conversely, those who have active and satisfying sex tend to fantasize more, meaning that fantasies do not compensate for a lack of sex life, but rather enhance it.[8]

Younger unmarried women were found to fantasize more often about their current partner, in contrast to married women, who were more likely to report fantasies outside of their relationship.[9] As a relationship lengthened and presumably familiarity and boredom crept into the bedroom, both men and women fantasied about people other than their partners, which may have been actual experiences in the past or current illicit relationships.

Men and women appear to experience sexual fantasies differently.[10] Unsurprisingly, women are inclined to take a more passive role in erotic and emotional fantasy encounters with emphasis on feelings, romance, intimacy, and relationships, whereas men's fantasies focus more on their immediate sexual needs and gratification. Men were also found to fantasize more than women and to enjoy a more dominant role with more explicit imaginings.[11]

Double the number of women to men had submissive fantasies (although few wanted to enact these in real life). Men, however, were far keener to have their fantasies materialize. Men were also more keen to watch their partner having sex with another man.[12]

Attaching fantasies to Enneagram types is tricky because we can shift from the fantasies of our conscious selves to those of our shadow selves, which can be very different—for example, not all fantasies of domination are experienced by Eights, and it's common for people who have submissive fantasies to also have ones where they are dominating. This was from a study of 1,517 Quebec adults (799 men and 718 women), who were asked to rank 55 different sexual fantasies, as well as to describe their own favorite fantasy in detail. The results were rated on a scale varying from 2.3% or less of the sample (rare), 15.9% or less (unusual), more than 50% (common), and more than 84.1% (typical). The results varied hugely, meaning that few could be thought of as being rare or unusual. So, in fantasies, clearly anything goes![13]

The whole subject of fantasies and the Enneagram is a subject waiting for deeper exploration.

Why are there so many different names for the types and other aspects of the Enneagram? It makes things confusing.

As the Enneagram developed, new teachers and writers emerged, and either because of copyright issues, new developments, or their understanding, they chose to call the same concepts different names. So, a Type One may be referred to as The Reformer, Perfectionist, Purist, Organizer, Idealistic, Perspective, Crusader and no doubt other terms as well.[14]

How do I know what type I am?

If prior to reading the book you didn't know your type and haven't discovered it in reading these pages, there are many online resources available to help. Some are more accurate than others so I'd suggest you do a few and then see which resonates most with you. I'd also ask partners, friends, family, and colleagues, who may see things about you which you don't. Finding your type can take longer for some, but keep an open mind to what arises and remember that finding your type is only the start of your journey.

Acknowledgments

This book has been a journey and there are many who have accompanied me along the way—some physically and some who I have never met. Your input has been gratefully received.

The first part of the journey, that of acceptance, was due to Sabine Weeke from Findhorn Press who, together with Inner Traditions, sent that magical "Yes" email. I am hugely grateful for your support throughout. Sabine, your touches of humor were a welcome delight during months of serious research, and your gentle support was a joy.

Although I have never met Oscar Ichazo, Hameed Ali (A.H. Almaas), Helen Palmer, Beatrice Chestnut, Sandra Maitri and the late Don Riso, I am hugely grateful for their and others' teachings, which have helped me gain a much deeper understanding of the Enneagrams in general. In particular, I'd like to thank Claudio Naranjo. His book *Character and Neurosis* was hugely helpful in this project, as was Anodah Offit's writings on sexual types. The late Dr Daniel's talk with Dr Ron Levine on sexuality was both warm and insightful, and the research by leadership-training organization Aephoria on sex and love, which they generously shared, was a huge bonus. Russ Hudson, I am deeply grateful for the universal generosity that allowed me the privilege of doing workshops with you.

To my editor, Nicola Rijsdijk, I am most grateful for your open and always enthusiastic approach to this subject. Your probing questions led me to better and clearer answers than my initial offerings. You lovingly crafted the book to make it far better than the "treatise" that arrived in your inbox. (And I apologize for my excessive comma usage!)

To John Luckovitch who, living on that small island where the Hudson River meets the Atlantic, so warmly and humbly received a request from a stranger at the bottom of Africa to write the Foreword. Your open, honest, and insightful feedback gently nudged me to make some necessary changes, particularly in naming the three groups. Thank you.

Monika Adelfang, my fellow Nine, who despite a hectic schedule found the time (and had the kindness) to read the manuscript and discuss it with me. Your wisdom came through in my words. I am enormously grateful to you for having connected me with John and other Enneagram personalities. Your generosity is a true gift.

To those who have been my students and clients, I've no doubt made innumerable mistakes, but I thank you for sticking with me (and occasionally for kindly pointing them out). Your personal stories and insights, together with those of my psychologist friends, have helped make this book richer.

My family, although you're possibly confused as to why I needed to write this book, I thank you for the support I had in knowing you were there for me, even if, in my enthusiasm, I did go on a bit at family gatherings.

To my dear friends, for coffee and laughter—which helped lighten the load of research—I thank you. (We never did get to discuss your fantasies though.)

Finally, to Anthony, my life partner—our experiences together have taken us down and up the integration spectrum, but I wouldn't have wanted it any other way. I'm grateful for your delight and encouragement in my addressing this topic, our debates about my approach, your doing the shopping in my writing absence, and the way you'd happily forgo your paintbrush to act as a sounding board.

Thank you, all, for knowingly and unknowingly walking this road with me. I hope that together we'll make a positive difference.

Notes

Introduction: A Bit of Foreplay

1. Clellan S. Ford and Frank A. Beach. *Patterns of Sexual Behavior*. (Harper & Brothers, New York, 1951), pp. 22-24.

2. Dr David Daniels and Dr Ron Levin. "Sexuality, Sensuousness and the Enneagram" http://drdaviddaniels.com/products. Accessed and purchased May 2018.

3. Comment by Russ Hudson at the 2018 Enneagram Global Summit, "Instincts Panel, Part 1."

4. Logue, Jeff. https://www.sagu.edu/thoughthub/pornography-statistics-who-uses -pornography. Accessed November 2018.

5. https://www.pornhub.com/insights/2018-year-in-review. Accessed March 2019.

6. https://www.pornhub.com/insights/2017-year-in-review. Accessed July 2018.

7. Dr Dan Siegal. 2018 Enneagram Global Summit. Interview with Jessica Dibb entitled "The Three Centers, the Essence of Life, and the Plane of Possibility: Expanding the Journey for Ourselves, Others, and the World."

8. A.H. Almaas and Karen Johnson. *The Power of Divine Eros*. (Shambhala Publications, Boston, 2013) p.137-138.

9. Brian Mustansk, https://www.psychologytoday.com/intl/blog/the-sexual -continuum/201112/how-often-do-men-and-women-think-about-sex. Accessed August 2018.

10. Steven Stack, Ira Wasserman, and Roger Kern. "Adult social bonds and use of Internet pornography". *Social Science Quarterly 85* (March 2004): 75-88. Accessed March 2018 from: Covenant Eyes. *Porn Stats*. 2015. http://covenant eyes.com/pornstats.

11. Ogi Ogasa and Sai Gaddam. *A Billion Wicked Thoughts: What the Internet Tells Us About Sexual Relationships*. (New York: Plume, 2011). Accessed March 2018 from: Covenant Eyes. *Porn Stats*. 2015. http://covenanteyes.com/pornstats.

1. So, What Exactly is the Enneagram?

1. P.D. Ouspensky. *In Search of the Miraculous*. Here he quotes Gurdjieff. Sourced from Claudio Naranjo. *Character and Neurosis*. p. 13.

2. George I. Gurdjieff was a mid-20th-century philosopher and spiritual teacher. *The Fourth Way* enneagram symbol was published in 1949 in *In Search of the Miraculous* by P.D. Ouspensky, and is an integral part of the Fourth Way esoteric system associated with George Gurdjieff. The Law of Three determines the character and nature of a vibration—active, passive, and neutralizing. https://www.ouspenskytoday.org/wp/about-teaching-today/the-law-of-three. Accessed September 2018.

3. Gurdjieff's Law of Seven determines how vibrations develop, interact, and change and is related to the musical scale. https://www.ouspenskytoday.org/wp /about-teaching-today/the-law-of-seven. Accessed September 2018.

4. https://www.enneagraminstitute.com/how-the-enneagram-system-works. Accessed October 2019.

5. Oscar Ichazo. *Interviews with Oscar Ichazo.* (Arica Institute Press, New York, 1982). p.19.

6. https://www.etymonline.com/word/passion. Accessed August 2018.

7. Claudio Naranjo, M.D. *Character and Neurosis.* (Nevada City: Gateways/ IDHHB, Inc, 2003). p. 25.

8. https://www.etymonline.com/word/passion. Accessed August 2018.

9. Don Riso and Russ Hudson. *RH Enneagram At-A-Glance Chart 1 Personality Elements.* The Enneagram Institute.

10. Terminology used by the Integrative 9 Enneagram Solutions (iEQ9).

11. Don Riso and Russ Hudson. *Understanding the Enneagram.* Rev. ed. (Boston, MA: Houghton Mifflin Company, 2000). p. 29.

2. Getting Intimate with the Enneagram

1. From iEQ9 certification training with iEQ9.

2. From iEQ9 certification training, *Understanding the Integrative Enneagram Workbook.* p. 168. Jerome Wagner – *Dialectics*: "Each core is the synthesis of its two neighbors."

3. John Luckovich. https://ieaninepoints.com/2018/09/21/instinctual-excitement -passion-and-intensity/#!biz/id/5817cd71178f4e845c57e97c. Also the New York Enneagram. https://newyorkenneagram.com. Accessed November 2018.

4. John Luckovich. https://ieaninepoints.com/2018/09/21/instinctual-excitement -passion-and-intensity/#!biz/id/5817cd71178f4e845c57e97c. Accessed November 2018.

5. Gloria Davenport, Ph.D. http://www.enneagram-monthly.com/subtypes -revisited.html. Accessed 20 May 2018.

6. John Luckovich. https://ieaninepoints.com/2018/09/21/instinctual-excitement -passion-and-intensity/#!biz/id/5817cd71178f4e845c57e97c. Accessed November 2018.

7. Ibid.

3. Triads: A Different Kind of Threesome

1. Karen Horney. *The Distrust Between the Sexes,* Feminine Psychology. 1931b/1967. p. 117.

2. John Luckovich. https://ieaninepoints.com/2018/09/21/instinctual-excitement -passion-and-intensity/#!biz/id/5817cd71178f4e845c57e97c. Accessed November 2018. Also the New York Enneagram. https://newyorkenneagram.com. Accessed November 2018.

3. Don Riso and Russ Hudson. *The Wisdom of the Enneagram.* (Bantam Books, New York, 1999). p. 51.

4. Claudio Naranjo. 2017 Enneagram Global Summit: *Trinity & Multiplicity.* p. 8.

5. Don Riso and Russ Hudson *Understanding the Enneagram.* (Houghton Mifflin, Boston, 2000). p. 254.

6. Riso, Hudson. *The Wisdom of the Enneagram*. p. 53.

7. Gilbert Schacter, Wegner, Daniel. *Psychology* (1. publ., 3. print. ed. Worth Publishers, Cambridge, 2011). p. 180.

8. Naranjo. *Character and Neurosis*. p. *xxvii*. Also Riso, Hudson. *The Wisdom of the Enneagram*. pp. 60-63.

9. Correspondence with John Luckovitch.

10. Correspondence with John Luckovitch.

11. Naranjo. 2017 Enneagram Global Summit: *Trinity & Multiplicity*. p. 8.

12. Ibid. pp. 8-10.

13. Ibid.

14. Ibid. pp. 8-9.

4. Type One: The Sinning Saint

1. Naranjo. *Character and Neurosis*. Introduction: *A Theoretical Panorama*.

2. Helen Palmer. *The Enneagram in Love and Work*, (New York: Harper One, 2007). p. 36.

3. Michael Ryan. *Prostitution in London, with a comparative view of that in Paris, New York, etc.* (H.Balliere *London*, 1839).

4. For example, the Bowden device used a cup fitted over the head of the penis, together with several chains clipped to groin hairs. Should the unfortunate man get an erection (heaven forbid!) then he would wake to the pain of his pubic hairs being ripped out. Likewise, the Jugnum device was a spiked ring meant to wake the sleeper should he happen to get an erection.

5. https://en.wikipedia.org/wiki/History_of_masturbation. Accessed March 2018.

6. Dr. Marlene Wasserman ("Dr Eve"). *Pillowbook*, (Cape Town: Oshun Books, 2007) p. 104.

7. Ibid. p. 39.

8. Claudio Naranjo. *Character and Neurosis*. (Gateways / IDHHB, Inc. Nevada, 1994). p. 41.

9. Study of 457 couples and their Enneagram partners: http://www.9types.com /writeup/enneagram_relationships.php. Accessed August 2018.

10. Avodah Offit. *The Sexual Self: How Character Shapes Sexual Experience*. (Beckham Publications Group Inc., Silver Spring. 2016. Kindle Edition). Location 981-1051.

11. http://www.9types.com/writeup/enneagram_relationships.php. Accessed June 2018.

12. Naranjo. *Character and Neurosis*. p. 61.

13. Offit. *The Sexual Self*. Location 981-1051.

14. Naranjo. *Character and Neurosis*. p. 47.

15. Naranjo. *Trinity and Multiplicity*. 2017 Enneagram Global Summit. Lecture notes pp. 8-9.

16. Palmer. *The Enneagram in Love and Work*. p. 44.

17. Naranjo. *Character and Neurosis*. p. 59.

18. Ibid. p. 46.
19. Palmer. *The Enneagram in Love and Work.* p. 43.
20. Ibid. p. 43.
21. From a research questionnaire by Aephoria (http://aephoria.co.za/) in which respondents were asked to write down their thoughts on love and sex.
22. Ibid.
23. Ibid.
24. Don Riso and Russ Hudson, *Discovering Your Personality Type*, (New York: Houghton Mifflin Company, 2007). p. 91.
25. Daniels and Levine. "Sexuality, Sensuousness and the Enneagram," Part 2. Dr Daniels used the word "artificial" in relation to Type One, which I would normally have placed at the door of a Type Three. Yet, when we are not being ourselves (in sex or any other interaction), then we will come across as artificial and, in the instance of Type Ones, as trying to be good and worthy partners. As he explains, the result will be artificial.

5. Type Two: The Sexy Seducer

1. Naranjo. *Character and Neurosis.* p. 180.
2. Don Riso and Russ Hudson. *Personality Types* (Boston, MA: Houghton Mifflin Company, 1996). p. 85.
3. Lewis C.S., *Mere Christianity*. (New York: Simon & Schuster Touchstone edition, 1996). pp. 109 and 111.
4. Naranjo. *Character and Neurosis.* p. 175.
5. Beatrice Chestnut. *The Complete Enneagram.* p. 352. and Naranjo, Claudio. *Character and Neurosis.* p. 184.
6. Naranjo. *Character and Neurosis.* p. 181.
7. David Bienenfeld. https://en.wikipedia.org/wiki/Histrionic_personality_disorder. Accessed July 2018. Information on clusters of behavior from: *Personality Disorders*. Medscape Reference. WebMD (2006). Accessed April 2018.
8. Offit. *The Sexual Self.* Location 792. Kindle edition.
9. Naranjo. *Character and Neurosis.* p. 27.
10. Carl Gustav Jung. *Psychological Types* (Eastford: Martino Fine Books, 2016), Ch. 10.
11. http://www.9types.com/writeup/enneagram_relationships.php In the study of 457 couples, Two men comprised the smallest percentage of all types (4%). Accessed August 2018.
12. Naranjo. *Character and Neurosis.* p. 192.
13. Male Twos chose female Four wives mostly, followed by Type Ones. http://www.9types.com/writeup/enneagram_relationships.php.
14. http://drpetermilhado.com/hysterical. Accessed July 2018.
15. Offit. *The Sexual Self.* Location 792
16. Judith Searle. "Sexuality, Gender Roles and the Enneagram," published in the May 1996 issue of *Enneagram Monthly*. http://www.judithsearle.com/articles/sexuality-gender-roles.html. Accessed June 2018.

17. Marie-Louise Von Franz. *Process*. pp. 205-6.

18. Offit. *The Sexual Self.* Location 808.

19. Ibid. Location 866.

20. Naranjo. *Character and Neurosis*. p. 182.

21. Aephoria questionnaire.

22. Ibid.

23. Palmer. *The Enneagram in Love and Work*. p. 72.

24. Searle. "Sexuality, Gender Roles and the Enneagram."

25. Naranjo. *Character and Neurosis*. p. 33.

26. Palmer. *The Enneagram of Love and Work*. p. 65.

27. Searle. "Sexuality, Gender Roles and the Enneagram."

28. "Key characteristics: Reactive types get off on making their partners the center of attention. Pertot divides this category into two sub-types: those that genuinely enjoy making sex all about their partner, and those that self-sacrifice their own pleasure as a means to keep their partner satisfied. There's a big difference!" https://lifehacker.com/how-to-identify-your-partners-libido-type-and-get -bet-1692431142. Accessed March 2018.

29. Chestnut. *The Complete Enneagram*. pp. 367-8.

30. iEQ9 *Understanding the Integrative Enneagram Workbook*. p. 142. and Helen Palmer. *The Enneagram*. p. 132.

31. Aephoria questionnaire

32. Chestnut. *The Complete Enneagram*. p. 368.

33. Ibid. p. 371.

34. Riso, Hudson. *The Wisdom of the Enneagram*. p. 133.

35. Chestnut. *The Complete Enneagram*. p. 372.

36. Aephoria questionnaire.

37. Chestnut. *The Complete Enneagram*. p. 375.

38. Naranjo. *Character and Neurosis*. p. 186.

39. Aephoria questionnaire.

40. Ibid.

41. Ibid.

42. Hudson, Riso. *Personality Types*. p. 91.

43. Naranjo. *Character and Neurosis*. p. 176.

6. Type Six: The Loyal Lover

1. Palmer. *The Enneagram in Love and Work*. p. 159.

2. Ibid. p. 164.

3. A Buddhist term referring to an unsettled, busy, indecisive, capricious state of mind.

4. Riso, Hudson. *The Wisdom of the Enneagram*. p. 250

5. Jerome Wagner. *The Enneagram Spectrum*. (Portland: Metamorphous Press, 1996). p. 90.

6. Sigmund Freud. *On Psychopathology* (Middlesex: Penguin, 1987). p. 198.

7. Offit. *The Sexual Self.* Location 1204.

8. Ibid. Location 1251.

9. G. E. Birnbaum, M. Mikulincer, and O. Gillath. "In and out of a daydream: Attachment orientations, daily couple interactions, and sexual fantasies." *Personality and Social Psychology Bulletin*, 37(10), 2011. pp. 1398-1410. doi:10.1177/0146167211410986

10. B. Edelman, "Red light states: Who buys online adult entertainment?" *Journal of Economic Perspectives*, 23, 2009. pp. 209-220.

    Also, Nigel Berber Ph.D. "The Sexual Obsession" https://www.psychology today.com/us/blog/the-human-beast/201206/the-sexual-obsession.

    "A new study has found that US states with a higher degree of religiosity are more likely to be searching for sex on the web. The study was compiled by researchers at Brock University in Ontario, Canada, and based on two years of data from Google Trends across US states."

    And https://www.christiantoday.com/article/americas-bible-belt-states -indulge-in-more-online-porn-than-other-less-religious-states/42045.htm. Both accessed August 2018.

11. From https://www.9types.com/writeup/enneagram_relationships.php after research on marriage choices in 457 couples. Accessed August 2018.

12. Offit. *The Sexual Self.* Location 1235-1251.

13. Palmer. *The Enneagram in Love and Work.* p. 163.

14. Naranjo. 2017 Enneagram Global Summit: *Trinity & Multiplicity.* Lecture notes p. 7.

15. Wagner. *The Enneagram Spectrum.* pp. 93-94.

16. Offit. *The Sexual Self.* Location 1204.

17. Riso, Hudson. *Personality Types.* p. 252.

18. Palmer. *The Enneagram in Love and Work.* p. 167.

19. Gert Holstege, professor at the University of Groningen in the Netherlands. https://www.newscientist.com/article/dn7548-orgasms-a-real-turn-off -for-women. Accessed September 2018.

20. Daniels, Levine, "Sexuality, Sensuousness and the Enneagram," Part 4.

21. Riso, Hudson. *The Wisdom of the Enneagrams.* p. 39

22. Naranjo. *Character and Neurosis.* p.243

23. Aephoria questionnaire.

24. Palmer. *The Enneagram in Love and Work.* p. 153.

25. Naranjo. 2017 Enneagram Global Summit: *Trinity & Multiplicity.* Lecture notes p. 8.

26. Udit Patel. https://sites.google.com/site/upatel8/personalitytype6. Accessed August 2018

27. Palmer. *The Enneagram in Love and Work.* p. 153.

28. Offit. *The Sexual Self.* Location 1251.

7. Type Three: Awesomely Orgasmic

1. Naranjo. *Character and Neurosis.* p.199. The term was originally used by Eric Fromm in *Man for Himself* (New York: Holt, Rinehart and Winston, 1964).

2. Naranjo. *Character and Neurosis.* p. 214.

3. Ibid. p. 210.

4. Naranjo. From an interview at the 2017 Enneagram Global Summit by Jessica Dibb. On p. 6 of the transcript he refers to a talk with Oscar Ichazo regarding the three centers, which he refers to as the Being (8,9,1, Body-centered), Doing (5,6,7, Head-centered) and Living (2,3,4, Heart-centred) groups. Each type has a problem with Being, Doing, or Living.

5. Riso, Hudson. *RH Enneagram At-A-Glance Chart 1 Personality Elements.*

6. Horney. *Neurosis and Human Growth* (New York: W.W .Norton & Company, 1991).

7. Riso, Hudson. *Personality Types.* pp. 126-7.

8. Riso, Hudson. *The Wisdom of the Enneagram.* p. 55.

9. Horney. *Neurosis and Human Growth.* pp. 198-208.

10. Ibid. Sourced from: https://en.wikipedia.org/wiki/Karen_Horney.

11. William Strauss, and Neil Howe. *Millennials Rising: The Next Great Generation.* (New York, NY: Vintage Originam, 2000). p. 370.

12. Jean Twenge, Ph.D. *Generation Me.* (New York: Simon & Schuster, 2006).

13. Peter Loffredo. http://fullpermissionliving.blogspot.com/2008/09/rigid-character -structure-we-are.html. Accessed July 2018.

14. Riso, Hudson. *The Wisdom of the Enneagram.* pp. 155-56.

15. Karen Horney. *Neurosis and Human Growth.* Sourced from http:// donemmerichnotes.blogspot.com/2011/09/neurosis-and-human-growth-by -karen.html?view=classic. Accessed June 2018.

16. Aephoria questionnaire

17. Horney. *Neurosis and Human Growth.* Sourced from http://donemmerich notes.blogspot.com/2011/09/neurosis-and-human-growth-by-karen.html? view=classic. Accessed July 2018.

18. Offit. *The Sexual Self.* Location 906.

19. Horney. *Neurosis and Human Growth.* Sourced from http://donemmerich notes.blogspot.com/2011/09/neurosis-and-human-growth-by-karen. html?view=classic. Accessed July 2018.

20. Horney. *Neurosis and Human Growth.* pp. 254-55.

21. Riso, Hudson. *Personality Types.* p. 123.

22. Riso, Hudson. *The Wisdom of the Enneagram.* p. 163.

23. Marie Robinson. *The Power of Sexual Surrender.* (New York: Signet, 1963). p. 158.

24. Horney. *Neurosis and Human Growth.* p. 17.

25. Robinson. *The Power of Sexual Surrender.* pp. 53-55.

26. Ibid. p. 11.

27. Ibid. p. 53.

28. Ibid. p. 158.

29. Peter Loffredo, LCSW. http://fullpermissionliving.blogspot.com/2008/09 /rigid-character-structure-we-are.html. Accessed July 2018.

30. Offit. *The Sexual Self.* Location 966.

31. Ibid. Location 970.

32. Naranjo. 2017 Enneagram Global Summit: *Trinity & Multiplicity.* Lecture notes p. 8.

33. Horney. *Neurosis and Human Growth.* ("Vulnerability in human relations. Self-contempt makes the neurotic hypersensitive to criticism and rejection.")

34. Naranjo. *Character and Neurosis.* p. 209.

35. Offit. *The Sexual Self.* Location 890.

36. Roughly 6% of the population has narcissistic personality disorder—7.7% of men versus 4.8% of women. http://uk.businessinsider.com/the-main-difference -between-narcissistic-men-and-women-2017-10?IR=T. Accessed July 2018.

37. Donald L Nathanson. *Shame and Pride: Affect, Sex, and the Birth of the Self.* (New York: W. W. Norton & Company, 1994). p. 235.

38. Donald L Nathanson. "Compass of Shame," http://www5.esc13.net/thescoop /behavior/files/2017/10/compassofshame.pdf.

39. Nathanson. *Shame and Pride.* pp. 305-77.

40. Chestnut. *The Complete Enneagram.* p. 355. Beatrice talks about Three Sexual / One-on-Ones: "…they use 'disconnection' from themselves as a way to forget, or to make up for or minimize past abuses."

41. Ibid. p. 328. "They have developed a special focus on autonomy in the face of a jeopardized sense of security."

42. Ibid. p. 331. "The Social Three is the most aggressive of the Threes, possessing a strong and assertive character."

43. Jeff Elison, Randy Lennon and Steven Pulos. "Investigating the Compass of Shame: The Development of the Compass of Shame Scale." *Social Behavior and Personality: An International Journal,* 2006, 34(3): 221-38 Sourced from https://www.researchgate.net/publication/233600755_Investigating_the _Compass_of_Shame_The_development_of_the_Compass_of_Shame_Scale.

44. Nathanson. *Shame and Pride.* pp. 340-41.

45. Donal Dorr, M.A., D.D. *Time for a Change.* Chapter 5: "Shame, Intimacy, and Spirituality." Dorr is a well-known facilitator, consultant, trainer, theologian, resource-person, and author.

46. Horney. *Neurosis and Human Growth*: "An attractive woman may think herself ugly because she doesn't live up to her idealized image of herself. The woman may respond by either devoting excess energy to beautifying herself or by having an 'I don't care' attitude."

47. Chestnut. *The Complete Enneagram.* p. 329.

48. Ibid. pp. 328-329.

49. Naranjo. *Character and Neurosis.* p. 205. (The late Dr Alexander Lowen was an American physician and psychotherapist and founder of Bioenergetics.)

50. Naranjo. *Character and Neurosis.* p. 205 and Beatrice Chestnut. *The Complete Enneagram*, p. 329.

51. Aephoria questionnaire.

52. Naranjo. *Character and Neurosis*, p. 217.

53. Chestnut. *The Complete Enneagram.* p. 331.

54. Jess Feist. *Theories of Personality.* (3rd. ed. Fort Worth, TX: Harcourt Brace, 1994, c.1985). p. 254

55. Aephoria questionnaire.

56. Chestnut. *The Complete Enneagram*. p. 334.

57. Aephoria. questionnaire.

8. Type Seven: The Spontaneous Suitor

1. Sigmund Freud. *Introductory Lectures*. 16.357.

2. Naranjo. *Character and Neurosis*. p. 163.

3. Karen Horney. *Our Inner Conflicts*. Sourced from http://davesenneagram.com/blog/the-idealized-image-and-enneagram-types-1-4-and-7. Accessed September 2018.

4. Naranjo. *Character and Neurosis*. p. 152.

5. Ibid. p. 162. Naranjo refers to a Seven's "playboy" orientation to life.

6. Von Franz. https://en.wikipedia.org/wiki/Anima_and_animus.*Process*. pp. 205-6.

7. Riso, Hudson. *The Wisdom of the Enneagram*. p. 265.

8. Naranjo. *Character and Neurosis*. p.168

9. Ibid. p.166

10. Riso, Hudson. *Personality Types*. p.268

11. Riso, Hudson. *The Wisdom of the Enneagram*. p.266.

12. Naranjo. *Character and Neurosis*, p. 164. Also Palmer. *The Enneagram in Love and Work*. p. 176.

13. Riso, Hudson. *Personality Types*. p. 275.

14. Naranjo. *Character and Neurosis*. p. 155.

15. Ibid. p. 156.

16. Riso, Hudson. *Personality Types*. p. 281.

17. Naranjo. *Character and Neurosis*. p. 164.

18. Riso, Hudson. *Personality Types*. p. 286.

19. Offit. *The Sexual Self*. Location 1511.

20. From the "Personality Elements" chart, Ichazo saw the Seven's Fixation as Planning, Riso and Hudson as Anticipation.

21. https://www.livescience.com/47023-sexy-thoughts-mind-female-orgasm.html. Accessed September 2018.

22. Offit. *The Sexual Self*. Location 1495.

23. Aephoria questionnaire.

24. Palmer. *The Enneagram in Love and Work*. p. 191.

25. Naranjo. *Character and Neurosis*. p. 153.

26. Emily C. Durbin, Benjamin D. Schalet, Elizabeth P. Hayden, Jennifer Simpson, Patricia L. Jordan. "Hypomanic personality traits: A multi-method exploration of their association with normal and abnormal dimensions of personality." *Journal of Research in Personality*. 43 (2009) 898–905. Available online May 3, 2009.

27. Michael Bader, D.M.H. https://www.psychologytoday.com/intl/blog/what-is-he-thinking/201712/why-do-some-men-engage-in-sexual-exhibitionism. Accessed October 2018.

28. Naranjo. *Character and Neurosis*. p. 163.

29. Chestnut. *The Complete Enneagram*. pp. 156-57.

30. Ibid. p. 159. In addition, regarding being vegan, Naranjo is quoted by Chestnut (2013).

31. Ibid. p. 160.
32. Ibid. p. 163.
33. Aephoria questionnaire.
34. Riso, Hudson. *The Wisdom of the Enneagram.* p. 269.
35. Ibid. p. 266.
36. Ibid.
37. Riso, Hudson. *RH Enneagram At-A-Glance Chart 1 Personality Elements.*

9. Type Eight: The Lusty Lover

1. Naranjo. *Character and Neurosis.* p. 129.
2. Ibid. p. 128.
3. Daniels, Levine, "Sexuality, Sensuousness and the Enneagram," Part 2.
4. Palmer. *The Enneagram in Love and Work.* p. 336
5. Katherine Fauvre. http://www.katherinefauvre.com/blog/2017/7/20/karen -horney-and-the-enneagram . Accessed May 22, 2018.
6. Robinson. *The Power of Sexual Surrender.* p. 123.
7. Palmer. *The Enneagram: Understanding Yourself and Others in Your Life.* (New York: Harper One, 1991). p. 316.
8. Russel E. Geen and Edward Donnerstein. *Human Aggression* (Academic Press; 1st ed, August 25, 1998) using research by Wilson and Herrnstein (1985), Berkowitz (1978) and Scully (1990). p. 112.
9. C. C. Joyal, A. Cossette, and V. Lapierre. (2015). "What exactly is an unusual sexual fantasy?" *Journal of Sexual Medicine,* 12, 328-340. Christian Joyal and colleagues (2015) asked over 1,500 women and men about their sexual fantasies. Of them, 64.6% of women and 53.3% of men reported fantasies about being dominated sexually, and 46.7% of women and 59.6% of men reported fantasies about dominating someone sexually.
   Also, Richters, J., de Visser, R. O., Rissel, C. E., Grulich, A. E., & Smith, A. M. A. (2008). *Journal of Sexual Medicine,* 5, 1660-1668. Juliet Richters and colleagues (2008) asked a large sample of Australians whether they had "been involved in B&D or S&M" in the past 12 months. Only 1.3% of women and 2.2% of men said yes.
10. Riso, Hudson. *Personality Types.* p. 318.
11. I see Reich's Phallic Narcissistic character and Lowen's Inspirer (psychopathic) character as being similar in many ways to Type Eights. https:// reichandlowentherapy.org/Content/Character/Psychopathic/psychopathic _inspirer.html. Accessed May 2018.
12. From a 2014 workshop with Russ Hudson in Cape Town.
13. Riso, Hudson. *Personality Types.* p. 318
14. https://reichandlowentherapy.org/Content/Character/Psychopathic /psychopathic_inspirer.html. Accessed May 2018.
15. Naranjo. Enneagram Global Summit 2017: *Trinity & Multiplicity.* Lecture notes. p. 8.
16. Naranjo. *Character and Neurosis.* p. 128.
17. http://www.medilexicon.com/dictionary/24201. Accessed May 2018
18. Naranjo. *Character and Neurosis.* p. 128.

19. Andreas Wismeijer and Marcel van Assen. (2013) *Study of Dutch BDSM practitioners* compared BDSM practitioners to non-BDSM practitioners on major personality traits. Their results showed that in comparison to non-practitioners, BDSM practitioners exhibited higher levels of extraversion, conscientiousness, openness to experience, and subjective well-being. Practitioners also showed lower levels of neuroticism and rejection sensitivity. The one negative trait that emerged? BDSM practitioners showed lower levels of agreeableness than non-practitioners.

20. Wismeijer and Van Assen. *Study of Dutch BDSM practitioners.*

21. Scott McGreal. MSc. www.psychologytoday.com/blog/unique-everybody-else/201502/personality-traits-bdsm-practitioners-another-look.
    https://www.psychologytoday.com/blog/unique-everybody-else/201307/bdsm-personality-and-mental-health.

22. Joris Lammers and Roland Imhoff. "Understanding the Antecedents of a Knotty Relationship." Department of Psychology, University of Cologne, Köln, Germany. Accessed via http://journals.sagepub.com/doi/pdf/10.1177/1948550615604452 17/4/2018.

23. William Reich. *Character Analysis.* pp. 217-18.

24. Reich. *Character Analysis.* Sourced from Naranjo. *Character and Neurosis.* p. 131.

25. Michael Samsel. *Finding Feeling and Purpose.* https://www.scribd.com/document/328233179/Finding-Feeling-and-Purpose-by-Michael-Samsel. And "The Male Achiever Character in Relationship." https://reichandlowentherapy.org/Content/Character/Rigid/Phallic/phallic_achiever.html. Accessed May 2018.

26. Samsel, *Finding Feeling and Purpose.* https://www.scribd.com/document/328233179/Finding-Feeling-and-Purpose-by-Michael-Samsel.

27. Chestnut. *The Complete Enneagram.* p. 13.

28. Riso, Hudson. *Personality Types.* p. 79.

29. Chestnut. *The Complete Enneagram.* p. 114.

30. Aephoria questionnaire.

31. Chestnut. *The Complete Enneagram.* p. 116.

32. https://www.enneagraminstitute.com/type-8. Accessed March 2019.

33. Daniels, Levine, "Sexuality, Sensuousness and the Enneagram," Part 2.

10. Type Four: The Romantic Romeo (or Juliet)

1. Naranjo. *Character and Neurosis.* p. 34.

2. Of the 457 couples tested, the female Four/male Nine was the highest at 16 couples, followed by the 15 couples who were male 9/female 1 at 15 couples. The opposite (male 4/female 9) was 5 couples. http://www.9types.com/writeup/enneagram_relationships.php.

3. Naranjo. *Character and Neurosis.* p. 103.

4. Ibid. Naranjo is quoting from Eric Berne, *Games People Play* (Ballantine Books, New York, 1985).

5. Riso, Hudson, *The Wisdom of the Enneagram.* p. 192.

6. Ibid. p. 191.

7. Naranjo. *Character and Neurosis.* p. 98.

8. Riso and Hudson name the Four's Fixation as "Fantasizing." Riso, Hudson. *RH Enneagram At-a-Glance Chart 1 Personality Elements.*

9. Tracey Cox. http://www.dailymail.co.uk/femail/article-3894882/What-does
-sex-fantasy-say-threesomes-dreaming-sleeping-raunchy-dreams-unravelled.
html#ixzz5EdiStprD. Accessed August 2018.

10. Riso, Hudson, *The Wisdom of the Enneagram.* p. 193.

11. *Enneagram Institute Pocket Guide:* Type Four, Delusion and Compulsion, Level 8
Security Point.

12. https://www.psychologytoday.com/us/blog/in-excess/201401/survival-the-fetish.
Accessed August 2018 from research led by Dr G. Scorolli (University of Bologna,
Italy) in 2007 from https://www.psychologytoday.com/us/blog/in-excess/201401
/survival-the-fetish.

13. C. Gosselin and G. Wilson. *Sexual variations.* (Faber & Faber, London, 1980).

14. From: https://www.sovhealth.com/health-and-wellness/the-psychology-behind
-sexual-fetishes/ August 2018 from the book *The Quick-Reference Guide to
Sexuality & Relationship Counselling* by Dr Tim Clinton and Dr Mark Laaser
(Wyoming: Baker Books, 2010).

15. Naranjo. *Character and Neurosis.* p. 112.

16. Searle. http://www.judithsearle.com/articles/sexuality-gender-roles.html. Accessed
July 2018.

17. Naranjo. *Character and Neurosis.* p. 97.

18. Ibid. p. 110.

19. Ibid. p. 105.

20. Ibid. p. 114.

21. Offit. *The Sexual Self.* Location 624.

22. Arnold Mitchell and Harold Kelman, "Masochism: Horney's View" in the
International Encyclopedia of Psychiatry, Psychology, Psychanalysis, and
Neurology, Vol. 7, pp. 34-35. (Van Nostrand / Reinhold, New York. 1977)
Sourced from Naranjo. *Character and Neurosis.* p. 108.

23. Ibid.

24. https://www.9types.com/writeup/enneagram_relationships.php. Accessed July
2018.

25. Chestnut. *The Complete Enneagram.* pp. 285-87.

26. Aephoria questionnaire.

27. Naranjo. *Character and Neurosis.* p. 115.

28. Ibid. p. 114.

29. Chestnut. *The Complete Enneagram.* p. 289.

30. Riso, Hudson, *The Wisdom of the Enneagram.* p.185.

31. Chestnut. *The Complete Enneagram.* pp. 289-90.

32. Riso, Hudson, *The Wisdom of the Enneagram.* p.185.

33. Chestnut. *The Complete Enneagram.* p. 292. Chestnut refers to this type as
"Competition."

34. Sandra Maitri. *The Enneagram of Passions and Virtues.* (New York: Penguin,
2005). p. 195.

35. Chestnut. *The Complete Enneagram.* p. 31.

36. http://www.katherinefauvre.com/instincts-1. Accessed August 2018.

37. Chestnut. *The Complete Enneagram.* p. 293.

38. Aephoria questionnaire.

39. Riso, Hudson, *The Wisdom of the Enneagram*. p. 186.

40. Palmer. *The Enneagram in Love and Work*. p. 115.

41. Daniels, Levine, "Sexuality, Sensuousness and the Enneagram," Part 3.

11. Type Five: The Lonely Lover

1. Maitri. *The Enneagram of Passions and Virtues*. p. 135

2. Maitri. *The Spiritual Dimension of the Enneagram*. (Penguin, New York, 2001). p. 205.

3. Ibid.

4. https://www.etymonline.com/word/avaricious.

5. Daniels, Levine, "Sexuality, Sensuousness and the Enneagram," Part 4.

6. Ibid.

7. Riso, Hudson. *Personality Types*. p. 174

8. https://www.pornhub.com/insights/2017-year-in-review. Accessed May 2018.

9. Ogi Ogasa and Sai Gaddam, *A Billion Wicked Thoughts: What the Internet Tell Us About Sexual Relationships*. (New York: Plume, 2011).

10. https://www.pornhub.com/insights/2017-year-in-review. Accessed May 2018.

11. IEQ9 Workshop on "Understanding the Enneagram". May 2018.

12. $L = 8 + .5Y - .2P + .9Hm + .3Mf + J - .3G - .5(Sm - Sf)2 + I + 1.5C$
    L: The predicted length in years of the relationship
    Y: The number of years the two people knew each other before the relationship became serious
    P: The number of previous partners of both people (added together)
    Hm: The importance the male partner attaches to honesty in the relationship
    Mf: The importance the female attaches to money in the relationship
    J: The importance both attach to humor (added together)
    G: The importance both attach to good looks (added together)
    Sm and Sf: The importance male and female attach to sex
    I: The importance attached to having good in-laws (added together)
    C: The importance attached to children in the relationship (added together)
    Note: All "importance" measures can be scaled from 1 to 5, where 1 is not important at all and 5 is very important.

13. Dr Amir Levine and Rachel Heller. *Attached* (London: Rodale, 2011). p. 24 and https://vle.stvincent.ac.uk/2014/pluginfile.php/33670/.../The%20Love%20quiz.docx. Accessed April 2018.

14. Ibid.

15. Ibid. and G. E. Birnbaum, M. Mikulincer and O. Gillath (2011). *In and out of a daydream: Attachment orientations, daily couple interactions, and sexual fantasies*. Personality and Social Psychology Bulletin, 37(10), pp. 1398-410. doi:10.1177/0146167211410986

16. Heidi Priebe. https://thoughtcatalog.com/heidi-priebe/2016/08/mbti-sexuality/5/. Accessed November 2018.

17. Naranjo. *Character and Neurosis*. p. 75

18. The Enneagram Institute.

19. Palmer. *The Enneagram in Love and Work*. p. 127. The name given by Helen Palmer to Type Five is the Observer.

20. https://www.psychologytoday.com/us/conditions/voyeuristic-disorder. Accessed April 2018.

21. Simon Le Vay, Janice I. Baldwin and John D. Baldwin. *Discovering Human Sexuality.* 2nd ed. (Sunderland, MA: Sinauer Associates, 2012).

22. Chestnut. *The Complete Enneagram.* p. 246.

23. Covenant Eyes.

24. Eric Johnston. "Kyoto law puts 'upskirt' photography in focus." *The Japan Times,* May 25, 2014.

25. James H. Jones. *Alfred C. Kinsey: A Public/Private Life.* (New York: Norton, 1997).

26. https://www.nytimes.com/1994/03/24/garden/an-afternoon-with-masters-and -johnson-divorced-yes-but-not-split.html.

27. iEQ9. *Understanding the Integrative Enneagram* Workbook.

28. Naranjo. *Character and Neurosis.* p. 92.

29. Chestnut. *The Complete Enneagram.* p. 252.

30. Ibid. p. 246.

31. Ibid.

32. Aephoria questionnaire.

33. https://www.psychologytoday.com/us/conditions/voyeuristic-disorder. Accessed April 2018.

34. Aephoria questionnaire.

35. Aephoria questionnaire.

36. https://www.vanityfair.com/hollywood/2018/03/fx-trust-john-paul-getty -girlfriends and https://life.spectator.co.uk/2018/01/john-paul-getty-a-life -of-miserliness-mistresses-and-hotel-hopping. Both accessed March 2018.

37. Riso, Hudson. *The Wisdom of the Enneagram.* p. 212.

38. Riso, Hudson. *Personality Types.* p. 213.

39. Naranjo. *Character and Neurosis.* p. 85.

12. Type Nine: The Sensual Sweetheart

1. Naranjo. *Character and Neurosis.* p. 265

2. Riso, Hudson. *Personality Types.* p. 349.

3. Ibid. p. 355.

4. Palmer. *The Enneagram in Love and Work.* p. 231.

5. Naranjo. *Character and Neurosis.* p. 258.

6. D. Moreault and D.R. Follingstad. "Sexual fantasies of females as a function of sex guilt and experimental response cues." *Journal of Consulting and Clinical Psychology,* 46(6), 1385-93. (1978) http://dx.doi.org/10.1037/0022 -006X.46.6.1385

7. https://www.9types.com/writeup/enneagram_relationships.php. Accessed October 2018.

8. https://www.enneagraminstitute.com/relationship-type-6-with-type-9. Accessed October 2018.

9. https://www.9types.com/writeup/enneagram_relationships.php. Accessed October 2018.

10. iEQ9. *Understanding the Integrative Enneagram* Workbook. p. 140.

11. Offit. *The Sexual Self: How Character Shapes Sexual Experience.* Location 1161-77.

12. Ibid. Location 1193.

13. Riso, Hudson. *The Wisdom of the Enneagram.* p. 324.

14. Jean Adeler. http://structuralenneagram.com/?p=37. Accessed October 2018.

15. Riso, Hudson. *The Wisdom of the Enneagram.* p. 329.

16. Aephoria questionnaire.

17. Chestnut. *The Complete Enneagram.* p.72.

18. Riso, Hudson. *The Wisdom of the Enneagram.* p. 320.

19. Chestnut. *The Complete Enneagram.* pp. 74-75.

20. Aephoria questionnaire.

21. Chestnut. *The Complete Enneagram.* p. 77.

22. Naranjo. *Character and Neurosis.* p. 254.

23. Daniels, Levine, "Sexuality, Sensuousness and the Enneagram," Part 2.

24. Maitri. *The Enneagram of Passions and Virtues.* p. 46

13. Why You'd be Attracted to Different Types

1. Offit. *The Sexual Self.* ("Histrionic Display: Sexual Theatre", Ch.4.) Offit's description of the "Histrionic Display: Sexual Theatre" personality matches Type Two and the Histrionic personality is also described by Claudio Naranjo as being the Type Two Enneagram type (*Character and Neurosis* pp. 174-98). Wilhelm Reich's *Character Analysis* describes the hysterical character in ways that match Type Twos.

2. The Phallic stage is the third of five Freudian psychosexual development stages.

3. Naranjo. *Character and Neurosis.* p. 70.

4. Palmer. *The Enneagram in Love and Work.* p. 167.

5. Naranjo. *Character and Neurosis.* p. 235.

6. J. S. Bourdage, K. Lee, M. C. Ashton, and A. Perry. 2007. "Big Five and HEXACO model personality correlates of sexuality." *Personality and Individual Differences, 43*(6), pp. 1506-16.

14. How to Engage with Different Types

1. Palmer. *The Enneagram in Love and Work.* p. 73. In my studies, Helen Palmer was the first to identify these three areas of attraction in Twos. Since reading this I have noticed how elements of the three show up repeatedly in Two's relationships: the Sexual Instinct Two being perhaps more attracted to beauty, the Social more to those on the up, and the Self-preservation to the victims.

2. Palmer. *The Personality Types in Love and Work.* p. 94.

3. https://reichandlowentherapy.org/Content/Character/Schizoid/schizoid_dreamer. html. Accessed April 2018.

4. Naranjo. *Character and Neurosis.* p.227.

5. Ibid.

6. Palmer. *The Enneagram in Love and Work.* p. 167.

7. Naranjo. *Character and Neurosis.* p. 237.

8. Ibid. p. 251.

15. What to Expect When Things Go Wrong

1. I would hazard a guess that Henry VIII was a Type Eight. This would make a Type Two his point of release—hence his ability to dispense with his six wives with such ease when they no longer pleased him.

2. Naranjo. *Character and Neurosis.* pp. 182 and 184.

3. Ibid. p. 195.

4. Horney. *Neurosis and Human Growth.* pp. 254-55

5. Marika Dentai. "Instinctual Types: Self-Preservation, Social and Sexual." *Enneagram Monthly #7*, September. 1995

6. Naranjo. *Character and Neurosis.* p. 18.

7. Wagner. *The Enneagram Spectrum.* p. 90.

8. Palmer. *The Enneagram in Love and Work.* p. 184.

9. Naranjo. *Character and Neurosis.* p. 250.

10. Offit. *The Sexual Self.* Location 1161.

11. Riso, Hudson. *Personality Types.* p. 349

Q&A with Ann

1. https://www.typologycentral.com/forums/myers-briggs-and-jungian-cognitive -functions/73348-type-lesbian-gay-bisexual.html; https://personalityjunkie .com/07/myers-briggs-enneagram-mbti-types-correlations-relationship/; https:// www.typologycentral.com/wiki/index.php/Enneagram_and_MBTI_Correlation. All accessed November 2018.

2. https://thoughtcatalog.com/heidi-priebe/2016/08/mbti-sexuality/14/. Accessed October 2018.

3. https://www.typologycentral.com/wiki/index.php/Enneagram_and_MBTI _Correlation. Accessed October 2018.

4. https://www.typologycentral.com/forums/myers-briggs-and-jungian-cognitive -functions/73348-type-lesbian-gay-bisexual.html. Accessed November 2018.

5. American Psychological Association: https://www.apa.org/topics/divorce. Accessed August 2018.

6. Brett Kahr. *Who's Been Sleeping in Your Head: The Secret World of Sexual Fantasies.* (Basic Books; First Edition, New York, 2008).

7. W.B. Arndt, J.C. Foehl and F.E. Good. (1985). "Specific sexual fantasy themes: A multidimensional study". *Journal of Personality and Social Psychology*, 48, pp. 472–80. And S.L. Lentz and A.M. Zeiss. (1983). *Fantasy and sexual arousal in college women: An empirical investigation. Imagination, Cognition, and Personality*, 3, pp. 185-202.

8. For a broad review of empirical work on sexual fantasy, see H. Leitenberg and K. Henning. "Sexual fantasy." *Psychological Bulletin*, 117, (1995). pp. 469–96.

9. Lisa A. Pelletier and Edward S. Herold, 1988. "The Relationship of Age, Sex Guilt, and Sexual Experience with Female Sexual Fantasies." *The Journal of Sex Research* Vol. 24, pp. 250–56.408;

10. Thomas V. Hicks and Harold Leitenberg, 2001. "Sexual fantasies about one's partner versus someone else: Gender differences in incidence and frequency." *The Journal of Sex Research* Vol. 38, pp. 43–50; D. Knafo and Y. Jaffe, 1984 "Sexual fantasizing in males and females." *Journal of Research in Personality, 18*(4), pp. 451–62; Glenn Wilson, 1997. "Gender Differences in Sexual Fantasy: An Evolutionary Analysis." *Personality and Individual Differences* Vol. 22, No. I. pp. 27–31.

11. B.J. Ellis and D. Symons. (1990). "Sex differences in sexual fantasy: An evolutionary psychological approach." *The Journal of Sex Research*, 27, pp. 527–55. Ellis and Symons; E.O. Laumann, J.H. Gagnon, R.T. Michael and S. Michaels, S. *The social organization of sexuality.* (Chicago: University of Chicago Press, 1994). Leitenberg and Henning "Sexual fantasy."

12. C.C. Joyal, A. Cossette and V. Lapierre. "What exactly is an unusual sexual fantasy?" pp. 328–40. University of Montreal's Christian Joyal said: "For example, people who have submission fantasies also often report domination fantasies. These two themes are therefore not exclusive, quite the contrary."

13. http://blogs.discovermagazine.com/seriouslyscience/2014/11/10/sexual-fantasies -least-popular-science-finally-weighs/#.XFb5CFwzapo. Accessed September 2018.

14. iEQ9 *Understanding the Integrative Enneagram.* p. 27.

Bibliography

Aldridge, Susan. *Seeing Red and Feeling Blue*. London: Arrow Books, 2001.

Almaas, A.H. and Karen Johnson. *The Divine Eros*. Boulder: Shambhala, 2017.

Anand, Margo. *The Art of Sexual Ecstasy*. London: Thorsons, 1999.

Bays, Brandon. *The Journey*. London: Thorsons, 1999.

Borysenko, Joan. *A Woman's Spiritual Journey*. London: Piatkus, 2000.

Caplan, Mariana. *Do You Need a Guru?* London: Thorsons, 2002.

Campling, Matthew. *The 12-Type Enneagram*. London: Watkins, 2015.

Chestnut, Beatrice, PhD. *The Complete Enneagram*. Berkeley: She Writes Press, 2013.

Daniels, David, Dr. and Dr Ron Levin. "Sexuality, Sensuousness and the Enneagram" http://drdaviddaniels.com/products.

Deida, David. *The Way of the Superior Man*. Louisville: Sounds True, 2017.

Enneagram Global Summit 2016-2018: 9 Essential Pathways for Transformation. The Shift Network. https://enneagramglobalsummit.com

Eve, Dr. (Dr Marlene Wasserman) *Pillowbook*. Cape Town: Oshun Books, 2007.

Friday, Nancy. *Forbidden Flowers*. London: Arrow Books, 1993.

Ford, Clellan S. and Frank A. Beach. *Patterns of Sexual Behavior*. New York: Harper & Brothers, 1951.

Fortune, Dion. *The Mystical Qabalah*. Wellingborough: The Aquarian Press, 1987.

Ford, Debbie. *The Dark Side of the Light Chasers*. London: Hodder & Stoughton, 2001.

Freud, Sigmund. *On Psychopathology*. Middlesex: Penguin, 1987.

Hanh, Thich Nhat. *The Heart of the Buddha's Teachings*. Berkeley, CA: Broadway Books, 1998.

Hay, Louise. *Heal Your Body*. Cape Town, South Africa: Hay House/Paradigm Press, 1993.

Horney, Karen, M.D. *Neurosis and Human Growth*. New York: W.W. Norton & Company, 1991.

Horsley, Mary. *The Enneagram for the Spirit*. New York: Barron's Educational Series inc., 2005.

iEQ9. *Understanding the Integrative Enneagram Workbook*. www.integrative9.com

Johnson, Robert A. *Owning Your Own Shadow*. San Francisco, CA: HarperCollins, 1993.

Judith, Anodea. *Eastern Body, Western Mind*. Berkeley, CA: Celestial Arts, 1996.

Jung, Carl. *Psychology of the Unconscious*. London: Kegan Paul Trench Trubner, 1916.

———. *Psychological Types*. Eastford: Martino Fine Books, 2016.

Kahr, Brett. *Who's Been Sleeping in Your Head: The Secret World of Sexual Fantasies*. New York: Basic Books, 2008.

Kornfield, Jack. *A Path with a Heart*. New York: Bantam, 1993.

Levine, Dr Amir and Rachel Heller. *Attached*. London: Pan Macmillan. 2011.

Lytton, Edward Bulwer. *Zanoni: A Rosicrucian Tale*. Whitefish, MT: Kessinger Publishing.

Lipton, Bruce H. *The Biology of Belief*. Santa Rosa, CA: Mountain of Love/Elite Books, 2005.

Kamphuis, Albert. *Egowise Leadership & the Nine Creating Forces of the Innovation Circle*. Self-published. Netherlands: Egowise Leadership Academy. 2011.

Maitri, Sandra. *The Spiritual Dimension of the Enneagram*. New York: Penguin Putnam Inc. 2001.

_____ . *The Enneagram of Passions and Virtues*. New York: Penguin Random House. 2009.

Millman, Dan. *The Life You Were Born to Live*. Novato, CA: HJ Kramer in a joint venture with New World Library, 1993.

Murphy, Joseph. *The Power of Your Subconscious Mind*. New York: The Penguin Group, 2008.

Myss, Caroline. *Anatomy of the Spirit*. London: Bantam, 1998.

_____ . *Why People Don't Heal and How They Can*. London. Bantam, 1998.

Naranjo, Claudio, M.D. *Character and Neurosis*. Nevada City. Gateways/IDHHB, Inc. 2003.

Nathanson, Donald L. *Shame and Pride: Affect, Sex, and the Birth of the Self*. New York: W. W. Norton & Company, 1994.

_____ . *Ennea-type Structures – Self-Analysis for the Seeker*. Nevada City: Gateways/IDHHB, Inc., 1990.

Offit, Avodah. *The Sexual Self: How Character Shapes Sexual Experience*. Memorial Series Book 3: Kindle Version, 2016.

Palmer, Helen. *The Enneagram in Love and Work*. New York: Harper One, 1995.

_____ . *The Enneagram: Understanding Yourself and Others in Your Life*. New York: Harper One, 1991.

Pearson, Carol S. *Awakening the Heroes Within*. New York: HarperCollins, 1991.

_____ . *The Heroes Within*. New York: HarperCollins, 1998.

Perel, Esther. *Mating in Captivity*. New York: Harper Paperbacks, 1997.

Reich, Wilhelm. (trans. Vincent R. Carfagno), *Character Analysis*, New York: Farrar, Straus & Giroux, 1990.

Reich, Wilhelm. *The Function of Orgasm*. London: Souvenir Press, 2016.

Riso, Don Richard and Russ Hudson. *The Wisdom of the Enneagram*. New York: Bantam Books, 1999.

_____ . *Understanding the Enneagram*. Rev. ed. Boston, MA: Houghton Mifflin Company, 2000.

_____ . *Discovering Your Personality Type*. Boston, MA: Houghton Mifflin Company, 2003.

_____ . *Personality Types*. Boston, MA: Houghton Mifflin Company, 1996.

Robinson, Marie N. *The Power of Sexual Surrender*. New York: Signet, 1963.

Searle, Judith. "Sexuality, Gender Roles and the Enneagram," *Enneagram Monthly*, May 1996

Shealy Norman C. and Caroline Myss. *The Creation of Health*. Walpole, NH: Stillpoint Publishing, 1998.

Shapiro, Debbie. *Your Body Speaks Your Mind*. London: Piatkus, 1996.

Spiegelhalter, David. *Sex by Numbers*. London: Profile Books, 2015.

Stone, Joshua David. *Soul Psychology*. New York: Ballantine Wellspring, 1999.

Surya Das, Lama. *Awakening to the Sacred*. New York: Broadway Books, 1999.

Tannahill, Reay. *Sex in History*. ABACUS. London, 1981.

Thondup, Tukulu. *The Healing Power of the Mind*. Boston, MA: Shambhala Publications, 1996.

Trees, Andrew. *Decoding Love*. Hay House. London, 2009.

Tolle, Eckhart. *The Power of Now*. London: Hodder & Stoughton, 2005.

Von Franz, Marie-Louise. "The Individuation Process". From *Archetypal Dimensions of the Psyche*. London: Shambhala,1997.

Wagner, Jerome, Ph.D. *The Enneagram Spectrum of Personality Styles*. Portland: Metamorphous Press, 1996.

Wasserman, Marlene. Pillowbook. Cape Town: Oshun Books, 2007

Zuercher, Suzanne. *Enneagram Spirituality*. Notre Dame: IN: Ave Maria Press, 1992.

About the Author

Ann Gadd is an accredited Enneagram practitioner (iEQ9 certified), holistic therapist, artist, workshop facilitator, author, and journalist. An avid, long-term student of the Enneagram, she offers Enneagram workshops for beginners and advanced students. The author of 22 books, including *The Enneagram of Eating*, *The Girl Who Bites Her Nails*, and *Finding Your Feet*, Ann lives in Cape Town, South Africa.

For more information visit: **http://www.anngadd.co.za**

Also of Interest from Findhorn Press

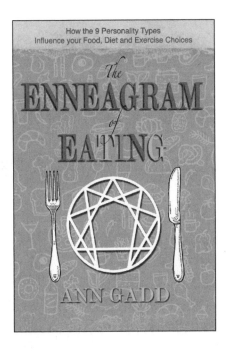

The Enneagram of Eating
by Ann Gadd

HAVE YOU EVER WONDERED why some people seem to adore food, while others find eating simply a need? Why some people just love to work out and others absolutely abhor anything to do with physical exercise?

Drawing on the 9 personality types of the Enneagram system, Ann Gadd explains your relationship to food and exercise. *The Enneagram of Eating* includes an easy food-personality test to find your type, this book provides an understanding of each type's emotional eating triggers, what exercise method will keep you motivated, and the best methods for weight loss or gain. Understanding yourself better through the Enneagram allows you to alter your subconscious programming and become not only physically, but emotionally healthier.

978-1-62055-827-0